AF556337

POVERTY, INEQUALITY AND FOOD SECURITY

POVERTY, INEQUALITY AND FOOD SECURITY

Edited by

Dr. Ram Krishna Mandal

Head & Associate Professor of Economics
Dera Natung Govt. College
Itanagar-791 113
Arunachal Pradesh
(India)
e-mail: *rkm_1966@yahoo.co.in*

DISCOVERY PUBLISHING HOUSE PVT. LTD.
NEW DELHI-110 002

Published by:
Tilak Wasan
DISCOVERY PUBLISHING HOUSE PVT. LTD.
4383/4B, Ansari Road, Darya Ganj
New Delhi-110 002 (India)
Phone : +91-11-23279245, 43596064-65
Fax : +91-11-23253475
E-mail : discoverypublishinghouse@gmail.com
sales@discoverypublishinggroup.com
web : www.discoverypublishinggroup.com

First Edition: **2015**

ISBN: 978-93-5056-710-4

Poverty, Inequality and Food Security

Printed at:
Infinity Imaging Systems
Delhi

Dedicated

To

Miss Anusree Krishna Mandal

Acknowledgements

The present study is an attempt at a comprehensive and critical analysis for the role of women in socio-economic development with special reference to educational levels, entrepreneurship, attitude of the society towards women, social and religious taboos, women's own awareness and political attainments in society.

The present volume is a collection of twenty two papers contributed by eminent scholars, academicians, policy makers, bureaucrats and thinkers from different parts of India. The publication of this book would not have been possible without their contributions. Their work is based on diverse source materials which consist of official reports, published journals, books and findings of field work. Most of their writings are based either on the social structural aspects or on the social dynamism and rapid regional socio-economic transformation or on the empowerment of women. I have felt the need to put some of their writings together so as to enable the readers to get an overall idea about the same aspect. Some of their writings have been updated, revised and edited for the purpose. I hope that the readers will find it relevant for understanding the features of women in a better way. I hope, this book will benefit immensely the students, teachers, young scholars, planners and administrators in the area of women study in particular and society of our country in general. I am conscious of the bulk of the work which becomes largely inevitable on account of the intrinsic sweep of the subject. I acknowledge my gratitude to all contributors, whose works are consulted in the preparation of this volume.

I would be falling in my duty if I do not extend my gratitude to our Principal, Shri Tomar Ete, Dera Natung Govt. College, Itanagar, Arunachal Pradesh, India for generating in me an interest to edit this book.

I also acknowledge the inspiration received from my beloved teacher and guide, Prof. Chandan Kumar Mukhopadyaya, Department of Economics, University of North Bengal, West Bengal. I express my deep sense of gratitude to him.

I have received supports and cooperation from my colleagues Dr. Madhuparna Bhattacharjee, Dr. A.I.Singh, Dr. Suparna Bhattacharya and Miss Anjali Biswas, my Research Assistant, I express a deep sense of gratitude to them.

I am also taking the opportunity to thank profusely to Shri Tilak Wasan, Managing Director, Discovery Publishing House Pvt. Ltd., New Delhi, for publication this book.

Lastly, I am grateful to the members of my family: Mrs. Archana Mandal (wife) and Miss Anusree Krishna Mandal, KVPY Fellow (Daughter) and Master Avinandan Krishna Mandal (son) for their untiring support and patience during the work of this volume.

Dr. Ram Krishna Mandal

Contents

List of Contributors

1. **Dr. Prof C.K. Roy**, F-632, Delta-1, Greater Noida, State No. 11, G.V. Nagar, U P, India. Pin - 201 306.
2. **Dr. Manoj Kumar Agarwal,** Coordinator, Centre of Excellence, Associate Professor, Department of Economics, University of Lucknow, Lucknow - 226 007, India.
3. **Dr. K. Sambasivam**, Associate Professor, Dept. of Economics, Bharathidhasan Govt. College for Women, Pondy - 3.
4. **Dr. Sanjaya Kumar Das**, Research Officer, Jadavpur Univerisity, Kolkatta, West Bengal, India.
5. **Mary Princess Lavanya**, Asst. Professor, Dept. of Social Work, Plot No: 3062, New No. 54, 14th Main Road, Anna Nagar, Chennai - 34, Tamil Nadu, India.
6. **Mriganka Saikia**, Assistant Professor, Dhing College, Dhing, Nagaon, Assam - 782 123, India.
7. **Pankaj Saikia**, Assistant Professor, Dhing College, Dhing, Nagaon, Assam - 782 123, India.
8. **Dr. Sailajananda Saikia**, Assistant Prof., Department of Geography, Madhab Chaudhury College, Barpeta, Dist. Barpeta, Assam - 781 301, India.
9. **Mrs. Shivani Mohan**, Assistant Professor (Economics), National Law University, Nyaya Nagar, Mithapur, Patna - 800 001, India.
10. **Shambhavi Mishra**, B.A. L.L.B.(Hons.), 2rd Year, Chanakaya National Law University, Nyaya Nagar, Mithapur, Patna - 800 001, India.
11. **Dr. Abhishek Tripathi**, (Manager/Sectary) Chintans Samagra Vikas Simit, Mahanagar, Lucknow, Uttar Pradesh - 226 006, India.
12. **Dr. Nanjunda**, Centre for the Study of Social Exclusion and Inclusive Policy (CSSEIP). Humanities Block, University of Mysore, Mysore-570006 Karnataka, India.
13. **S. Jyothi lakshmi**, Dept. of Economics, KSOU University, Mysore, India.
14. **Dr. G. Vanithamani**, Guest Faculty, Department of Economics, APA College for Women Chinnakalayamputhur, Palani - 624 615, Tamil Nadu, India.

15. **Niteesh Kumar Upadhayay**, (Ph.D. Scholar, WBNUJS), Chanakya National Law University, Yaya Nagar, Mithapur, Patna - 800 001, Bihar, India.

16. **Kuhumita Laha,** Student, LL.M., WBNUJS, Chanakya National Law University, Yaya Nagar, Mithapur, Patna - 800 001, Bihar, India.

17. **Ashok Das Gupta**, Research Scholar (UGC Fellow), Department of Anthropology, University of North Bengal, India.

18. **Francis Kuriakose**, 3rd Floor, 22 A, Manakula Vinayagar Koil Street, Puducherry - 605 001, India.

19. **Deepa Kylasam Iyer**, 3rd Floor, 22 A, Manakula Vinayagar Koil Street, Puducherry - 605 001, India.

20. **Dr. (Mrs.) Asha Sharma,** Assistant Professor, Department of Commerce, Mahila PG Mahavidyalaya, Jai Narain Vyas University, Jodhpur, India.

21. **Dr. Mithilesh Kumar Jha**, Asst. Prof. & Head, Dept. of Economics, Yingli Govt. College, Longleng, Nagaland , Pin - 798 625, India.

22. **Vineeth Sahadevan**, Asst. Professor, De Paul Degree College, Belagola Post, Mysore, Karnataka - 571 606, India.

23. **Dr. N.K. Patra, Assistant Professor,** Department of Agricultural Extension, School of Agricultural Sciences and Rural Development, Nagaland University, Nagaland - 797 106.

24. **M.N. Odyuo,** Assistant Professor, Department of Rural Development and Planning, School of Agricultural Sciences and Rural Development, Nagaland University, Nagaland - 797 106.

25. **S. Das,** Assistant Professor, Department of Agricultural Economics, School of Agricultural Sciences and Rural Development, Nagaland University, Nagaland - 797 106.

26. **Dr. L.Y. Longchar,** Associate Professor and Head, Department of Agricultural Extension, School of Agricultural Sciences and Rural Development, Nagaland University, Nagaland - 797 106.

27. **Dr. Surojit Sen Gupta**, Assistant Professor, Department of Sociology, Maharaja Bir Bikram College, Agartala - 799 004, Tripura.

28. **Kaniska Sarkar**, Assistant Registrar, 4/2 Block- H, Officers' Quarters, Jadavpur University Main Campus, 188, Raja S.C. Mallick Road, Kolkata - 700 032.

29. **M.N. Odyuo,** Assistant Professor, Department of Rural Development and Planning, School of Agricultural Sciences and Rural Development, Nagaland University, Nagaland - 797 106.

30. **Dr. N.K. Patra**, Assistant Professor, and **Dr. L.Y. Longchar,** Associate Professor and Head, Department of Agricultural Extension, School of Agricultural Sciences and Rural Development, Nagaland University, Nagaland - 797 106.

31. **S. Das,** Assistant Professor, Department of Agricultural Economics, School of Agricultural Sciences and Rural Development, Nagaland University, Nagaland - 797 106.
32. **Dr. N.K. Patra**, Assistant Professor, Department of Agricultural Extension, School of Agricultural Sciences and Rural Development, Nagaland University, Nagaland - 797 106.

Introduction

Ram Krishna Mandal

A pertinent question that has often emerged in the context of Indian Economic planning is: Whether the gap between the haves and have-nots has narrowed or widened since the launching of the planned economic development in India? To examine this, a number of governmental, institutional and individual studies have been made from time to time. All studies have arrived at the conclusion that this gap has actually widened and there has been a concentration of wealth and economic power in a few hands to the detriment of the underprivileged and the common people. Before we analyse the findings of these studies, the cause of the perpetuation of inequalities, and suggestions to overcome them, it is instructive to have a theoretical interlude on the compatibility of growth and equality (or income distribution).

Earlier, the classical economists were also in favour of income inequality. According to them, income equality discourages savings. Income inequality means a higher income for the working classes and a rise in their consumption. This, in turn, means a rise in population. The classical, therefore, believed that inequalities of incomes were necessary to provide the incentive for economic growth.

But Marx thought otherwise. According to him, it was income inequality that would bring the doom of capitalism. He argued that income inequality meant less consumption for the poor masses. This would lead to unsold stocks of goods and to a stop of further production. In this way, there would be cumulative over-production and under-consumption and the capitalist economy would move towards secular stagnation.

It was Lord Keynes who pleaded for income equality to sustain economic growth. He wrote: "In contemporary conditions the growth of wealth far from being dependent on the abstinence of the rich as is commonly supposed, is more likely to be imposed by it. One of the chief social justifications of great inequality of wealth is, therefore, removed." According to Keynes, a society which saves more due to inequalities of income and wealth, bring secular stagnation, because inequalities would reduce its consumption capacity and bring contraction in demand. Ultimately, it would lead to fall in production and slowing down the economic activity. Keynes, therefore, favoured income equality which might lead to sustained economic growth via the multiplier effect.

Of the post-Keynesian economists, Professor Kurihara has carried Keynes' views further. Keynes believed that encouraging consumption is alternative to saving. But Kurihara shows that they are complementary. When there is income inequality it leads to excessive thriftiness and fall in inducement to invest as a result of declining marginal efficiency of capital. Economic growth requires the balancing of the two factors which is possible in a "high-wage, low profit economy and investment-free society."

In the 1950s and 1960s, the thinking on income equality and growth was influenced by Kuznets' U-shaped Curve. Kuznets suggested on the experience of the developed countries that historically there was a tendency for income inequalities to increase first, and then to be reduced as countries developed from low level. Accordingly, it was believed that a high degree of inequality in the distribution of income had a favourable effect on economic growth in the early stages of development gained momentum, its benefits would automatically "trickle down" to the lower income groups over the long run. So this approach emphasized the maximization of the growth rate of the economy by building up capital, infrastructure and productive capacity of the economy, and leaving the income distribution untouched.

Lewis was the principal supporter of this view. He outlined the process through which income inequality led to the economic growth of the 18th century England, the 19th century Western Europe and the early 20th century Japan. He advocates the same for underdeveloped countries. Lewis contends that voluntary savings from a significantly large share of national income only where inequality of income distribution is such that profits are a relatively large share of national income. When growth is taking place, the modern sector grows faster than the traditional sector and the relative share of profits in national income also increases. This tends to perpetuate income inequalities. In the long run, however, when employment opportunities increase all round and the traditional sector also develops, the distribution of income tends to stabilize. But this is an automatic process and is only a side-effect of the growth of the economy.

According to Lewis, the share of profits in national income should be increased by expanding the capitalist sector of the economy deliberately. For this, he suggests that those who lived on unearned incomes, particularly ground rents, should be taxed heavily and the proceeds given to capitalists who live on profits. Profits can also be increased by giving subsidies and tax rebates by providing adequate supplies of raw materials and capital equipment, by restricting imports of competitive products, by controlling wages and trade unions, and by government purchases of the goods of the industries. Thus it is contended that larger profits accruing to the capitalist sector will mean larger savings which will be invested for larger capital formation and growth rates.

But this is not a correct view in the context of developing countries. Perpetuation of income inequalities is no condition for rapid economic growth. Unlike the developed countries, the conditions in developing countries are such that income inequalities are not necessary for their economic development. A number of arguments are given in support in support of view.

Perpetuation of income inequalities is not feasible under the system of parliamentary democracy and the political climatic prevailing in such countries. The policy of raising profits to increase savings for capital formation may lead to social unrest and may even fail to produce socially desirable investment since the profit making classes are not necessarily increased in the welfare of the masses. Thus income inequalities may hamper economic development.

The policy of increasing profits of the capitalist sector through subsidies, tax rebates, controlling wages and trade unions, etc. creates vested interests and leads to maldistribution of resources within a developing economy.

Moreover, there is no guarantee that the wealthy classes in such economies will utilize their savings in productive channels. Rather, businessmen, landlords and other rich elites spend much of their incomes on conspicuous consumption, gold hoards, jewelers, estates and expensive houses, speculation, foreign travel, etc. In certain cases, it leads to the fight of capital in the form of deposits in bank abroad and hoardings of foreign currencies and gold in the safe vaults of Western banks. Thus such savings and investments do not serve any fruitful purpose. They do not add to the productive resource of the economy but are a drain on them.

On the other hand, the perpetuation of income inequalities brings more harm to the economy. Inequalities retard development. Therefore, prudence demands that effort should be made to raise the income of the majority of the people who are poor.

Further, inequalities lead to great economic waste. The waste is caused by inefficient management. Businessmen who are rich may be efficient entrepreneurs themselves, but their children who inherit their wealth may not be as efficient as their fathers. Thus starts a process of inefficient management thereby lowering the rate of economic development.

Another cause of economic waste due to inequality is loss of human capital. As the majority of people are poor with low levels of income and low levels of living, they cannot provide themselves with nutritional diet, formal education and training. Consequently, their productive efficiency is low which, in turn, leads to a slower growth of economy. Thus the reduction of inequalities and raising the incomes and levels of living to the poor would raise not only their productive efficiency but also that of the economy.

The prominent cause for this unequal distribution of income and wealth in India are poverty, inadequate development, economic concentration, tax evasion, inequitable distribution of means of production, capital intensive technology, unemployment and underemployment etc. (Jhingan, 2004, pp. 745-748).

Balanced regional development does not mean equal development of regions in the country. It simply implies the fullest development of the potentialities of an area according to its capacity so that the benefits of overall economic growth are shared by the inhabitants of all the regions. Balanced regional development does not mean self sufficiency in each State or region. Neither does it mean equal level of industrialization nor a uniform economic pattern for each State. Rather, it means widespread diffusion of industry in backward areas so far as it is economically feasible. The ultimate aim is to raise the living standards of the people in backward regions to those of the advanced. It may be through the development of agriculture, industry, trade and commerce. According to Mumford, it is "a problem of increasing habitability- a problem of social and economic renewal.

Underdeveloped countries are characterized by regional differences in income and employment. According to Professor Myrdal, the main cause of regional inequality has been the strong backwash effects and the weak spread effects in such economies. The genesis of regional inequalities has a non-economic basis which is associated with the capitalist system guided by the profit motive. The profit motive results in the development of those regions where the prospects of profit are high while other regions remain underdeveloped. Myrdal attributes the phenomenon to the free play of market forces. The latter tend to concentrate economic and social overheads in certain regions leaving the rest of the country. These inequalities are accentuated by migration, capital movement and trade. Migration of young and active people from backward region will favour the advanced region and depressed economic activity in the former; capital will move into the developed regions thereby creating capital shortage in the backward. The development of industries in former region may ruin the existing industries of the latter regions. So the backwash effects though the deliberate State action for a balanced regional development (Jhingan 2004, p.727).

Globalization, as a consequence of WTO, linked with the international trade liberalization, opening up of economies, and a free flow of capital, labour, information and technology is a major paradigm shift making significant changes in the world economy. It has a considerable potential to significantly influence both the food/nutritional security and poverty for better or worse, but its implications and consequences are not yet fully understood (Singh, 2004).

Distribution of operational land holdings is highly skewed. There are about 119,931 thousand holding spread over 159,436 thousand hectares with average size as 1.33 hectares. More than four-fifths of the holdings have area less than two hectares each and are spread over two-fifths of operated area. Only 1 per cent of holdings are large with area greater than 10 hectares each but account for more than 13 per cent of operated area. Thus there is huge inequity in land distribution.

Definitely, the volume will explore the present scenario of poverty and income inequality as well as the strategy for economic equality among the masses. It consists of twenty two papers collected from different scholars from different corners of the country.

Innovation and Research on Food Habits (Indian Philosophy and Modern Research)

Prof. C.K. Roy

Introduction

For an efficient and effective human resource the people of a nation should feel calmer, happier and more energetic in their daily life. In this context the Indian concept which is oldest is quite clear. In case we refer *Shrimadbhagwat Geeta* Lord Krishna had given his teaching about classes of the people on this earth and their way of living starting from YOGA to food habits.

There are three types of human nature (character) 'GUNA'.

- **SATWIK (Pure):** Those who think positive and are calm, happier and more energetic. They do not opt "Sin" and perform their *Karma* (duty) in a perfect order with an attitude of selflessness. *Satwik* is the pleasant form of people who perform their work with nearly zero error and without greed. They are dedicated persons. This was applicable to saints and people with positive thinking who dedicated their life for future betterment of the society. They were fully harmonized with self, their family and society as a whole.
- **RAJAS (Normal/average- to live):** They are at a lower level than *Satwik* and are normal people to live and work. This was applicable for kings (*Raja*) who had to perform their duty with adequate effort and political approach to get work done in their kingdom with normalcyand fordevelopment of their area of command. Today it is applicable to corporate and business groups where total purity in work is not possible. It is a middle path to perform. They feel proud of their position and work as commanders.

- **TAMAS (Extra egoists and impure in dealings):** These people are not fit to work on the true democratic pattern and adopt mostly unethical approach. *Tamas* was applicable to "*Rakshas* (devils). These people are selfish and selflessness in absent in them. They act like devils and are self styled people. They care for their own good and do not work positively in favor of the society.They have ugly look and adopt practices to harm others. In another term they behaved like a beast.
- The earth has all these three types of people but by adopting yoga and changing food habits and living style it is possible to convert them from *Tamas* to *Rajash* or at least *Satwik* stages.

Food habits recommend in *Geeta* and its impact chapter 17 (7-22) of *Geeta* prescribes different food habits for three categories of people mentioned above and its impact on their behaviour.

The '*Shradha*'(faith/reliance)is of three types and on similar ground foods are also of three types which are liked by each type of person. *Satwik* persons prefer *Satwik* food which are juicyvegetables and soft and durable food. *Rajas* people prefer, beater, sour, and softy, very hot and rough food. *Tamsy* people prefer half cooked '*Kachha*' non-juicy full of bad smell and stalk food.. Due to these three different types of food intake by the three classes of the people, described above the nature of each will be different which are being elaborated here under:

SATWIK – unconditional love, hard working, and faithful, peaceful and energetic are the major nature of such people.

RAJASY – Are proudly in nature and follow the path of conditional love, they perform worship or their work with certain conditions and are not very peaceful or calm. They are vain with false doctrine. They rule over people over their span of command. Behave like a king and perform their work mostly with application of 'X' theory.

These are expressions in *Srimadbhagwat Geeta* which is an Indian ideology in existence since past more than 3000 gears, but the world has been searching and doing researches on impact of food habits and preferred food types today. A study report (refers TOI, dt. 25.01.2013) in which a research has been published. This research related to food habits of the people and impact of it on the human behavior. It wasbased on eating fruits, veggies that means vegetarian's food impact on the sample size selected vis a vis others eating non vegetarian and junk food. The finding was that these items of food lifts mood and makes you calmer and more energetic. The details of this report follows:.

"**Melbourne**: Eating more fruit and vegetables may make young people calmer, happier and more energetic in their daily life, according to a new research. Researchers from the University of Otago in New Zealand investigated the relationship between day-to-day emotions and food consumption.

Researcher TamlinConnner, Caroline Horwath and Bonnie White analyzed a total of 281 young adults (with a mean age of 20 years) who completed an internet-based daily food diary for 21 consecutive days.

The results showed a strong day-to-day relationship between more positive mood and higher fruit and vegetable consumption, but not other foods. "On days when people ate more fruits and vegetables, they reported feeling calmer, happier and more energetic than they normally did," Conner said in a statement.

To understand which comes first - feeling positive or eating healthier foods Corner and her team ran additional analysis and found that eating fruits and vegetables predicted improvements in positive mood the next day, suggesting that healthy foods may improve mood."

Another report TOI dated 1st Feb, 2013, has given its opinion about the value of vegetarian diet recommending cuts heart disease risk. The details are as under:

London: This should make a majority of Indians happy.

The risk of hospitalization or death from heart disease has been found to be 32 per cent lower in vegetarians, than people who eat meat and fish.

New insight brought out on Wednesday by researchers at the University of Oxford through the largest study ever conducted in the UK comparing rates of heart disease between vegetarians and non-vegetarians suggests that a vegetarian diet can reduce risk of heart disease by up to a third.

The researchers found that vegetarians had significantly lower blood pressures and cholesterol levels than non vegetarians, which is thought to be the main reason behind their reduced risk of heart disease.

The new findings, published in the American Journal of Clinical Nutrition, also showed that vegetarians typically had lower body mass indices (BMI) and fewer cases of diabetes as a result of their diets.

In India, a significant chunk of the population is vegetarians. Also, more youngsters are also turning to a vegan diet.

According to India's health ministry, the leading cause of deaths in India among non-communicable diseases is cardiovascular disease (29.89 lakh).

Dr. Francesca Crowe, lead author of the study at the Cancer Epidemiology Unit, University of Oxford said, "Most of the difference in risk is probably caused by effects on cholesterol and blood pressure, and shows the important role of diet in the prevention of heart disease."

The analysis looked at almost 45,000 volunteers from England and Scotland enrolled in the European Prospective Investigation into Cancer and Nutrition (EPIC)-Oxford study, of whom 34 per cent were vegetarian."

The purpose of this comparison is that what the world is searching today is already available in our Vedas, upnishada and sastras. Today we are lured of what others are searching and re-searching and hardly care for our traditional thoughts' and findings which are already in existence.. If yoga and food habits are followed as mentioned in our shastras (*Geeta*) the outcome of today's research by a foreign agency could have been challenged. The above analysis explains about the richness of Indian old culture and ideology about food habits already prescribed in our Vedas and shastras and the world after research arrive at the similar decisions that too after several researches and investing huge funds.. This should alarm us that our traditional findings and practices have value which needs to be challenged at world level and it is the right time that it needs to be adopted not only in India but at global level.

Learning from the Nature

In relation to the food intake if we analyze the nature we are living in the outcome will be similar to the researches conducted all over the world and the lesson provided in our *Vedas* and *Srimadbhagwat Geeta*. It is said that nature around us is the best teacher freely available.

In case we compare an elephant with that of a lion or tiger we find that the elephant is an animal which is vegetarian and is the strongest and most powerful in its strength where as a tiger or lion is next to it. The elephant is possible to be tamed. Its nature is calm and is also used as a domestic animal. It is one of the most sensible animal and possesses better intelligence than any other meat eaters. In older days it was used for transportation of men and heavy goods including wooden logs in forest and heavy building materials used in construction of forts and palaces. Compared to it most of the beasts which are depending on non vegetarian food are furious in nature and they live to 'KILL'. It was not possible to tame them and convert it in to useful purposes. It is said that lions fight with other lions and never live together. They have an extreme nature of *'Tamas'* full of anger, selfishness and fighting for self existence. The nature of a lion or tiger can be compared with the description of a *"Tamsi"* person full of anger and destruction. These differences appear to be the impact of vegetarian and non vegetarian food habits.

Another observation is of two animals *'Ganda'* (rhino) and hypo (*Dariai Ghora*) which are totally vegetarian that are most powerful and live together like a family. Have less anger and have better calm than those which eat meat.

Another example is the camel which has very high strength and power in their jaws.

In earlier days (before year1960's) in a marriage procession of jamindars in rural areas the elephants were inducted and their number was an indication of the might of those jamindars..To maintain safety in case of elephants going mad or out of control a few camels were included in the procession to have a control over such elephants. The camels catch the ear of the elephants and punish them to maintain discipline. Here again the camel is a vegetarian animal which is most peaceful and wise.

In case we compare the researches, *Geeta's* saying and learning's from the nature the conclusion is that a vegetarian food provides calm,respect, vigor, and strength to perform better and reducesdiseases and sufferings in our life. It is therefore suggested that some agency (government owned) or NGO should take the challenge to implement these innovations and researches which will help the efficiency of the people of the country and turning the people more calm,co-operative and peaceful leading to a greater harmony at global level. To get a more positive result this theme may be included in the primary level curriculum because tender the age of a child greater shall be the chance of acceptance.

The vegetarian system, in case popularized among the people of not only India but of the entire globe will help in raising the average life expectancy on this globe. Also the behavior of the people will change from *Tamas* (cruel) to *Satwik* (gentle man) and will help in reducing the crime at global level. The level of killing diseases will come down resulting in to higher productivity due to lesser losses of manpower and higher individual efficiency to work. A healthy person will be able to earn more due to his higher efficiency to work. Also he or she will be able to save more due to lesser expenditure on his food bill and medical bill due to lower sickness. The extra savings will improve the quality of life and the standard of living.

Exploring Economic Differentials Among the Bhotia and Raji Tribes in Uttarakhand

Dr. Manoj Kumar Agarwal

ABSTRACT

At a time when the barriers across community and the nations are being dismantled by the onslaught of the globalization that emphasizes upon economic routes to human well beings, we should analyze the pattern of economic changes taking place in the isolated communities. Such communities might be strong within itself but they need to share the cake of economic progress. It is a well known fact that the Indian economy has been demonstrating its economic strength through sustained economic growth at rapid rates particularly since the 1980s that got strengthened since the process of economic reforms were initiated since 1991. This has led to many types of technological advancements which have been helpful in raising the living standards of the masses as well. However, for gaining economically in such circumstances, it is as much the responsibility of the government as it is for the communities themselves. Here, we take up the case of the two tribes of Uttaranchal (now renamed as Uttarakhand) in Pithoragarh district, that is, Bhotia and Raji. In this paper, we would be taking stock of the economic status of these tribes that would be reflecting wide gaps prevailing between the two tribes' economic achievements. It can be further reiterated that economic parameters seem to influence the other parameters and thus the economic variables might initiate the process of overall change and well being in any society.

Introduction

We present here an economic study of the Bhotia tribe and Raji tribe in the Pithoragarh district of Uttaranchal, a state which was carved out of Uttar

Pradesh in 2000 keeping in mind that there is need for special attention to this hilly state encompassing some of the terai areas as well. Bhotia people are found in rural areas as well as in towns, cities and at prominent places elsewhere. There has been a common refrain that Bhotia people generally are leading a lifestyle just like any other group or community and they have intense interactions with the outside world as at one time or the other some member (s) of their family is (are) living outside their native place. They generally would go out for higher studies, preparing for jobs, for business purposes, doing jobs or exploring for jobs or business opportunities, being in the armed forces or frequenting their native places in the extreme situations of Pithoragarh or even crossing the border and going to Tibet and using the opportunity to do some business out of that from both the sides. Socially and culturally, the Bhotia tribe seems to be at much higher level.

Raji people are still very closed in the sense that they shy away from the outside world and their exposure and interaction with the outside world has been highly restricted. They are generally confined to few villages of the Pithoragarh district and that too mainly in two blocks – Dharchula and Didihat. They reside in villages which are not easily accessible. These are mainly surrounded by the forests. Their villages are generally at the top of the mountain instead of being in the valleys. It is found that the land on which Raji people live belongs to the Forest Department and the latter do not object over them as the government policy is to provide them help in many ways including their dependence on the forest resources. These people generally would not like to interact with the strangers and even the localities from the other communities. Raji men are quite lazy and generally the outside job is done by their female counterparts. Houses of the Raji tribal people are generally small and not very clean. Generally, some improved conditions of the houses are due to support received for the house construction under some governmental schemes like Indira Awaas Yojana (IAY). Economic activities of the Raji households are quite limited. They will undertake some farm activities in their villages or nearby their villages. It is mainly the responsibility of the Raji females to take care of the agricultural operations right from the stage of the ploughing and sowing to harvesting and processing. Females would also go to collect forest woods for their own consumption as well as to collect some surplus to be sold in the markets which happen to be few kilometres away from their villages. In this regard, it can be stated that generally males would not go to market for sale and purchase activities. They will collect firewood from the jungle and take these to homes to be taken care of by the female members in the families. Unlike Bhotia households, Raji households seem to prefer nuclear family structure.

Nature of Study

The present paper is based on the primary data collected for a research project during 2005 and 2006[1]. Now we can deal with some common features that have been found about the respondents during the course of this study that would help us in making the further analysis more meaningful for deriving inferences. The entire fieldwork was to be organised in such a manner that adverse weather conditions could be avoided. In all, around twenty villages of the Pithoragarh district in different blocks were covered. For Raji, we covered only one block of Dharchula where there is maximum concentration of the Raji households. Our study is based upon 330 households and out of this 285 were Bhotia households and the remaining 45 belonged to Raji households. This can be considered a large sample size considering the tough mountains and tough situations faced during the interviews, particularly among the Raji tribe where they will not give sufficient time and where it was not possible to work for more than 3-4 hours of a day. That also required climbing up on foot for more than one hour and then getting back to the road in almost one hour while at that moment being conscious about the safety in going up and coming down. Moreover, winning the confidence of the Raji respondents was not an easy affair besides confronting the problems due to poor communication quality in many ways.

Table 2.1: Nature of Houses of the Respondents

Tribe	Income Group (Rs.)	Kuchcha	Hut	Semi-Pucca	Pucca	Total
Bhotia	< 12000	4.4	2.2	11.1	82.2	100.0
	12000-36000	1.1	–	16.9	82.0	100.0
	36000-60000	4.2	–	10.4	85.4	100.0
	>60000	3.9	–	12.6	83.5	100.0
	Total	3.2	0.4	13.3	83.2	100.0
Raji	< 12000	5.9	41.2	11.8	41.2	100.0
	12000-36000	9.1	18.2	45.5	27.3	100.0
	Total	6.7	35.6	20.0	37.8	100.0
All	< 12000	5.1	19.0	11.4	64.6	100.0
	12000-36000	2.0	2.0	20.0	76.0	100.0
	36000-60000	4.2	–	10.4	85.4	100.0
	>60000	3.9	–	12.6	83.5	100.0
	Grand Total	3.6	5.2	14.2	77.0	100.0

It is found that the Bhotia tribe is more progressive. The Raji tribe, despite government's increasing thrust to provide opportunities and assistance, remains far away from development. This is, initially, confirmed from the fact that the house condition of the Raji respondents has been highly deplorable whereas it has been far better among the Bhotia respondents although in the case of the latter too there is need for much to be done (Table 2.1). Household amenities have been far away from the desired norms as in most of the houses of the Raji respondents, there have not been in-house toilet facilities or the electricity connections in their houses. Raji households are highly backward as in the case of almost 87 per cent of the households, the status was that of illiterate unlike among the Bhotia where it was quite low at less than 10 per cent. More than two-third of the Bhotia respondent households had high level of education of more than high school whereas it was just 2 per cent in the case of the Raji respondents. This shows that Raji people are quite low in terms of basic human development variable. In terms of the access over telephone and mobile facilities, none of the Raji respondents was found to have it even though among the Bhotia also it was confined to less than one-third of the respondents (Table 2.2).

Table 2.2: Basic Amentias in the Houses of the Tribal Respondents

Tribe	In-House-Toilet				Electricity			Mobile/Telephones		
	Yes	No	Limited Use	Total	Yes	No	Total	Yes	No	Total
Bhotia	201 (70.5)	75 (26.3)	9 (3.2)	285 (100.0)	249 (87.4)	36 (12.6)	285 (100.0)	83 (29.1)	202 (70.9)	285 (100.0)
Raji	6 (13.3)	37 (82.3)	2 (4.4)	45 (100.0)	9 (20.0)	36 (80.0)	45 (100.0)	--	45 (100.0)	45 (100.0)
All	207 (62.7)	112 (33.9)	11 (3.3)	330 (100.0)	258 (78.2)	72 (21.8)	330 (100.0)	83 (25.2)	247 (74.8)	330 (100.0)

It could be seen through Table 2.3 that there is wide income gap between the Bhotia and Raji households. Raji households have been mostly poor and at subsistence level only as 86.7 per cent households lived with an annual income of up to only Rs. 12000. This is very low level of income as we know that during 2004-05, per capita income of India was Rs. 22946 whereas it was lower at Rs. 17707 in the case of Uttaranchal showing very poor economic status of the Raji households. On the other hand only 13.3 per cent of the households had income level ranging from Rs. 12000 to 36000 per annum only. Thus, among the five classified groups of income, the Raji households remained confined to only the bottom two groups only. It could be shared that even in the second group of income, the Raji households remained generally towards the lower side of the range and they generally were far below the upper cap of the second group. As against this, the Bhotia households seem to be at much higher levels of income as only 17.9 per cent of these lived in the lowest income group of Rs 12000 per annum. Another 33 per cent were found to be in the range of Rs. 12000 to 36000. Thus the remaining households enjoyed higher income levels. It is derived that 16.1 per cent were grouped in the income range of Rs. 36000 to 60000 whereas in the further higher level of income, that is Rs. 60000 to 120000, 23.9 per cent of the Bhotia households were classified. Thus, the remaining 9.1 per cent Bhotia households enjoyed very high level of income which was more than Rs. 1.2

lakhs. This clearly demonstrates that in a comparative analysis, Bhotia population has been better off economically as compared to the Raji households that were suffering from the low level of economic attainments.[2]

Table 2.3: Distribution of households in terms of annual income (Rs.)

Tribe	Less than 12,000/-	12,000/- to	36,000/- to 36,000/-	60,000/- to 60,000/-	Above 1,20,000/-	Total 1,20,000/-
Bhotia	51 (17.9)	94 (33.0)	46 (16.1)	68 (23.9)	26 (9.1)	285 (100.0)
Raji	39 (86.7)	6 (13.3)	–	–	–	45 (100.0)
All	90 (27.3)	100 (30.3)	46 (13.9)	68 (20.6)	26 (7.9)	330 (100.0)

Note: Figures in parentheses show percentage share in the total respondents of the tribe.

Pattern of Occupation

Occupation structure of any population suggests about its economic role and its economic prospect. Generally, a poor and backward population's occupation remains confined to traditional activities which have low productivity and where the prospect of growth is limited. Unlike this, if the occupational structure is well diversified towards the modern activities, the level of economic attainments becomes high along with the sufficient prospect about the future because such activities are more rewarding due to high productivity. This in turn requires that there is increased wealth and capital formation – human and material.

We can find the pattern of engagement in primary and secondary occupations of males and females of the two tribes (Table 2.4). We have taken a very practical and liberal definition of the two levels of occupations. Primary occupation implies that people use it necessary to engage in any economically gainful occupation whereas in the secondary occupation, people use it to supplement the income from the primary occupation or they do it as part time or hobby or traditional work which is economically also helpful. However, in case the two are same then the primary work is one where the person earns relatively more income with greater regularity. It could be seen from the table that Bhotia people have more commitment for the primary occupation alone as compared with the Raji counterparts as in the case of the former 69.4 per cent workers are only in the primary occupation unlike for the Raji people where the ratio is much lower at 38.9 per cent. Although in both the tribes similar trend could be seen with regard to men and women taken separately as well, it is also true that in both the tribes women have lower proportions in primary occupation as compared to the men. What needs to be watched is it that people including men folk also join the category of only secondary occupation.

Table 2.4: Pattern of Occupation Among the Men and Women of Bhotia and Raji Tribes

Tribe	Gender	Primary	Secondary	Both	Total
Bhotia	Men	255 (72.6)	34 (9.7)	62 (17.7)	351 (100.0)
	Women	169 (65.0)	69 (26.5)	22 (8.5)	260 (100.0)
	Total	424 (69.4)	103 (16.9)	84 (13.7)	611 (100.0)
Raji	Men	28 (41.2)	18 (26.5)	22 (32.4)	68 (100.0)
	Women	14 (35.0)	10 (25.0)	16 (40.0)	40 (100.0)
	Total	42 (38.9)	28 (25.9)	38 (35.2)	108 (100.0)
All	Men	283 (67.5)	52 (12.4)	84 (20.0)	419 (100.0)
	Women	183 (61.0)	79 (26.3)	38 (12.7)	300 (100.0)
	Total	466 (64.8)	131 (18.2)	122 (17.0)	719 (100.0)

Note: Figures in brackets are the percentage distribution.

This clearly suggests that the occupation pattern is showing economic backwardness among the Raji people as compared to the Bhotia because the former do not have assured primary occupation or they don't like to explore the avenue. Moreover, there is no doubt the participation of women in the economic spheres in both the occupations, but the Raji men are low performers as is evident from large share of these being engaged only in the secondary occupation and leaving the job of economic functioning to women. Moreover, Raji people's share is more with regard to engagements in the primary and secondary occupations together (35.2) than of the Bhotia (13.7%). It may be argued that this high trend for the Raji is due to distress and not due to much economic prudence.

(A) Members engaged in primary occupation only

It is shown earlier that the Bhotia have the highest share of primary occupations (69.4%) like the Raji workers but the ratio for the latter has been very low (38.9%) as shown in Table 2.5. Thus, the former's ratio has been slightly less than the double of the former. The members of both the tribes engaged in the primary occupations only shows that the distribution is widely spread in the case of the Bhotia whereas it remains highly confined for the Raji. A comparison between the men of the two tribes reveals that there have been only two occupations for the Raji men engaged in primary occupations alone, that is working as farmers (10.7) or as labourers (89.3%).

Table 2.5: Members Engaged in Primary Occupation Only

Tribe	Male								Female							
	Farming	Drivers	Woolen Work	Labour	Contractor	Govern-ment Service	Private Service	Total	Farming	Drivers	Woolen Work	Labour	Contractor	Govern-ment Service	Private Service	Total
Bhotia	20.0	17.3	13.7	3.9	0.4	43.9	0.8	100.0 (255)	16.0	–	76.9	–	–	7.1	–	100.0 (169)
Raji	10.7	–	–	89.3	–	–	–	100.0 (28)	85.7	–	–	14.3	–	–	–	100.0 (14)
All	19.1	15.5	12.4	12.4	0.4	39.6	0.7	100.0 (283)	21.3	–	71.0	1.1	–	6.6	–	100.0 (183)

Table 2.6: Average Monthly Earnings of Members Engaged in Primary Occupation Only (%)

Tribe	Male							Female						
	< 1000	1001-2000	2001-4000	4001-8000	8001-12000	> 12000	Total	< 1000	1001-2000	2001-4000	4001-8000	8001-12000	> 12000	Total
Bhotia	10.2	13.3	22.0	42.4	3.9	8.2	100.0 (255)	52.1	30.8	8.9	7.1	1.2	–	100.0 (169)
Raji	89.3	10.7	–	–	–	–	100.0 (28)	85.7	14.3	–	–	–	–	100.0 (14)
All	18.0	13.1	20.0	38.2	3.5	7.4	100.0 (283)	54.6	29.5	8.2	6.6	1.1	–	100.0 (183)

In contrast, the occupational structure of the Bhotia men engaged only in the primary occupations has been highly distributed among various activities and towards modern activities where they are not found to engage in business activities. However, the government service occupies the top list with 43.9 per cent followed by farming (20.0%) and working as vehicle drivers (17.3%). What is unique to them is it that 13.7 per cent of the Bhotia men have taken up the work of woollens as the main activity which, in fact, has been their traditional economic activity and it is generally pursued by all the Bhotia households even if they have scaled up to any height of economic status. They have also somewhat diversified to private services and contractor but it is also seen that a small fraction (3.9%) works as labour also.

Thus, Bhotia people have taken advantage of the government's policy of job reservation and their own level of education to get high share in the government jobs and thus the agriculture has been left to others in the family. Generally they do not accept business as the primary occupation alone although they originally belonged to business class. Therefore, Bhotia has diversified and taken advantage of the diversification in the economy. On the other hand, the Raji men mainly abstain from agriculture and engage only as labourers or petty work of wood cutting etc. A comparison of the women of the two tribes engaged only in any primary occupation reveals that the diversification of the Bhotia women has been more because of their engagement in the woollen works (76.9%). The rest is filled by farming activities (16.0%) or the government jobs (7.1%). The position of the Raji women has been not so forward looking as they work mainly as farmers (85.7%) or work as labourers (14.3%). Thus, Raji men do not primarily engage in agricultural pursuit which is left to women in the family. Bhotia women have also shifted their priorities towards the government jobs. With regard to farming, it can also be added that it has not been the mainstay for Bhotia. Rather they seem to have diversified towards the service sector activities besides their traditional manufacturing business of woollens[3].

We can now get estimates of the income earned by the members engaged in the various types of the primary occupation (Table 2.6). That these are indicative income ranges because the people generally avoid telling exact income ranges and most of the times they prefer to give only underestimated income just as a precautionary measure from their sides. Still, we can take these income estimates to reflect the pattern of differences that would have prevailed among them. It is found that as usual, the Raji people, both males and females remain confined to the lowest income ranges which might be termed as the bare subsistence levels and this is matched with the types of occupations, being low paid and casual, where they were engaged. Bhotia men seem to be definitely far better as generally they seem to be well off and mostly in the middle income ranges and they have spread to high income ranges. Even female workers engaged exclusively in some primary occupation only seem to earn better than the Raji men or women although they also remain confined to the lowest income levels. Thus, whereas the Bhotia households are making vertical economic movements in terms of the profession and the consequent income earnings, the Raji households still seem to remain trapped in low income ranges just to somehow manage their survivals.[4]

(B) Members engaged in secondary occupation only

According to SEEDS (2006),

> Though tribal economy is mostly depending upon farming, these tribals over generations inherited their traditional art. This art is still continuing despite all odds faced by these tribal households. This chapter mainly brings out with various types of handicrafts made by these tribals in different states and in different districts and problems faced by these households. Craftsmen produce a variety of utilitarian items using natural material like cane and bamboo. Not only these materials, readily available, they are also easy to work with and hardly require the use of specialized tools or equipment. (p. S-4)

Now we analyze the secondary occupations of the Bhotia and Raji tribes. As made clear earlier, the secondary occupation is one with which people get engaged as a source of some supplementary income; earning while taking it as pastime; or taking it as a stop gap arrangements and these activities may fetch cash income or not. Such activities are helpful in managing the household having economic implications and such activities have been thus estimated in monetary terms to the best possible extent although these may not be sufficiently close to market valuations for so many reasons. We can find that the income earned through the secondary occupations has been far lower than those from the primary occupations (Table 2.7). Activities under the secondary occupations get confined to few and generally the traditional activities or the household activities like woollen and animal husbandry for the Bhotia men and women while it has been wood & forest, labour, and animal husbandry in the case of the Raji people. Interestingly the reported activities are such that which have been their old traditional activities. It is found that 65.3 per cent of the Bhotia men engaged in the secondary occupations alone and 89.9 per cent of the Bhotia women engaged in the secondary occupations alone were found to be associated with the woollen activities through which they manufacture many useful items like sweaters, *loi*, *punkhi*, blankets, carpets and other such items through the hands or handlooms[5]. Similarly, 22.2 per cent of the Raji men and 60.0 per cent of the Raji women were found to take upon the wood & forest products as the secondary occupations showing that they depended on the forest a lot for their subsistence and survival[6]. However, since the forest products are not sufficient for them, the Raji men (77.8%) and Raji women (20.0%) also casually take upon the work as labourers in hours of need in their local surroundings.

Table 2.7: Members Engaged in Secondary Occupation Only (%)

Tribe	Male						Female					
	Woolen	Animal Husbandry	Labour	Wood & Forest	Contractor	Total	Woolen	Animal Husbandry	Labour	Wood & Forest	Contractor	Total
Bhotia	85.3	5.9	8.8	–	–	100.0 (34)	89.9	10.1	–	–	–	100.0 (69)
Raji	–	–	77.8	22.2	–	100.0 (18)	–	20.0	20.0	60.0	–	100.0 (10)
All	85.3	3.8	32.7	7.7	–	100.0 (52)	78.5	11.4	2.5	7.6	–	100.0 (79)

Table 2.8: Average Monthly Earning of Members Engaged in Only Secondary Occupation (%)

Tribe	Male					Female				
	< 400	401-800	801-1200	>1200	Total	< 400	401-800	801-1200	>1200	Total
Bhotia	23.5	17.6	11.8	47.1	100.0 (34)	30.4	24.6	15.9	29.0	100.0 (69)
Raji	16.7	44.4	27.8	11.1	100.0 (18)	70.0	20.0	10.0	–	100.0 (10)
All	21.2	26.9	17.3	34.6	100.0 (52)	35.4	24.1	15.2	25.3	100.0 (79)

Earnings from the secondary occupations have not been substantial. But definitely it could have much marginal significance for women, old-aged and poor households. Now, the differences in the earnings of the two tribes and their men and women are quite evident that could be attributed to mainly the nature of activities they selected in their given circumstances (Table 2.8). It is clearly discernible that a large ratio of the Bhotia men (47.1%) and women (29.0%) joined the top income group of more than Rs 1200 a month from the secondary occupations. However, not even a single Raji woman could join that group and the Raji men were only 11 per cent in that category. Otherwise, majority of the Raji men and women remained confined to the lowest income groups. Thus, to raise the earnings of the tribes, their occupational shift from the traditional and low productivity activities to modern and high productivity occupations becomes indispensable that may also require capacity to invest for which state support can play important role.

(C) Members engaged in both primary and secondary occupations

It has already been noted above that Bhotia people are generally engaged less in both the occupations, primary and secondary, as compared to Raji people in the Pithoragarh district of Uttaranchal. Pattern of occupations of such people shows that it is not much in the formal and modern sector activities. As could be seen from Table 2.9 that like earlier, here also the Bhotia men have largely diversified occupational structure in case of the primary occupation where farming seems to dominate (40.3%) followed by the woollen works (21.0%) and the government service (16.1%). In the remaining, they are occupied in the business, pension, labourers, private service, etc. Unlike this diversification, the Bhotia women remain stuck with the woollen work (72.7%) and the farming (27.3%). However, in the case of the Raji men and women they were mainly engaged in the farming and then only as casual labourers. Thus, the diversification was found lacking in the case of Raji tribe and their occupations remained localized. Moreover these occupations were not found to be economically much assuring. Such things get prominently reflected in the form of income levels.

It is found again that the Raji people remained contented with the lowest earnings that could not be always in cash as the values derived here are even for the items which were for self consumption as well. Both males and females remained confined to the lowest income group of less that Rs. 1000 a month 86.4 per cent men and all the women) while another 15.6 per cent men were confined to another slightly higher, but not much different, income group of Rs. 1000-2000. Again, the Bhotia people seem to be better off as majority had joined higher income groups than the Raji counterparts although in a large segment they also needed improvements in their incomes as around 40 per cent Bhotia men remained in the income groups of up to Rs. 2000 a month and their women were having larger share of up to two-thirds.

Table 2.9: Nature of Primary Occupation of those Engaged in Both Primary & Secondary Occupation

Tribe	Male									Female								
	Farming	Business	Woolen Work	Labour	Contr-actor	Govt. Service	Private Service	Pension	Total	Farming	Business	Woolen Work	Labour	Contr-actor	Govt. Service	Private Service	Pension	Total
Bhotia	40.3	6.5	21.0	4.8	1.6	16.1	3.2	6.5	**100.0** (62)	27.3	–	72.7	–	–	–	–	–	**100.0** (22)
Raji	72.7	–	–	27.3	–	–	–	–	**100.0** (22)	87.5	–	–	12.5	–	–	–	–	**100.0** (16)
All	48.8	4.8	15.5	10.7	1.2	11.9	2.4	4.8	**100.0 (84)**	52.6	–	42.1	5.3	–	–	–	–	**100.0 (38)**

Table 2.10: Monthly Earnings from Primary Occupation of Members Engaged in Both Occupations (%)

Tribe	Male							Female						
	< 1000	1001-2000	2001-4000	4001-8000	8001-12000	> 12000	Total	< 1000	1001-2000	2001-4000	4001-8000	8001-12000	> 12000	Total
Bhotia	19.4	21.0	27.4	19.4	11.3	1.6	100.0 (62)	45.5	22.7	22.7	4.5	4.5	–	100.0 (22)
Raji	86.4	13.6	–	–	–	–	100.0 (22)	100.0	–	–	–	–	–	100.0 (16)
All	36.9	19.0	20.2	14.3	8.3	1.2	100.0 (84)	68.4	13.2	13.2	2.6	2.6	–	100.0 (38)

It is noteworthy that the Bhotia men who were engaged only in the primary occupation were better placed as their income levels were found to be higher as could be compared with Table 2.6 where relatively lower proportion of the Bhotia men remained in the lowest income groups. On the other hand, for others, that is Raji men and women or even Bhotia women, situation was not found to be much different in both the situations.

Now looking at the activities of the people engaged in the secondary occupation, it is found that as usual the Bhotia men and women have diversified economic activities. Interestingly, even the Raji men and women seemingly have more diversified economic activities that earlier. However, what remains to be underlined is it that men and women of Bhotia or the Raji tribes have been engaging in the traditional activities which are not much rewarding. Rather it seems that they were inclined towards such secondary activities only generally out of distress and in highly distressing situations because these are such activities where they could associate themselves at any time without prior planning and without much additional economic investments. However, economic gains from associating with such activities, cash or kind, could be that as usual the Bhotia people have higher income earnings even from the secondary occupations. Raji people again remained restricted to the lowest income groups showing their low capacity to get earnings from the traditional activities.

Land Holding and Farming by the Tribes

There have been much economic changes noticed among the tribal people of Uttarakhand. Still, agriculture continues to dominate the scenario for the reasons that when they don't have any alternative and better opportunity, they may fall back on it and related activities like the animal husbandry. Besides, in a rural economy, it is well known that the agricultural land holding is an important economic security by virtue of being a production asset. Given this, we can analyze the land holdings and the likely production. We first take upon the pattern of land holding by the respondent households of the two tribes (Table 2.11). It is found that the landless respondents are more among the Bhotia as compared to the Raji because 38.6 per cent of the former were without any farm land unlike only 2.2 per cent among the latter. This also shows that the Raji people are almost fully dependent on the farming for subsistence whereas the Bhotia have better alternatives as is evident from the earlier analysis. What is really more interesting here is the fact that the Raji people on an average seemingly possessed more land than the Bhotia respondents. Thus, the Raji tribe has better access over the land resources. But it would be really deceptive if we take it to be final word because there are many more things that need to be taken care of.

Table 2.11: Pattern of Land Holdings

Land size (in *nali*)	Bhotia		Raji		All	
	Number of Holdings	%	Number of Holdings	%	Number of Holdings	%
Nil	110	38.6	1	2.2	111	33.6
<5	78	27.4	20	44.4	98	29.7
5-10	47	16.5	15	33.3	62	18.8
10-20	30	10.5	5	11.1	35	10.6
20-50	18	6.3	3	6.7	21	6.4
>50	2	0.7	1	2.2	3	0.9
Total	285	100.0	45	100.0	330	100.0

Table 2.12: Status of Irrigation and Cropping Intensity of the Farm Land

Tribe	Land Size	Number of Holdings	Whether Irrigated		Area Sown more than Once	
			Yes	No	Yes	No
Bhotia	< 5	78	35.9	64.1	47.4	52.6
	5-10	47	14.9	85.1	25.5	74.5
	10-20	30	100.0	0.0	33.3	66.7
	20-50	18	61.1	38.9	50.0	50.0
	>50	2	–	100.0	–	100.0
	Total	175	37.7	62.3	38.9	61.1
Raji	< 5	20	15.0	85.0	25.0	75.0
	5-10	15	13.3	86.7	20.0	80.0
	10-20	5	20.0	80.0	60.0	40.0
	20-50	3	–	100.0	–	100.0
	>50	1	100.0	–	–	100.0
	Total	44	15.9	84.1	25.0	75.0
All	< 5	98	21.4	78.6	42.9	57.1
	5-10	62	14.5	85.5	24.2	75.8
	10-20	35	88.6	11.4	37.1	62.9
	20-50	21	52.4	47.6	42.9	57.1
	>50	3	33.3	66.7	–	100.0
	Total	219	33.3	66.7	36.1	63.9

Looking into the qualitative dimensions of the land use, Table 2.12 reveals that the Raji respondents are found lagging behind the Bhotia respondents. Status of irrigation on Bhotia farmland is much better than on the farmland of the Raji people. Among all the Bhotia respondents' landholdings, it is found that in 37.7 per cent cases the land was reportedly irrigated whereas this ratio has been far lower at just 15.9 per cent. Similarly, we can take up the case of cropping intensity which mainly depends upon the enterprising skills of the farmers and resource endowments with them that might involve cash expenditures along with the capital stock for this purpose. High degree of cropping intensity, thus, suggests modernization of the farming operations. It is found that in more than 38 per cent instances the Bhotia respondents having farmlands reported that they had crops more than once in year on their lands whereas the ratio was lower at only 25 per cent in the case of the Raji respondents. Although there has not been any specific trend to be observed with regard to size of landholdings and cropping intensity, still one could find that it is high at the lowest size of the landholdings or at the big sizes. Higher cropping intensity at the lower side might be attributed to subsistence farming whereas towards the big landholdings could be attributed to the capacity of the farmers to manage it relatively more effectively. It could be found that despite having better size of landholdings, the Raji farmers have not been better off in terms of better farming operations.

Table 2.13: Nature of Crops Grown on Cultivated Area by the Farmers (%)

Tribe	Rice & Wheat	Coarse Cereals	Pulses	Vegetables	Fruits	Fodder	Total
Bhotia	72 (24.7)	40 (13.7)	35 (12.0)	135 (46.4)	3 (1.0)	6 (2.1)	291 (100.0)
Raji	41 (73.2)	10 (17.9)	1 (1.8)	4 (7.1)	–	–	56 (100.0)
All	113 (32.6)	50 (14.4)	36 (10.4)	139 (40.1)	3 (0.9)	6 (1.7)	347 (100.0)

Better farming operations evident for the Bhotia respondents get further support from Tables 2.13, 2.14 and 2.15. Progressive farming is one which is not only modernized in terms of production structure, rather one where there is diversification from mainly the traditional crops for subsistence towards fruits and vegetables etc. Table 2.13 brings out that the farming of the Bhotia tribe has been well diversified unlike that of the Raji respondents. The latter mainly depended on the cultivation of cereal crops (91%) while the remaining was mainly the vegetables (7.1%) and pulses (1.8%). Due to better farm strategy, Bhotia farmers preferred the vegetables the most (46.4%) followed with sufficient gaps by wheat and rice (24.7%), course cereals (13.7%) and pulses (12%). Better and efficient farm strategies also get reflected through better output. It is quite revealing that despite having larger farmlands, Raji respondents seem to suffer due to lower farm productivity and poor returns. We have derived that the Bhotia farmers have shown better farm productivity as is seen from Table 2.14 where it is mentioned that the ratio of the Bhotia farmers demonstrating higher crop and vegetables & fruits outputs has been significantly higher than what has been the case with the Raji farmers who generally remained confined towards the lower size outputs. This definitely gets translated into the monetary value that has been an approximation of the estimates based on the prevailing market prices.[7]

Table 2.14: Quantity of Agricultural Output (in quintals)

Tribe	Crop Output					Vegetable Output				
	<1	1-5	5-10	>10	Total	<1	1-5	5-10	>10	Total
Bhotia	47 (31.8)	64 (43.2)	15 (10.1)	22 (14.9)	148 (100.0)	58 (53.7)	36 (33.3)	8 (7.4)	6 (5.6)	108 (100.0)
Raji	7 (16.3)	29 (67.4)	4 (9.3)	3 (7.0)	43 (100.0)	26 (96.3)	1 (3.7)	–	–	27 (100.0)
All	54 (28.3)	93 (48.7)	19 (9.9)	25 (13.1)	191 (100.0)	84 (62.2)	37 (27.4)	8 (5.9)	6 (4.4)	135 (100.0)

Note: Figures in parentheses show per cent distribution.

Table 2.15: Total Value of Agriculture Output (Rs.)

Tribe	<2000	2000-5000	5000-10000	10000-20000	>20000	Total
Bhotia	30 (17.1)	47 (26.9)	33 (18.9)	40 (22.9)	25 (14.3)	175 (100.0)
Raji	9 (20.9)	22 (51.2)	10 (23.3)	2 (4.6)	–	43 (100.0)
Total	39 (17.9)	69 (31.7)	43 (19.7)	42 (19.3)	25 (11.5)	218 (100.0)

Note: Figures in parentheses show per cent distribution.

What has been a further source of farm disparities between the two tribes are the still poorer returns if estimated in monetary terms. It is because the Raji people undertake cultivations for the crops which had lower value additions unlike the Bhotia people who preferred crops and vegetables having better market prices. This is the reason the lower side concentration of the farm output in monetary terms has been still larger as compared to the size of outputs in volume terms. In fact, this also paves the way for deriving the inference that the Raji people generally undertake farm operation with the subsistence as main guiding force whereas the Bhotia undertake the farming for remunerative returns as well. But, if some help could be extended to the Raji people for improving and diversifying their farming, they can also turn this profession into a more rewarding one.

Respondents' Desire to Change the Profession

Generally, a person would like to change her/his profession for two broad reasons. One, if a person is engaged in low paid profession, (s)he will like to improve the economic status and avail the better opportunity that (s)he finds around. Second, the person is more ambitious and would like to switchover to still better economic opportunities. In either circumstances, the person needs to have awareness and motivation to improve the economic status by availing the better opportunities which are found in the close vicinities or which are in the reach that may sometimes require some helping hand. A careful analysis in this regard would reveal that such a tendency is visible among the tribes under study. There are many noteworthy features in this regard that can be derived from Table 2.16. It shows desire to change the existing profession and this has been done for various income – groups respondents. Interestingly, Raji respondents have shown greater inclination for change in the existing profession (37.8%) than demonstrated by the Bhotia respondents (30.2%). This at the outset hints that the Raji people were getting conscious about their poor state of affairs and they wished to get it changed by using the opportunities available, which in fact would have induced them to think so. However, majority of the Bhotia respondents refused to change the existing profession (48.4%) or they felt that there was no need for this (8.8%). But among the Raji respondents there was no large ratio disapproving the change of the existing profession. Thus, the Bhotia people were satisfied with the existing profession and their act can be justified as it has already been established that they have been relatively more progressive and well off besides being educated and professionally highly diversified. Unlike this, lack of such categorical denial to change the profession can be attributed to their low level traps and their lack of awareness and illiteracy could be held responsible in a cumulative manner.

Table 2.16: Respondents' Preference to Change the Existing Profession

Tribe	Income Group (Rs.)	Yes	No	No need	Can't say	Total
Bhotia	< 12000	28.9	55.6	2.2	13.3	100.0 (32)
	12000-36000	41.6	41.6	3.4	13.5	100.0 (96)
	36000-60000	33.3	50.0	4.2	12.5	100.0 (45)
	>60000	19.4	50.5	18.4	11.7	100.0 (97)
	Total	30.2	48.4	8.8	12.6	100.0 (270)
Raji	< 12000	32.4	17.6	5.9	44.1	100.0 (29)
	12000-36000	54.5	36.4	9.1	–	100.0 (10)
	Total	37.8	22.2	6.7	33.3	100.0 (39)
All	< 12000	30.4	39.2	3.8	26.6	100.0 (61)
	12000-36000	43.0	41.0	4.0	12.0	100.0 (106)
	36000-60000	33.3	50.0	4.2	12.5	100.0 (45)
	>60000	19.4	50.5	18.4	11.7	100.0 (97)
	Grand Total	31.2	44.8	8.5	15.5	100.0 (309)

Now, an analysis in terms of effect of income level on the change in the existing profession shows results as per expectation during the stage of economic development. It can be seen here that among the Raji, low income respondents showed low tendency to shift their profession whereas the higher income people showed significantly higher inclination to change. Among the Bhotia respondents, higher variations in income groups have been noted. As far as effect of income level on inclination to change the profession is seen, we find that the lowest income group respondents and the highest income group respondents have shown the least inclination to change the profession as their respective shares have been 28.9 and 19.4 per cent. Moreover, these income groups have shown the highest disapproval for the change. However, the difference in the behaviour of these two groups needs to be interpreted carefully. It is because the lowest income has shown still greater inclination towards the change basically due to their urge to improve their economic lots while others in the society and the community are doing better in other professions. The highest income groups felt little need to change from the existing activities as they were happy from the current profession that has been more rewarding in the given circumstances. These arguments get confirmed as the highest income group respondents have shown the maximum disapproval for the changes whereas this has been still lower in the case of the lowest income group Bhotia respondents. Given this, it is easier to derive that the middle income Bhotia respondents have been the most interested group in this tribe to change the existing profession as they have moved to some extent in terms of achievements which has further induced them to look for better opportunities. As far as the difference in the behaviour between the two tribes in terms of desire to change the profession is concerned, qualitatively the Bhotia have been better due to their higher economic achievements and social development. Just as an indicator, we can look at the degree of indecisiveness in the two tribes and it is found that it has been much higher among the Raji people whereas it has been there among the Bhotia as well but in lower proportions.

Furthermore, the causes of desire for change in the existing profession by the two tribes (Table 2.17) show that the Raji respondents were guided mainly by the economic considerations of raising their economic levels through better employment opportunities or simply for economic reasons. On the contrary, the Bhotia respondents were guided by other reasons as well and these were loss in the existing professions (24.8%) and for better life style, which is living standard. In fact, this narration of the loss should be read not simply the loss, but their way of estimation as they found that they could have earned better elsewhere given their competence and efforts. Thus, the Bhotia had shown somewhat broader reasons for the change as they were already ahead of the Raji people in terms of economic and social attainments. But still the attitudes of the Raji respondents have shown their desire to improve their economic and social lots but which are still at early stages.

Table 2.17: Reasons for Desire to Change the Profession

Tribe	Income Group (Rs.)	For Better Employment	To Increase Income	For Better Life Style	Loss in Existing Profession	For Higher Position in Society	Total
Bhotia	< 12000	11.8	29.4	17.6	29.4	11.8	100.0 (17)
	12000-36000	17.6	37.3	11.8	25.5	7.8	100.0 (51)
	36000-60000	21.1	47.4	10.5	10.5	10.5	100.0 (19)
	>60000	13.6	31.8	18.2	31.8	4.5	100.0 (22)
	Total	16.5	36.7	13.8	24.8	8.3	100.0 (109)
Raji	< 12000	7.1	71.4	7.1	–	14.3	100.0 (14)
	12000-36000	14.3	71.4	14.3	–	–	100.0 (7)
	Total	9.5	71.4	9.5	–	9.5	100.0 (21)
All	< 12000	9.8	48.4	12.9	16.1	12.9	100.0 (31)
	12000-36000	17.2	41.4	12.1	22.4	6.9	100.0 (58)
	36000-60000	21.1	47.4	10.5	10.5	10.5	100.0 (19)
	>60000	13.6	31.8	18.2	31.8	4.5	100.0 (22)
	Grand Total	15.4	42.3	13.1	20.8	8.5	100.0 (130)

Conclusion

Analysis has been done so as to establish the fact that the Bhotia people have been far better than the Raji respondents. There has been more occupational diversification among the Bhotia people as compared to the Raji who have been confined to traditional low paid works like the farming, forest products and wood, labourers etc whereas the Bhotia respondents have been engaged more towards modern occupations like the government service, private service, farming and their traditional work like woollens etc. The latter have been earning much higher than the Raji people who generally remained confined to their villages and the vicinity of their villages. A comparative analysis of the farming operations shows that in terms of the land holdings, the position of the Raji seems to be better. Still, due to better farm operations and use of better farm strategies, the farm diversification has been undertaken efficiently by the Bhotia where the productivity and returns have been much higher. Moreover, the cropping intensity has been higher on Bhotia landholdings than that of the Raji. But, it also needs to be emphasized that the Raji respondents have also been now learning the need for opportunities and it is for this reason that there is a significant proportions among them who would like to change their professions for better economic returns for better and improved lifestyle given the availability of opportunities in the surroundings which could have been due to some demonstration effect. Although, Bhotia people have also expressed their desire to change the professions, but they have lower proportions as the better-off people would not like to change the existing profession. On the whole, Bhotia tribe of Uttarakhand is economically better off and more progressive. However, if the lagging Raji tribe is offered some sustained support, they can also move forward gradually.

NOTES

1 *Comparative Analysis of Socio-economic and Demographic Features Among the Tribes of Uttaranchal: A Study of the Bhotia and Raji Tribes of Pithoragarh District;* Report Submitted to the Indian Council of Social Science Research (ICSSR), New Delhi (India), 2007.

2 It has been well Presented by a Thorough Empirical Studies by Meenakshi et al (2000) that "Poverty Rates are Uniformly Higher for the SC and ST Communities, Irrespective of the Deprivation Measure used." Furthermore, "Relative Deprivation Among SC and ST Communities is seen to be much Greater when the Adjusted Head Count Ratios are Used as Compared to that Indicated by the Usual HCR based on the OPL". (p. 2754)

3 G S Mehta (1999) Observes that "Prominent Among the Various Household-based Manufacturing Activities are the Wool and Wool Related Activities Functioning in the Middle and High Mountainous and Hill Areas of Uttarakhand" (p. 88).

"However, it has been well realised that the Development of Woollen Activities is taking Place at much below the Level of Expectations. Several Factors have been Reported Behind the Unsatisfactory Progress of these Activities by Various Institutions which are Engaged in Woollen Work in Uttarakhand." (pp. 88-89)

4 It is brought out by Jena (2008) that "when Women earn Better, the Household Spends more on Food and Health Needs. Meleka Daiamma, 50, says 'we Buy Eggs, have Beefs ... and Pig Meat when we Earn'. 'We add Goats to our Herds' adds Tulasi, the SHG President...Another Indicator of Improved well-being ... owing to Increased Earning of Women is that from the 54 Households Only Two Elderly Persons are Listed for the Government's Emergency Feeding Scheme at the Anganwadi Centre." (p. 19)

5 It has been Observed by SEEDS (2006) that 'Uttaranchal Besides Spiritual and Cultural Heredity is Traditionally well known for its Artistic Tribal Crafts. The Age Old Woolen Carpets, Woolen Items due to Climatic Need Continue to be Dominant in all the Districts of Uttaranchal but Predominantly in the Districts of Pithoragarh, Chamoli, Uttarkashi. This is inhabited by 5 Categories of Tribes but the Maximum Number of Tribal Community Belongs to "Bhotias". Living in Highly Hilly Regions of these Districts. The Hand Knitted Carpets of Various Sizes, Shawls are being Prepared by Ten Thousand Artisans in these Areas. They Roughly Produce Woolens Worth Rs. 5 crores annually'. (p. 39)

6 The Raji Men Seem to Climb the Big Long Trees as if they are moving on the Elevators so is their Proximity and Deftness with the Forest and such Products are then sold by the Raji Women in the Market to Fetch the Household Essentials in Return. This one can see even today.

7 Meenakshi et al (2000) have Concluded in a Study on Poverty Among the SC, ST and Female Headed Households that "Poverty is a Multifaceted Phenomenon, a fact Highlighted by the Lack of an Economically meaningful one-to-one Correspondence Between Education and Landholding Size on the One Hand, and Conventional Measures of Poverty on the Other. There is need for more Research on which Indicators are best able to Identify the Food-insecure." (p. 2754)

REFERENCES

Agarwal, Manoj Kumar and Sameera Maiti (2005): 'A Study of Demographic Structure and Fertility Among the Bhotia Tribe of Uttaranchal (India)'; *Demography India;* Vol. 34(1); January-June.

Bailey, F. (1960): *Tribe, Caste and Nation;* Manchester University Press, Manchester.

Bateille, Andre (1974): 'Tribes and Peasantry' in *Six Essays on Contemporary Sociology;* Oxford University Press, Delhi.

EPW (2007): 'Forests and Tribals – Restoring Rights'; *Economic and Political Weekly;* XLII (1); January 6; 4-5.

Government of India (2006): *The Scheduled Tribes and Other Traditional Forest Dwellers (Recognition of Forest Rights) Act, 2006;* Ministry of Law and Justice, New Delhi.

Jena, Manipadma (2008): 'Food Insecurity Among Tribal Communities of Orissa'; *Economic and Political Weekly;* XLIII (6); February 9; 18-21.

Maiti, Sameera and Manoj Kumar Agarwal (2007): 'Demographic Analysis of a Small Community with Reference to Fertility Trends: The Karen of Andaman Islands (India); *Journal of the Indian Anthropological Society;* 42 (1); January - April.

Maiti, Sameera and Manoj Kumar Agarwal (2007): 'The Tolcha Bhotia of Uttaranchal: A Demographic Study with Special Reference to Mortality'; in K.K.N. Sharma (ed), *Reproductive and Child Health Problems in India;* Academic Excellence, Delhi.

Meenakshi, J V, Ranjan Ray and Souvik Gupta (2000): 'Estimates of Poverty for SC, ST and Female-Headed Households' *Economic and Political Weekly;* XXXV (31); July 29; 2746-2754.

Mehta, G S (1999): *Development of Uttarakhand: Issues and Perspectives*; APH Publishing Corporation, New Delhi.

Naswa, Samedha (2001): *Tribes of Uttar Pradesh and Uttaranchal*; Mittal Publications, New Delhi.

Pathy, Suguna (2003): 'Destitution, Deprivation and Tribal 'Development'; *Economic and Political Weekly*; XXXVIII (27); July 5; 2832-2836.

Pokharia, D. (2000): 'Sociological and Linguistic Study of the Raji Tribe of the Kumaon Himalaya'; Annual Report 1999-2000 of the UGC Sponsored Major Research Project; Kumaon University, Almora Campus; (Unpublished).

Saksena, H.S. *et al.* (1998): *Perspectives in Tribal Development – Focus on Uttar Pradesh*; Bharat Book Center, Lucknow.

Socio Economic and Educational Development Society (SEEDS) (2006): *Status Study of Tribal Handicrafts – An Option for Livelihood of Tribal Community in the States of Rajasthan, Uttaranchal, Chhattisgarh and Arunachal Pradesh*; Report submitted to the Planning Commission of India, New Delhi.

Socio Economic and Educational Development Society (SEEDS) (2007): *Research Study on Livelihood Options, Asset Creation out of Special Component Plan (SCP) & Tribal Sub Plan (TSP) Schemes and its Impact Among SCs and STs in India*; Report Submitted to the Planning Commission of India, New Delhi.

3 Financing Human Development and Poverty Alleviation, Housing, Social Welfare in Tamilnadu *An Assessment*

Dr. K. Sambasivam

ABSTRACT

Besides the two major sectors of education and health, human development also depends on basic social infrastructure like shelter and water, while the overarching consideration is the extent of poverty that shuts off the poor from the benefits of all improvement opportunities – including those provided free – that require even small amounts of complementary private expenditure. Mainstream poverty alleviation programmes address some dimensions of poverty; in particular those arising from lack of employment opportunities, but these have to be supplemented by other welfare programmes targeted at specific groups of beneficiaries such as the old and the infirm, destitute, widows who cannot support themselves, particular groups of underprivileged citizens, and the disabled. In general, there can be a vicious cycle of poverty and low human development, each reinforcing the other. Even considering the narrow area of public finances, a high level of poverty usually implies large expenditure obligations but a small resource base.

Introduction

Besides the two major sectors of education and health, human development also depends on basic social infrastructure like shelter and water, while the overarching consideration is the extent of poverty that shuts off the poor from the benefits of all improvement opportunities – including those provided free – that require even small amounts of complementary private expenditure. Mainstream poverty alleviation programmes address some dimensions of poverty; in particular those arising from lack of employment opportunities, but these have to be supplemented by other welfare programmes targeted at specific groups of beneficiaries such as the old and the infirm, destitute, widows who cannot support themselves, particular groups of underprivileged citizens, and the disabled. In general, there can be a vicious cycle of poverty and low human development, each reinforcing the other. Even considering the narrow area of public finances, a high level of poverty usually implies large expenditure obligations but a small resource base. Tamilnadu does not have such a debilitating level of poverty, which is below that for the country as a whole, and half that of the highest level estimated for any individual state. As such, the state can, in some sense, afford to attack the problem of poverty (in all its aspects) more vigorously than some other states. As a matter of fact, Tamilnadu does incur substantial expenditure on poverty alleviation under social sector heads and rural development that complements central government expenditures for poverty alleviation through the state budget as well as outside the state budget through local bodies, nongovernmental organisations and special organisations like, societies and boards. There are also direct interventions under other economic categories like agriculture and industry in the form of subsidies or incentives. Though the entire public expenditures are intended to benefit the poor in one form or the other, some direct interventions for poverty alleviation are through expenditure under rural development and social welfare heads. Of the total expenditure on social services, expenditure on social welfare, labour welfare, rural housing, social security and welfare, and rural development are some of the heads of expenditure incurred by the government specifically towards people below poverty line and special groups.

Poverty Alleviation and Rural Development

Poverty is generally defined as the state or condition of having little or no money, goods, or means of support; condition of being poor; indigence. Synonyms are penury, destitution, need, want; these words imply a state of deprivation and lack of necessities. Poverty denotes a serious lack of the means for a proper existence. Thus, poverty is an economic condition, and is, to some extent, relative to the prevalent levels of general prosperity. Poverty line is a minimum income level used as an official standard for determining the proportion of population living in poverty. The present official poverty line is based only on calories and hence accounts for little else but the satiation of one's hunger. This, in actual practice, provides a large scope for programmes other than the official poverty alleviation programmes. Of course, at least some of the centrally sponsored programmes in this area are proposed to be based on multi indicator surveys, but the official poverty statistics continue to be based on a poverty line defined largely on the basis of a minimum calorie intake. In 2004, the official poverty lines were Rs. 368 and Rs. 559 per person per month for rural and urban areas. However, it should be clear that the actual number of poor can be far larger than official estimates. There has been a lively debate on the methodology of estimating poverty and the resultant poverty estimates. Even official estimates are not always strictly comparable with each other because of different methodologies followed in both collection and estimation of data. Keeping this in view, we restrict our estimations of resource requirement for poverty alleviation to two alternatives – one taking the official estimates of 1999-2000 as the basis, and the other based on the extent of poverty in Tamilnadu worked out by us on the basis of NSSO data (60thRound – thin sample). Under rural development, major expenditures on poverty alleviation can be classified into wage-employment generating, self-employment generating and rural infrastructure creating schemes. *Sampoorna Grameena Rojgar Yojana, Swarnjayanti Gram Swarojgar Yojana, Indira Awas Yojana,* Drought Prone Area Programme, Desert Development Programmes and Augmented Rural Water Supply Programme are the prominent poverty alleviation programmes. Central transfers under these schemes are directly made to local bodies (*panchayats*/DRDA). Allocations made by the centre are now being transferred to local bodies directly since 1990-91 outside the state budget. Therefore, even as the state government incurs some expenditure on poverty alleviation, just looking at any states expenditure does not convey the entire picture.

The entire expenditure on poverty alleviation including that on social welfare as classified into various categories, such as, direct poverty alleviation (rural development) and other social service sectors like social welfare, rural housing is given in table 4.1. Per capita expenditure on poverty alleviation including welfare programes increased from Rs. 153 in 1990-91 to Rs. 370 in 1998-99 (not reported in the table); subsequently, it rose to Rs. 695 in 2004-05 and dropped a little to Rs. 529 in 2005-06. In real terms, there was little increase in the 1990s, while there has been some increase after that. The composition of this category of expenditures has changed over time; although rural development expenditures within this category outstripped social sector expenditures in the nineties, it reversed subsequently and the latter far outstripped the poverty alleviation expenditures by 2005-06. This could have happened partly because some of the poverty alleviation expenditures are not fully accounted for, being outside the budget (although we have included in the table such expenditures on the major schemes) and also because the reduction in poverty was substantial in terms of the official Planning Commission estimates. In contrast, expenditure on social services has increased since the pressure to expand coverage of social services usually increases as soon as the urgency of immediate relief from poverty diminishes; demand for basic services like education, health, and water supply are likely to increase with reduction in income poverty and deprivation in terms of food and shelter.

SGRY was one of the main programmes in poverty alleviation and constituted a major share of the total expenditure on poverty alleviation in a district. A similar pattern obtains for the state as a whole. Of the total expenditure on direct poverty alleviation programmes, wage employment programmes like SGRY and *Food for Work* constituted around 56 per cent in 2003-04 and 40 per cent in 2004-05. If one includes MPLAD and MLACDS, the percentage goes up substantially. Of all these, SGRY is the major programme for alleviating poverty through wage employment. In what follows, we concentrate on SGRY as the main scheme for poverty alleviation. Rural development expenditure under the centrally sponsored scheme, this scheme is a centrally sponsored wage employment generating programme with states sharing 25 per cent of cash expenditure. Wages under this programme are paid in cash and kind. The minimum wage as per the provisions of the scheme in Tamilnadu during 2004-05 was Rs. 54 per day. Of this, the cash component was Rs. 25.75 and the remaining wage was paid by distributing 5 kg of rice at the price of Rs 5.65 per kg. The central government supplied the rice or wheat in addition to 75 per cent of the cash expenditure. In 2004-05, all the three tiers of rural local bodies together generated employment amounting to 5.19 crore person days with cash expenditure of Rs. 309.6 crore in addition to food grains distributed. It is clear from table 4.3B that only 43 per cent of total expenditure of Rs. 309.6 crore has gone into wages and the remaining 57 per cent is absorbed by the material used in the works that are being taken up under these schemes.

Goals Ahead and Resource Requirements

The poverty lines as defined by the Planning Commission for the state of Tamilnadu were Rs. 07.64 per capita per month in rural areas and Rs. 475.60 in urban areas during 1999-00. If we update this rural poverty line by consumer price index for agricultural commodities,23 it works out to Rs. 368 per capita per month in rural areas in 2004-05. The MDG goals specify that half the proportion of people living below poverty line should be brought above the poverty line. The 10th Plan targets to reduce poverty ratio by 5 percentage points by 2007 (this might have been achieved, going by comparable estimates of poverty relating to 1999-2000 and 2004-05 that showed a reduction in that period of above 4 percentage points) and by 15 percentage points by 2012. *Common Minimum Programme* of the coalition government at the centre has laid down strategies through which poverty ratio can be brought down. *Employment Guarantee Act* works in this direction, by guaranteeing a minimum of 100 days wage employment in a year to tackle the unemployment in lean seasons of agriculture dominated rural India.

To achieve the 10th Plan target of reducing poverty ratio by 5 percentage points from the level of 2004-05 in 2007 i.e., from 76.5 lakh to 59.72 lakh people, around 16.78 lakh of the rural population had to be additionally covered under poverty alleviation programmes in Tamilnadu. To reduce it by 15 percentage points by 2012, another 33.55 lakh rural population has to be covered. To cover an additional 16.78 lakh population assuming a household size of 4.5, additional employment of (16.78 lakh/4.5 *100) 3.73 crore person days needs to be generated. With the present employment generation at 5.17 crore person days (that is expected to lift the beneficiaries above the poverty line by the end of the Tenth Plan), the first goal is assumed to have been met by now. To meet the second goal by 2012 of reducing the poverty level by 10 percentage points, an additional employment of 2.29 crore person days at the cost of Rs. 137.16 crore is necessary. Using the present official minimum wage of Rs. 60, the additional resources required can be derived as the product of the minimum wage and the additional person days of employment to be generated. The present employment generating scheme, SGRY is creating about 5 crore person days, with only 43 per cent of cash expenditure going towards wages. Considering the poverty ratio of 2004-05, an additional (7.46-5.17) 2.29 crore person days need to be generated at a cost of Rs. 137.17 crore to achieve the second goal.

Employment generating programmes need to be strengthened and targeted more towards people below poverty line in rural areas. Since the selfemployment generating programmes are directed toward the population closer to the poverty line, wage employment generating programmes need to be directed towards the poorest of the poor. Though information on implementation of SGRY/NREGS provides the extent of person days' employment generated, one needs to look at the number of households benefited and verify their status relative to the poverty line to ensure that the benefits are adequately targeted. As per our estimates, simply maintaining the past levels of expenditures should have achieved the short-term goal already and no additional resources would have been required. To achieve the long term goal, Rs.212 crore per annum will be needed to create wage employment to the poor. In addition to this, extant programmes towards self employment, rural housing and transfer payments to the aged and destitute people need to be continued to prevent swelling the ranks of the absolute poor.

Housing and Social Welfare

Public provisioning of various amenities like drinking water, sanitation, housing, and pensions for the aged and destitute persons are contributing factors to improve the well-being and, under certain circumstances, to eliminate poverty. In this section, we consider housing and social welfare issues.

Housing

The only available source for relatively recent information on housing conditions is *Census 2001*. In Tamilnadu, of the total population, nearly one lakh households are reported as living in dilapidated houses. If this number is juxtaposed against the number of houses being provided during a year, the task of covering these one lakh households does not appear to be adifficult one.

The major programme for provisioning of housing in Tamilnadu is the centrally sponsored scheme, *Indira Awas Yojana* (IAY). In 2003-04, nearly 57,000 houses have been constructed under IAY of which 33,000 houses for scheduled caste, 210 for scheduled tribe and the remaining for other communities. The Government of India provides Rs. 20,000 for SC and ST for each house constructed and Rs 10,000 for other communities. Total expenditure on provisioning of housing in Tamilnadu in 2003-04 was Rs. 119.89 crore. Even if the same level of expenditure were continued, the remaining population without proper housing should have been covered in the next two to three years. As such, there does not seem to be any additional requirement of resources in this area for Tamilnadu. In case there still remains a backlog, these can be taken care of within the normal expenditures. The only issue would then be, identification of appropriate beneficiaries; on this we have no new insight to offer.

Social Welfare

Pensions to the aged, destitute persons, and handicapped persons, and grants-in-aid to charitable institutions are the main expenditures under social security and welfare head. Of these, pensions are important in the context of social security. The 2001 census has shown that the elderly population of India aged 60 and above had reached 77 million. Of this number, nearly 25 per cent in all states and union territories benefit from National Old Age Pension Scheme and *Annapurna* scheme. Nearly 50 per cent of the elderly are dependent on others in Tamilnadu, usually their children or younger relatives. Most of the aged population who are unable to work and have been deserted by their children are covered under five different pension schemes in Tamilnadu. They are: (i) Old Age Pension Scheme (GoI sponsored); (ii) Destitute Physically Handicapped Pension Scheme; (iii) Destitute Widow Pension Scheme; (iv) Destitute Agricultural Labourers Pension scheme; and (v) Deserted Wives Pension Scheme. The beneficiaries under these schemes are entitled to a pension of Rs. 400 per month provided they are not habitual beggars, not having a major son or have been deserted by their children, and have no means of subsistence. The Government of India now allocates Rs. 400 (revised from Rs.75 and then Rs 200 paid earlier) per beneficiary per month towards these pensions under the first scheme called National Old Age Pension Scheme and allocates food grains. However, the Government of Tamilnadu has been paying Rs. 400 (revised from Rs. 200) per beneficiary to be on par with other state government sponsored schemes even before the rates were revised by the centre. While the total number of beneficiaries is around 12 lakhs, the expenditure is around Rs. 300 crore towards direct money transfers and another Rs. 50 crore towards other benefits. The Government of Tamilnadu claims 100 per cent coverage of all the aged and destitute who qualify. Unless and until the state government further revises the rate of pension per beneficiary (note that the Government of India norm is now equal to the pensions granted by the Government of Tamilnadu), or expands coverage, additional funds should not be larger than the Rs. 300 crore that was required when the rate was half the current rate 26. However, it is generally recognised that for the elderly persons that are not supported by their family, the most important problem is often physical debilities that prevents them from undertaking even routine chores properly, something that the younger lot takes for granted. In other words, they require care and support, even when financial problems may not be as acute. This argues for establishment of homes for the elderly, of both 'paid' and 'free' variety. Such homes are apparently in short supply in the state, and the government could perhaps pay greater attention to this aspect of the care for the elderly, particularly in view of the twin facts of rising percentage of the elderly in the total population, and increasing life expectancy of those being categorised as the elderly.

Apart from the pension schemes for the aged, there are other welfare schemes for the organised and the unorganised sector. For the organised sector, the usual pension, insurance, and provident fund schemes are operated by the state government. For the unorganised sector also, there are several welfare boards that have been set up by the government. There are also survivor benefit schemes like Family Distress Relief Scheme and Accident Relief Scheme for the unorganised sector labour. In addition, there are other social welfare schemes such as marriage and maternity assistance for poor women. Most of these schemes have fairly low coverage, and the actual expenditure is small compared to the total government expenditure.

Conclusion

Poverty being a multidimensional concept, the measurement of poverty in terms of minimum nutritional requirements has been controversial ever since its inception. Even while accepting this basic premise, there are many more problems in applying this concept in a large country like India, with major differences in almost every parameter that one cares to look into between different regions. Application of the concept for actual implementation of policy to alleviate poverty naturally aggravates the related controversies, particularly when transfer of funds from one level of government to another is concerned. The official system has tried to respond to some of the critical observations, but the responses have generated further controversy. In this background, the policy tools for poverty alleviation have essentially consisted of either providing wage employment or facilitating asset ownership that could generate self-employment. For those with minimal assets, conditions were sought to be created through various schemes that would facilitate generation of a stream of earnings from those assets. Other schemes, usually with very short-term impact, included responding to the symptoms of poverty (free clothing, shelter, subsidised food etc.).

While each of these types of interventions have a place in the overall scheme of public response to the problem of poverty, sustained impact is probably the greatest on the poorest through the wage employment route, provided such employment is adequate and is available on a sustained basis for a minimum period of time. Else, its impact is temporary, and even those lifted out of poverty can relapse into poverty. The most successful schemes have been those effectively combining wage employment creation with creation of durable social assets like rural roads that actually cause an upward shift in rural incomes in general, and result in better access to other publicly provided services. It is thus not surprising that a programme like SGRY is the major thrust of poverty alleviation strategy. One important requirement for this scheme to have the desired impact, however, is full coverage of the identified poor. Otherwise, individual poor households cannot be targeted on a sustained basis; there is a likelihood that 'A' gets the benefit today and 'B' gets the benefit tomorrow and so on, with few of them getting enough out of the scheme to pull them out of poverty, and keep them out of it. In Tamilnadu, this task is now manageable, because the size of the problem that remains to be tackled has shrunk. In our estimates of resource requirements, we have tried to allow for complete coverage of the estimated poor. It should be fairly easy to build in synergy between poverty alleviation and policy interventions in other areas through the type of assets that is created. Apart from the rural roads mentioned above, other assets like drainage systems for better sanitation, and consequent improvement in health, water conservation tanks for better water availability and other environmental benefits, and construction of educational or health facilities can provide multiple benefits to the rural community.27 There is obviously a larger role for decentralisation in the choice of desirable assets to be created, apart from the identification of the beneficiaries and monitoring of actual implementation. In Tamilnadu, the success of interventions to reduce birth and death rates over a period has resulted in the phenomenon of aging of the population of the state and an increase in the dependency ratio. In this situation, it becomes important to devise interventions for the benefit of the aged, not only those who are poor, but also for those who can pay for the services. While the market can perhaps respond to the demand for the paid services, the concerned group is a vulnerable one whose welfare needs to be carefully monitored to prevent exploitation. For those who cannot pay, both financial and other kinds of help (like old age homes) are needed; the government should not consider its duty done by only providing financial assistance. Because of their vulnerability, financial assistance can easily be misappropriated.

REFERENCES

Beegle, K. (2008). 'Health Facility and School Surveys in the Indonesia Family Life Survey', in S. Amin, J. Das, and M. Goldstein (eds), *Are You Being Served? New Tools for Measuring Service Delivery*. Washington DC: Th e World Bank: pp. 343-64.

Abbas, A.A. and G.J. Walker (1986). 'Determinants of the Utilization of Maternal and Child Health Services in Jordan', *International Journal of Epidemiology*, 15(3): 404-7.

Abdelrahman, A.I. and S.P. Morgan (1987). 'Socioeconomic and Institutional Correlates of Family Formation: Khartoum, Sudan, 1945–75',*Journal of Marriage and the Family*, 49(2): 401-12.

Aghion, P. and J.G. Williamson (1998). *Growth, Inequality and Globalization:Th eory, History and Policy*. Cambridge, Cambridge University Press.

Arya, S. and A. Roy (eds) (2006). *Poverty, Gender and Migration*, New Delhi, Sage Publications.

Asian Development Bank [ADB] (2007). *Key Indicators 2007: Inequality in Asia*, Manila, ADB.

Bardhan, P.K. and T.N. Srinivasan (1974). *Poverty and Income Distribution in India*, Calcutta, Statistical Publishing Society.

Bhalla, Surjit, Singh (2002). 'Growth and Poverty in India—Myth and Reality', in Govinda Rao (ed.), *Poverty and Public Policy: Essays in Honour of Raja Chelliah* (forthcoming).

Dandekar, V.M. and N. Rath (1971). 'Poverty in India-1: Dimensions and Trends', *Economic and Political Weekly*, January: 25–146.

Dantwala, M.L. (1950). 'India's Progress in Agrarian Reforms', *Far Eastern Survey*, 19(22): 239-44.

Government of India [GoI] (2002). *National Human Development Report 2001*, Planning Commission, Government of India, New Delhi,Oxford University Press.

Land Acquisition and its Impact on Tribals Livelihood in Jajpur District, Odisha

Dr. Sanjaya Kumar Das

ABSTRACT

Impact of land acquisition on tribal people, affected by development project, has been overwhelmingly negative in India. In almost all the resettlement operations, for which reliable information is available, the majority of oustees have ended with lower incomes; less land than before; less work opportunities, inferior housing; less access to the resources of the commons such as fuel-wood and fodder; and worse nutrition and physical and mental health. In order to examine the livelihood restoration of the displace, this paper is based on an empirical study conducted on the displaced persons of the major industrial project namely the Kalinga Nagar industrial project located in tribal two tribal dominated blocks, Danagadi and Sukinda of Jajpur district of Orissa.

Introduction

Impact of land acquisition on tribal people, affected by development project, has been overwhelmingly negative in India. In almost all the resettlement operations, for which reliable information is available, the majority of oustees have ended with lower incomes; less land than before; less work opportunities, inferior housing; less access to the resources of the commons such as fuel-wood and fodder; and worse nutrition and physical and mental health (McCully, P., 1996: 77). This is how the Indian experience, particularly of the tribal communities can be stated. I will try and take a broad overview of the available evidence from empirical research experiences of the affected people in Kalinga Nagar Industrial project in the Jajpur District and various issues which emerge from the Indian experience of displacing and rehabilitating adivasi communities. The estimates show that no fewer than 40 per cent of the displace people and project affected person of five decades of planned development are from the tribal communities that formed only 8.08 per cent of the country's population in 1991 (Walter Fernandes, 1998: 265). In Orissa, they are 22 per cent of the population but 42 per cent of its DPs/PAPs (Fernandes, Walter and Mohammed Asif, 1997: 112). Similar data come from other States like Jharkhand, West Bengal and Kerala.

In order to examine the livelihood restoration of the displace, this chapter is based on an empirical study conducted on the displaced persons of the major industrial project namely the Kalinga Nagar industrial project located in tribal two tribal dominated blocks, Danagadi and Sukinda of Jajpur district of Orissa. The acquisition of land for Kalinga Nagar Industrial complex began in early 90s, in different phases. Till now, about 13000 acres of land have been acquired covering 83 revenue villages that falls under 10 Gram Panchayats of Sukinda and Danagadi Block of Jajpur district. Of these, 6900 acres are private land and the remaining area is said to be 'government land. However, in reality, people are cultivating most of these 'government land', for generations, over which they do not have *patta* (legal deeds). According to the official data, 814 families have been displaced, so far, in Kalinga Nagar. The number of families, likely to be displaced/affected in the near future is said to be about 5000. The displacement got over about 13 years ago and this is the appropriate time to examine and assess the status of rehabilitation of these displaced people and to note whether they have restored their pre-displaced living standards at the minimum. There are about three colonies where the minimum number of displaced families has resettled, while other have resettled in scattered manner.

The present study has been carried out in three rehabilitation colonies and 10 most affected village covering 300 sample displaced families. All the three colonies as well as the 10 village are located in the two tribal dominated block of Jajpur District of Orissa and hence the geographical coverage of the study is restricted to the three colonies and 10 village of the Jajpur district. In addition to this, some of the affected areas from where the affected people were displaced have been covered in the study; this is mainly due to farm an idea about the quality of life of the displaced people during the pre-displaced stage in the affected villages. Thus, some of the affected area falling under the remaining village was also covered for the study.

Methodology

For the study, three colonies and 10 villages have been covered and a total number of 300 Displaced Families were selected on the basis of random sampling method. Information pertaining to the civic amenities, infrastructure facilities, common property resources available to the Displaced Families in the colonies/village, health care facilities, educational institutions, religious institutions etc. Similarly, information from individual family level pertaining to the socio-economic condition, health & education status and information of the like were also collected by using a family Schedule from the 280 sample families covering three colonies and 10 villages. To be more specific, about 10 per cent of the total Displaced Families of the project were covered for the study. Also due care has been taken to ensure that aspect of social composition has been taken consideration in the selection of the sample, to make the sample more representative.

The various methods used for the empirical data collection in this study are: Schedule Method, Participatory Rural Appraisal Method, Focused Group Discussion Method, Participatory Walk through Method and Social Mapping. To substantiate the findings, Case Study Method has also been used. But in this study, at all stages effort has been made to draw a comparative account of the quality of living of the displaced families during the pre-displacement stage and post-displacement stage with a view to examine how and to what extent the displaced families have been able to reconstruct/restore their pre-displacement standard of living.

Livelihood Prior to and Following Land Acquisition

Before analysing the impact of land acquisition on tribals after displacement, a brief socio-economic character of the sample house-hold has been presented. The socio-economic profile of the sample households can be broadly classified in term of demographic profile, caste, gender and literacy level and age structure of the respondents. These socio-economic, variables are important indicators of the impact of displacement through land acquisition on different sections and age groups. Table 4.1 gives the socio-economic characteristic of sample households.

Table 4.1: Sample Village and Resettlement Colony Selected for Study in Kalinga Nagar Industrial Area

Name of the Village	Company	No. of Person Displaced	No of Sample Taken for Study
1	2	3	4
Kashikudi	Nilachal Ispat Nigam Ltd.	634	90
Siari	Mesco Steel and Jindal	59	13
Chandia	TISCO and Moharastra seamless	331	36
Gobarghati	TISCO and Moharastra seamless	558	60
Gadapur	TISCO and Moharastra seamless	140	27
Khurunti	M/S Jindal Stainless Steel	55	10

(Contd...)

1	2	3	4
Jakhapura	M/S VISA Industries Ltd. M/S K.J.Ispat Ltd.	18	4
Mangalpur	M/S VISA Industries Ltd. M/S K.J.Ispat Ltd.	43	9
Kacherigaon	M/S Dinabandhu Steel & Power Ltd. M/S Rohit Ferro Tech. Limited	27	5
Chandia	M/S Dinabandhu Steel & Power Ltd. M/S Rohit Ferro Tech. Limited	17	4
Name of the Colony		**No of People Staying**	**No of Sample Taken for Study**
Gobarghati	Nilachal Ispat Nigam Ltd.	120	24
Trijanga Rehabilitation	Mesco Steel	40	10
Anji Rehabilitation	TISCO	35	8
Total		2077	300

The socio-economic profile of the sample house-hold given in table 4.2 shows that out of 300 sample household have been drawn from two social groups, 270 (96.42%) belong to scheduled tribe, 10 (3.58%) belong to schedule caste groups. As far as gender is concerned 194 (69.29) household respondents are male and 86 (30.71%) are female. The table also shows the level of education of respondent 125 (44.64%) are illiterate, 122 (40%) are from primary level and only 43 (15.36%) are from secondary and above. As far as the age group is concerned, 94 (33.57%) are in the age group of 18-30, 98 (35%) in the age group of 31-50, 76 (27.14%) is the age group of 51-65, and only 12 (4.29%) are from age group of 66 and above. Due to unavailability, all the sample house hold included in the study are not head of the family but some of them are the member of the project affected family.

Table 4.2: Socio-economic Profile of Sample Households (Number 280)

Sample Variables	Sample Components	No. of Households	Percentage of Total Numbers of Samples
Caste	Scheduled Tribe	270	96.42
	Scheduled Caste	10	3.58
Gender	Male	194	69.29
	Female	86	30.71
Education	Illiterate	125	44.64
	Primary	112	40.00
	Secondary and above	43	15.36
Age	18-30	94	33.57
	31-50	98	35.00
	50-65	76	27.14
	66 and above	12	4.29

In the empirical study, an attempt has been made to find out whether the displaced families of the Kalinga Nagar Project, after a lapse of 13 years of displacement have been able to reconstruct and restore back their pre-displaced living standards, and if not then to what extent they have been able to, and what extent they have failed to restore back their former standards of living. For assessing this aspect, certain parameters have been used under 10 Broad Heads.

Land Holding Status

It has been a tested truth that expropriation of land removes the main foundation upon which a person's productive systems, commercial activities and livelihoods are constructed. Michael Cernea (2005), therefore rightly states that this is the principal form of decapitalisation and pauperization of displaced people through loss of both physical & man made capital. Since land is considered as the most long standing productive asset, this parameter has been taken for analyzing the standard of living of the displaced people in the post-displacement stage as compared to their former standards of living before displacement. For analyzing this, three indicators have been taken in-to consideration. They are: legal average land holding size of a displaced family, average encroached land of a displaced family and percentage of landless family.

Table 4.3: Land Holding Size during Pre and Post Displacement

Sl.No.	Parameter Used	Status in the Pre-displacement Stage	Status in the Post-displacement Stage
1.	Average legal land holding per family	2.64 acres	0.62 acres
2.	Average encroached forest/govt. land per family	About 1.5 acres	Less than 0.20 acres
3.	Percentage of families landless (as per the government definition of landless)	48.98%	85.25%
4.	Average operational land holding per family	3.69 acers	0.90 acers

As showing in table 4.3, the average land holding of the Displaced Families, which was 2.64 acres before displacement has substantially come down to 0.62 acres in the Post-displacement stage. Similarly, the data further indicates that the encroached land which, the Displaced Families were enjoying before displacement was about 1.5 Acres per family and as is revealed from the study, this has considerably reduced to 0.20 acres in the Post displacement stage. As regards the third indicator, it has been observed that while 48.98 per cent displaced families were landless before displacement, it has increased to 85.25 per cent. When the aforementioned three indicators of land holding size is taken into consideration, it is observed that it has reduced considerably in the post-displacement stage in case of the displaced people. This is as an important parameter that has been responsible for non-restoration of the livelihood of the Displaced Families of Kalinga Nagar Industrial Project. This also has contributed to the further impoverishment of the displaced families.

The analysis of the study further indicate that the following reasons are mainly responsible for the non-restoration of the former landholding status of the displaced families, even 13 years after displacement. Encroached land acquired from the displaced Persons, but which is of unobjectionable category and could have been settled in favour of the encroachers as per law, should have been settled in favour of the there so that they could have at least got the compensation for such land. This money would have enabled the displaced families to purchase some land and increase their landholding size near their relocation site.

Usually in rural and tribal pockets like, the resettlement sites of Kalinga Nagar Industrial project, there are huge extent of revenue land, which is leasable. Such lands are available in small patches in large number as reported from the revenue officials records in the study area. If this possibility would have been explored by the project authorities in co-ordination with the revenue officials, land-based rehabilitation would have been possible in about two-fifth of displaced families. Thus families would have actually been able to improve in their landholding size as compared to their pre-displacement stage. But no such initiative was taken in this direction.

If measure of land settlement/consolidation had been undertaken in the proposed command area of the project, simultaneously land would have been acquired from the benefited persons, and could have been allotted land based rehabilitation possible. One step would have ensured increase in the land holding size of the displaced persons. Such a step has been successfully made in the dam Projects of Madhya Pradesh.

Access to Common Property Resources

Tribal people suffer from physical displacement mainly because law does not recognize communal customary rights of tribal people to their lands. The resettlement literature is full of case studies of how development projects ignore the customary rights of the tribal people and treat them as illegal occupants of government land. Such an approach invariably leads to the impoverishment of once settled communities. In addition, they were given no compensation for losing their common resources—pastures, forest lands, water bodies, burial grounds, and quarries. Without those resources, their income and quality of life significantly deteriorated.

Displacement from common property resources has its harshest effects on the tribals. In Kalinga Nagar tribal areas, it is women who generally control farm production and household economy, and hence their dependence on common property resources for earning or saving income is greater than that of men. The loss of access to these resources "results in the emergence of an unemployed and unemployable 'housewife' who is, increasingly, not only perceived to be but becomes almost solely dependent on her husband. Additionally, access to resources in the post-displacement scenario is almost always mediated via husbands, who now assume the role of 'sole' bread earners. This puts serious drains on the household budgets.

The project-affected area of Kalinga Nagar Industrial Project, which has been taken for study was a very thickly forest area and a large extent of the forest has come under acquisition because of this project. Most of the displaced Persons belonged to the scheduled tribe, population and majority of the displaced People depended on the agriculture and forest for their survival. Besides, most of the displaced persons have encroached a sizable area of either forest or government land, which they were cultivating for ages. The earning from this source was essential for their livelihood. Because of the acquisition of these lands, the displaced people lost very precious land, but could neither get replacement of the land nor could get any compensation whatsoever for this land as there was no record of right over such encroached land. This, in fact, contributed to the impoverishment of the displaced people in the project area. Besides, forest as a major common property resource, there are a number of other resources like grazing land, wood lot, burial ground, waste land and space for cultural shows, which were very meaningfully used by the displaced people in their original villages before displacement. But most of these facilities were not available to the displaced people in the relocated places. Besides, for sharing the common property resources, in most of the resettlement places, feuds/conflicts of very serious nature has been reported between the hosts and the resettlers.Besides, the fruits, roots, tubers and other forest produces consumed, collected and sold by the people were also stopped in the new relocation sites, which contributed to the impoverishment of the displaced persons.

According to table 4.4, while 75.85 per cent of the displaced Families had encroached land before displacement, it has substantially reduced to 23 per cent in the post-displacement stage, as most of the forest/government land encroached by them got acquired, and secondly, in the new relocated place there were no vacant unencroached government/forest land. Further, it is also seen that due to the acquisition of encroached land, the average encroached land per family, which was 1.50 acres in the pre-displacement stage, got reduced to only 0.20 acres in the Post-displacement stage. In addition to the above status, it is also revealed that in the pre-displacement phase people had easy accessibility to the forest and about 34.65 per cent of family depended on Minor Forest Produce (MFP) for their survival, accessibility to forest got reduced considerably and this resulted in reducing the percentage of displaced families depending on MFP for survival to only

14.20 per cent. It was also observed that while all the displaced families before displacement had access to grazing land as well as to the burial ground, in the post displacement stage, only about 25 per cent and 26.66 per cent had access to grazing land and burial ground respectively. It has been seen that in the relocation sites, since the displaced families did not have any earmarked places for burial and grazing land, while trying to share these places which the host population, there have been often conflict which have led to feuds in a large number of instances.Access to common property resources has been considerably reduced in case of the displaced People in the Post-displacement stage and this to a large extent has disrupted the livelihood restoration.

Table 4.4: Access to Common Property Resources during Pre and Post Displacement

Sl. No.	Parameter Used	Status in the Pre-displacment Stage	Status in the Post-displacment Stage
1.	% of families having encroached forest/govt. land	75.85%	23%
2.	Average encroached land for family	About 1.50 Acres	Less than 0.20 Acres
3.	Accessability to forest for mfp & fuel wood	Easily accessible	Accessibility has been restricted
4.	% of families whoes primary source of earning is mfp	34.65%	14.20%
5.	% of families having access to grazing land	100%	About 25%
6.	% of families who have access to burial ground	100%	26.66% have earmarked burial space & others use vacant space as burial of the dead.

Table 4.4 shows that in most of the cases in the relocated place, access to forest is limited and similarly in very limited places access to common property like burial ground and grazing land is available where as in most of the places no earmarked places are there for such purposes in and around the place of relocation. Thus, due to substantial reduction of access of the displaced persons to most of the common property resources- especially to the forest, the displaced families receive adverse effects from various fronts. Critical analysis in the project affected as well as the relocation places in the study area indicate that number of factors are responsible for lack of access to common property resources for the displaced persons, in the project affected area. If such factors would have been taken care of, loss of access could have been reduced to a large extent. However, the following are the main factors responsible.

Space for burial ground, grazing land and waste land has not been provided to the displaced families close to the relocation sites. Due to this, the displaced families in the post relocation stage have faced a lot of inconveniences and have picked up feuds and quarrels with each other for sharing such places, which are meant for them.

Also, most of the time the displaced families have been relocated far off from the forests and therefore the displaced families have lost access to the forest/natural resources. In fact, during the study I could not find places close to the forest which are leasable and had such land been selected for the relocation of the displaced families, they could have got better access to the forest and this would have helped them a lot in rebuilding/reconstructing their former standards of living.

It also has been found out that, although, some sort of forest or the other is there near the relocation sites where the displaced families have been resettled, and are denying the access of the displaced families to such forests.

Access to Health Care Services, Morbidity and Mortality

Apart from economic status, health is a major indicator to gauge the quality of living. Studies suggest that in most of the disasters including displacement in development projects, vulnerability to illness normally increases, unsafe drinking water supply and waste water tends to proliferate infectious diseases, diarrhea, dysentery, increased morbidity, mortality rate and decreases in health levels take place in the relocated site after Displacement. In the present study, eight indicators have been taken for analyzing the Health Status of the Displaced Persons of Kalinga Nagar Industrial Project in the Post Displacement stage. The parameters are: average distance of medical centre from the habitat, birth attendant at the point of delivery, frequency of the visit of the health worker, Quality of ICDS Services, Immunization Status of the Pregnant Mother, Immunization Status of the Children, M.M.R. and I.M.R.

Table 4.5 shows that in the post-displacement stage, the distance of the medical centers from the place of stay has become less, immunization rate of the pregnant women and children have increased and consequently the Infant Mortality & Maternal Mortality Rates have decreased quite considerably as compared to the pre-displacement stage. But, on the other hand, there has been no change in the irregular visit of the health worker, irregular ICDS services in the post-displacement place and the indigenous untrained birth attendants continues to assist at the point of delivery.

Thus, when one looks at all the health indicators, it appears that there has been some improvement in the health status of the displaced people in their rehabilitated site as compared to their pre-displaced health standards.

Table 4.5: Access to Health Services, Morbidity & Mortality during Pre & Post Displacement

Sl. No.	Parameter Used	Status in the Pre-displacement Stage	Status in the Post-displacement Stage
1.	Average distance of medical center from the habitat	about 10 kilometres	about 6 kilometres
2.	Birth attendant at the point of delivery	Mostly indigenous untrained *dhai*	Mostly indigenous untrained *dhai*, but in some cases trained *dhais* are conducting delivery
3.	Frequency of the visit of the health worker	4-5 times a month (casual & irregular)	4-5 times a month (casual & irregular)
4.	ICDS service and its regularity	Is available, but irregular	is available, but irregular
5.	Immunisation status of the pregnant mother	Pregnant mother were invariably not immunised	About 30% mother are immunised
6.	Immunisation status of the children	Children and infants were very rarely immunised	About 40% of children & infants immunised
7.	M.M.R.	Much higher than now	About 18 per thousand delivery
8.	I.M.R.	Much higher than now	16.5% infant mortality have occurred

As far as the access to health services, morbidity and mortality is concerned, it is observed that while the distance of the hospitals from the habitational sites has marginally reduced and the MMR, IMR, Immunization of the mother and the children have marginally improved, deplorable health conditions of the displaced persons in general still persists even in the new place of relocation after the displacement. However, the various important reasons for the continued deplorable health status of the displaced persons and their family members still continues due to the following important reasons.

There is no drainage system in the relocation sites and the rainwater accumulates in and around the relocation places which the mosquitoes breed leading total diseases among the children. Besides, there are no sanitary latrines in the houses of the displaced families and they defecate in the open field and often near the habitational sites. This also results in unhealthy condition. Therefore, septic latrine must be insisted in the houses of each displaced family either through some intervention or the other to ensure the people a healthy living.

Absence of safety drinking water also has contributed to the deteriorating health of the people belonging to the displaced families in the relocation place. Although the project official have installed the required number of tube wells as per the stipulation of the provisions, yet the tube wells have been defunct and are drying out much before the summer season.

Thus, people are taking contaminated water, which is adversely affecting their health condition of the people. In most of the dispensaries the doctors are not staying for most part of the year and the ICDS supervisors as well as the health workers are becoming highly irregular for which the health status of the displaced people are in a very bad state in the post relocation stage.

Here is some observation regarding health condition of surveyed villages, and I found out that in the last six years alone, 188 people had died due to various illnesses. This number excludes death due to aging and those killed in the ongoing repression; the 188 deaths are of people below the age of 45. In the last six months alone, 14 people from just about three villages have died since there was no medical aid to reach them, neither were they allowed to leave the area. And the illnesses are due to the diseases of malaria, jaundice, tuberculosis, fever and several other illnesses piled together. This list is not comprehensive; it is only from few of the nine villages within Chandia Panchayat. These nine villages are the ones affected directly by Tata Company.

The villagers told me that the medical centre was empty as no patient would visit there. There are no doctors here. Just one medical in-charge, who sits in the OPD till 12 noon and doesn't wait a minute more even if there are patients lined outside. He runs to his private clinic which he operates from his quarters. He just holds a post-graduate degree in Medicine, but he handles all sorts of cases because there is no other doctor here. He will check a patient coming in, and will promptly refer him to Cuttack.

Mena Mohanty who was an '*Asha* Madam'. The Orissa state government had roped in midwives from villages to be *Asha* Madams who would be responsible for all the pregnant women in the village. She was responsible for bringing in the women in labour to medical centres. On doing so, she would receive Rs 250. "So you must be travelling to other villages too, to see if there are more pregnant women. I ask Mena didi. She smiled widely to reveal her paan-stained teeth. "I am responsible only for the women in my village. In a year, there are just about 10 pregnancies. So I can earn only that much," she replied. Mena didi said that she had been working as a midwife in her village since 30 years and was an expert in her work.

Food Security

Food security is regarded as one of the most important indicators of livelihood. Therefore, this indicator has been taken in the present study to find out to what extent displaced people have food security in the post-displacement stage as compared to their pre-displacement period. In fact, it has been invariably observed that forced uprooting increases the risk that people will fall into chronic food insecurity, defined as caloric protein intake levels below the minimum requirement for normal growth and work. Sudden drops in food crops availability and/or incomes are certain during physical relocation. To analyse this food security level among the displaced families, six indicators have been used. They are average crop yield per family, principal source of livelihood of the family, secondary source of livelihood, principal diet of the family, supplementary diet of the family and average surplus food grains per year per family.

Table 4.6 analysis on the basis of the empirical data collected from the displaced families, indicate that while the average crop yield per family has declined significantly in the post- displacement stage as compared to their pre-displacement time, the average surplus food grains per family per year has reduced very sharply in the post-displacement period. Further, while during the pre-displacement stage along with rice, forest produces were used as the principal diet, due to the acquisition of forest in the affected villages and forest being almost inaccessible in the new of resettlement place, the principal diet has been restricted to only rice among the displaced persons in the post displacement stage. Analysis of the above indicators with regard to food security indicates that the displaced families have become more food insecure after the displacement as compared to the pre-displacement period. This is also a indicator of impoverishment of the displaced families.

Table 4.6: Status of Food Security during Pre and Post Displacement

Sl. No.	Parameter used	Status in the Pre-displacement Stage	Status in the Post-displacement Stage
1.	Average crop yield per family	25-30 quintals	6-7 quintals
2.	Principal source of livelihood	Agriculture	Agriculture and wage earning (non agriculture)
3.	Secondary source of livelihood	Minor forest produce	Nil
4.	Principal diet	Rice, forest produces	Rice
5.	Supllmentary diet	Salap (juice of a tree) & other forest based edibles	Occasionally slap & very rarely forest based edibles
6.	Average surplus of food grains per family per year	1-2 quintals	Nil

In the previous section, the data analysis indicated that the displaced people by and large have become food insecure in the new place of relocation after the displacement. This is indicative of the fact that the average yield of paddy per family per year has reduced from about 15 quintals during the pre-displacement stage to about seven quintals in the post-displacement period. Secondly, while the average surplus food grains per family per year was 1 to 2 quintals prior to displacement, it became almost nil in the post-displacement period. In the empirical study, an effort was made to find out the various factors responsible increasing food insecurity among the displaced families after displacement. The study revealed the following main factors to be associated with food insecurity.

Land holding size has been reduced quite considerably in the post-displacement period decreasing thereby the per capita yield of foodstuff. Due to loss of employment opportunities in the place of relocation, the people have become further food insecure in the new place of stay after displacement. Access to forest has been stopped and dependence on it has also become very minimal in the new place of stay for which people have become increasingly food insecure.

Employment Opportunities

It has been invariably found out that in the post displacement stage, the displaced people of development Projects do not get employment, as employment opportunities reduces. This culminates into impoverishment of the displaced people and eventually a large number of such families migrate out to far off places in search of employment. Therefore, in order to examine whether the displaced population have been further impoverished, five parameters in respect to employment opportunities have been assessed. Table 7 shows that, while a person per day was getting about 300 days of work on an average per year, before displacement, in the post-displacement period, it has been reduced to 240 days a year. Like wise, while in the pre-displacement stage 65 per cent of DPs and 30 per cent DPs were engaged in the agricultural sector, wage earning respectively for their survival, it decreased to 23 per cent in the agricultural sector whereas it increased to 51 per cent in wage earning. On the other hand, it is really a matter of concern that people without gainful occupation increased from 5 per cent in the pre-displacement stage to 10 per cent in the post-displacement stage and it was also observed that 16 per cent displaced persons were found. Out migration takes place in the post-displacement stage. All these aspects put together indicate that employment opportunities have shrink in the post-displacement stage for the displaced people. As a result, they have migrated to far off places in search of migration. This is a clear indication of non-restoration of former standards of life impoverishment of the displaced people in the post-displacement stage.

It has been found that in most of the relocation places, the employment opportunities for the displaced people have decreased quite considerably and people are without employment for a good number of days as compared to the pre-displacement time. The study tried to reveal some of the key factors responsible for reduction in employment opportunities, some of which are as follows.

Before the displacement and acquisition of land, people by and large were engaged in farm labour for an appreciable number of days. But due to acquisition of land and relocation of the displaced families, mostly in the non-command areas, the displaced persons were deprived of this opportunity, which culminated in impoverishment.

Table 4.7: Employment Opportunities during Pre and Post Displacement

Sl. No.	Parameter Used	Status in the Pre-displacement Stage	Status in the Post-displacement Stage
1.	Average number of days a person gets work	About 300 days	About 240 days
2.	% of majors without gainful occupation	About 5%	About 10%
3.	% of DPS engaged in agricultural sector	65%	23%
4.	% of DPS engaged in wage earning (non agr.)	30%	51%
5.	% of DPS migrated out	Nil	16%

Besides, before the displacement, for about 5-6 years earth work, other unskilled work of the project generated employment for the displaced as well as non-displaced persons in the affected area. But after the displacement, the project activities/construction activities almost stopped, and hence the employment opportunities suddenly got stopped. This is one of the main reasons for the shrinkage in employment opportunities.

House Ownership and Housing Condition

It is known that due to acquisition of land and homestead in the development projects, a large number of people lose their homes. Hence, loss of housing shelter is temporary for most displaces, but for some it remains a chronic condition. In fact, in a broader sense, homelessness is also placelessness, loss of a group's cultural space, identity, or cultural impoverishment. For examining the extent to which house ownership/ homelessness has taken shape in the post-displacement period, in case of the displaced people five indicators have been examined (as may be seen in table no – 8). The data analysis states that while only 65 per cent displaced people had a house, which stood in their name prior to displacement, in the post-displacement stage it increased, and 87.25 per cent displaced families owned a house. Secondly, during the phase prior to displacement, 18 per cent DPs had a house, which was on encroached land, but in the post-displacement period it reduced substantially and only 4.5 per cent DPs were found to have constructed house on encroached land. The other indicators of housing show that the quality of house has improved quite considerably in the post-displacement stage. This is indicative of the fact that, while in the pre-displacement stage as high as 70 per cent families had thatched house, it got reduced to only 17.8 per cent in the post-displacement period. Similarly, while there were only 4.10 per cent concrete roofed houses before displacement, in the post-displacement stage it substantially increased to 34.35 per cent. The above analysis, thus, clearly shows that housing as a parameter of livelihood has improved quite considerably in the post-displacement period, in case of the displaced families of Kalinga Nagar Industrial Project.

Table 4.8: House Ownership during Pre and Post Displacement

Sl. No.	Parameter Used	Status in the Pre-displacement Stage	Status in the Post-displacement Stage
1.	% of DPS having their own house	About 65%	87.25%
2.	% of DPS having a house on encroached land	18%	4.5%
3.	% of DPS having a thatched house	69.30%	17.8%
4.	% of DPS having a tiled/asbestors house	09.60%	39.6%
5	% of DPS having a concrete roofed house	4.10%	34.35%

In fact, one of the positive livelihood parameters in the study, which has shown remarkable improvement/restoration in case of the displaced families in the post displacement stage, is the house ownership as compared to the pre-displacement stage. To be precise, more than 87 per cent of the displaced families became house owners in the post-displacement stage as against 65 per cent, prior to the displacement. Similarly, the quality of housing has also improved considerably in the post-displacement stage. Hence, this is the parameter, which has rather shown improvement as compared to the former standard, and therefore, needs no identification of non-restoration factors.

Access to Education

Educational level is taken as one of the most important livelihood indicators for assessing reconstruction of livelihood. But, unfortunately, it has been noted that after the displacement, educational losses are sustained by the children of the displaced families in a number of projects. In this context, in this study, access to education has been chosen as an indicator for assessing the relative livelihood restoration status of the displaced people in the post-displacement stage. For analyzing this, six parameters have been used, as may be seen in table 4.9. The analysis presented in the table indicate that the distance of the primary school from the habitation has decreased marginally in case of the displaced people in the post-displacement stage. But, on the other hand, the distance of the high school and college have become even more in the post-displacement stage. Likewise, the teachers in the school have become more irregular than before in the resettlement sites, drop out rates of students at primary level have remained unchanged in the post-displacement period. Thus, as far as displaced children are concerned education has been restricted in the post-displacement period as compared to the pre-displacement time.

Table 4.9: Access to Education during Pre & Post Displacement

Sl.No.	Parameter Used	Status in the Pre-displacment Stage	Status in the Post-displacment Stage
1.	Distance of primary school from the habitation	2-3 kilometers	within 1-2 kilometers
2.	Distance of high school from the habitation	About 5-6 kilometers	6-8 kilometers
3.	Distance of college from the habitation	About 25 kilometers	35 kilometers
5.	Regularity of the teachers in the school	Not very regular. Almost remained absent 10 days a month	Become further irregular. there are some schools where there is no teacher & rate of absence of the teacher has increased
6.	% drop outs at primary level	Around 40%	Almost remained unchanged

As far as access to education is concerned, the findings have revealed that while the distance of the primary schools have decreased from the habitational sites, in case of the post-displacement stage, the distance of the high school and colleges have increased and the teachers have become more irregular than before. In addition to this, the rate of drop outs have remained almost unchanged in the post-displacement period. Thus, taken as a whole, access to education continues to be the same as it was before. However, it can be certainly said that educational attainment has been much less than what was desired in the post-displacement stage.

Income Level and Access to Credit Institution

Income leveland economic condition of an individual is very widely used as the criteria for determining the standard of living of a person. Taking this fact into account, in this study an attempt has been made to make comparative assessment of the economic conditions of the displaced families pre and post displacement using five distinct indicators. The analysis has been presented in table 4.10.

Table 4.10 shows that income level of the displaced families have almost remained unchanged. It has marginally increased from Rs. 8,500/ per annum to Rs. 9,500, since the inflation rate has not been taken into consideration, the increase is not substantial. In respect of per cent of families below the poverty line, percentage of families borrowed money from the private money lenders, location of the credit institution from the habitat have almost remained unchanged in the post-displacement stage as compared to the pre-displacement phase.Thus, it is clear that the economic level of the displaced families have remained almost unchanged in the post-displacement stage as compared to the stage prior to displacement.

Thus, when the analysis is made in respect of the aforementioned 10 broad indicators, it is revealed that the living condition or the quality of living of the displaced people have deteriorated in the post-displacement stage with the exception of housing condition. The housing conditions has improved quite significantly. Even income level has remained almost unchanged as compared to the pre-displacement stage.

Table 4.10: Income Level & Access to Credit Institution during Pre & Post Displacement

Sl.No.	Parameter Used	Status in the Pre-displacement Stage	Status in the Post-displacement Stage
1.	Average income per family	Rs. 8,500/-	Rs. 9,500/-
2.	% of families below poverty line	About 85%	About 75%
3.	% of families borrowed money from private money lenders	About 65%	About 45%
4.	% of families borrowed money banking/credit institutions	About 10%	About 20%
5.	Distance of the banking/credit institution from the habitat	About 20 kms.	About 20 kms.

It has also been observed, from the findings of the study, that the income level of the displaced families in the post-displacement stage has marginally increased when compared with to post-displacement stage. But if the rate of inflation taken place in the last seven years is taken into consideration, it gives us an indication that the income level in the has declined. The study has revealed the following main factors responsible for such poor economic level, in case of the displaced people. Also, after the displacement, access to credit institution has also decreased.

As job opportunities have reduced drastically due to acquisition of land, non-replenishment of land by the project by way of land based rehabilitation, income level has declined in true sense of the term. Secondly, as no viable alternative for income generation of the displaced families has been tried out in the resettlement sites either by the project, or by the government or even by the people themselves, the income level of the displaced families could not be restored.

Thus, the above factors, indicated under each of the livelihood parameters clearly indicate that the factors that are responsible, directly or indirectly, for the non-restoration of the former standards of living of the displaced families could have been overcome in development projects, if certain safeguards or precautionary measures were taken in consideration. Keeping this in view, an exercise has been made in this paper to list out some steps, which should be followed by the project implementing agencies or policy-makers associated with resettlement so that impoverishment can be avoided in case of displaced families. This cannot only ensure regaining former standards of living, but can also improve the pre-displaced living standards at the post-displacement stage. And can also lead to sustainable resettlement.

Larger Social, Economic and Environmental Threats

Involuntary and forced displacement induced by development projects, besides the above discussed problems, pose certain larger social, economic, and above all, environmental threats, which has perpetual or irreversible impact on the project affected people, in particular, and their habitat, in general. Displacement forces people to leave their usual habitation to which they are used to, in doing so they leave behind, besides their personal belongings, the common utility assets, the social bondage and security, which are all an essential part of their life. Not only the land-owners are evacuated but the landless agricultural labourers, carpenters, blacksmith, cobbler, barber, tailor and so on those depended on these land and the village society loose their livelihood too. The common properties like grazing land, ponds, wells, sacred grooves, worship places, playgrounds, and fuel sources are lost in the village.

The worst form of social impoverishment is caused due to loss of networks which are built up over generations. People who are used to traditional way of living are exposed to entirely new and alien living conditions and environment that is hostile to them. They are forced to think and live individually, unlike the usual common living and dependency, wherein only the well-off sections of the community survive.

People start to confront and fight within family for compensation money, the callous settlement of different ethnic and caste groups develop inter community hostility. Many are rendered jobless and even if jobs are offered they find it beneath their dignity to work as labourers. The affected people have no political voice. As they are resettled in new fragmented conditions there is lack of uniformity, the living conditions at different places of resettlement are different, thus the common interest vanish is leaving the marginalized ones further to the periphery.

Not alone the social conditions of the project affected persons is deteriorated, it is same with the host community where these people are resettled. "The inflows of displaces increases pressure on resources and scarce social services, as well as competition for employment. Prices of commodities tend to rise and health risks in the host area increases. Cultural clashes are quite likely, and social tensions tend to endure long. Secondary adverse effects on the environment hurt both the hosts and the displaced (Cernea, 2000: 3659).

Conventionally, people had to worry about displacement caused due to big dams alone, which would affect the population of a region where the dam is being constructed or limited to the submergence area. However, contemporarily the cause of displacement has multiplied in numbers and dimensions with varied and enormous impact not only on the physical population of the nation but also affecting the social and economic fabric with serious threats to environment and the ecological balance. The fast-track industrialization has turned our cities inhabitable, forests barren and man-to-machine, a country, which was predominantly a sustained traditional economy has been transferred into modern growth-led economy devoid of human considerations. Those who cherished the new economic policy failed to wield the same in application. The long-hidden agenda inherent in the policy, best identified with the western culture. In a state once firmly based on the principles of socialism, the long over the process of privatisation of essential commodities.

The modern agents of development don't even leave the natural resources untouched. They are encroached upon by of foreign entities, wherein, the indigenous, the rightful owners, have to pay for the things once considered to be natural and common. Privatization of drinking water supply with vesting river rights in to the hands of private entity, the Seonath River in Chhattisgarh, the groundwater exploitation and contamination by Cola giants in (Plachimada in Palakkad) Kerala, privatization of water supply for Trivunanthapuram and Vizag to be facilitated (displacing millions) by constructing the Polavarm Multipurpose Dam, besides the already privatized electricity and water supply in number of metropolitan cities including Delhi and Mumbai are some of the many instances of this draconian run. The web of industrialisation, privatization, globalisation, liberalisation, and the excuse of development, has become a irreversibly complex. And this complexity has been integrated and seeped deep into the economic and in all the policies of the state. Development projects, nevertheless, symbolizing economic growth, an important component of development, cannot be a goal in itself, nor can go indefinitely. A project, howsoever technically perfect, will not bear the desired results if we keep the "substance" out of it. Development means the development of the "people".

Moreover, no development can be accepted at the cost of environment, which essentially means human survival, rather 'the survival of the humanity'. Unsystematic and piecemeal approach to development has cost us dearly in the form of depletion of the environment and loss of ecological balance. The large scale deforestation, due to mining and establishment of industries, has resulted in climate change and inconsistent weathers. Big dams submerge huge area of forest cover causing irreversible loss to varieties of flora and fauna besides the land area. The pollution (air, water, soil and noise) caused by the industries accentuate the miseries of the present as well as the generations to come, added to this pollution by industries and urban centers is the garbage and toxic waste that is generated over time. No wonder that the environmental impact assessment of most of the big and mega projects reveal that such hyped and appreciated mega ventures are nothing but surviving at human and environmental costs. It is high time we realize the need of transforming our developmental policies to answer the larger human and environmental requirements until it becomes too late.

Economic cost alone can never be the only consideration in a project that is going to affect the lives of lakhs of people, the ecology and the environment, not just in the short term but for centuries to come. Today, almost all the developmental projects are woven into economic fabric with the thread of liberalization, privatization and globalization (LPG), and up for sale in a market-driven economy, thus ruling out the commoners from being among the beneficiaries of such a development. On the contrary, the development is achieved at the cost of the commoners.

If we consider displacement as the factor responsible for causing impoverishment, then the maximum impoverishment is caused due to industrialization-induced displacement, next only to the displacement caused by dams. Since it creates a vicious circle of displacement, beginning with acquisition of land for the establishment of industry and culminating in mass slums, the existence of slum in every industrial city is a sufficient testimony to this fact. However, in the modern context, the extended threat is that all the activities are run and controlled by private entities. This result in the concentration of the natural and economic resources and wealth, belonging to the people, in limited hands, to an extent of excluding immediate institutional remedies from the state. In liberalisation, privatisation and globalisation (LPG) the sate has found a disguise to escape its social and welfare responsibilities. It is only when the state finds the situation out of control, coupled with peoples' movement, it aversely takes some steps for resettlement and rehabilitation only to subside and undermine the mass movements.

After the analysis of this study, it seems fair to conclude that the globalization has been depriving the people from their livelihood, harming the interests of the lakhs of tribals. The New Economic Policy and the package of LPG, and particularly the globalization has further deepened the problem of the displacement in India. The tribals, peasants, dalits, women, workers, and their organizations have a difficult task of resisting the interests of these new capitalist forces such as mass media, urban industries, which are supported by the state. The struggle against the displacement has, thus, become the struggle against the larger politics of globalization.

And, in the process, the civil society has to deal with varied forms of inconsistencies from within and out of the society. The answer may not be found in one-sided approach to the problems. We have to reach to a harmonious solution ensuring better management production and distribution of the resources with sustainable development as its end result. We will have to have a holistic view and consider in totality the needs, necessities and wants of different sections of the society, with state as the major stakeholder in the whole process; forming a fine balance between the 'right to development' and the 'right against displacement'.

The foregoing analysis clearly underlines the fact that, the development paradigm in tribal areas has ignored the aspirations and that has resulted in greater inequalities. The resource rich tribal regions are used as sources of raw material to the benefit of other classes. This contradiction has got intensified after globalisation with the Indian and foreign private sector wanting more of their land and other resources. The deep regional disparities and inequalities created and increased by the path of capitalist development in India is further accentuated in the case of tribals. Adivasi communities because of locations of habitations in remote and ecologically rigorous areas, away from the fertile river valleys, would have required a decentralized and location-specific approach to development which would have strengthened the democratic structures within the communities to enable tribals to take decisions about the requirements of protection of their land and livelihoods even while enabling them to access the rights to education, health, civic facilities and so on. But on the contrary the British colonial policies of placing and displacing tribal communities according to the perceived requirements of the State have been a continued feature, determined at present by the urgent corporate requirement of access to mineral wealth located in tribal areas. Democracy has been brutally butchered in tribal areas reflected in the arbitrary decisions taken by the State which virtually transformed tribal communities into encroachers on their own land and turned their traditional rights and common ownership of forest resources into gestures of generosity by the State "granting" them highly diluted and limited access to what rightfully belongs to the community.

It cannot be denied that the state needs industrial activities to boost the economy. But at the same time the fact cannot be ignored that the agents of "growth" have also surfaced as the ones contributing to the loss of resources livelihoods and ecological, and this industrialisation should not happen at the cost of life and livelihood of poor tribals and dalits. But we cannot cherish the profits of industrialization at the cost of fertile agricultural lands and critical ecological habitats. Development is not a condition that can be characterized just by economic growth; rather the measures should be largely qualitative, representing an overall wellbeing that includes social, economic as well as environmental indicators. The claim for development is only justified when deliberations of equity, justice and sustainability are taken into account. The process should also encourage democratic participation of various stakeholders in the decision making process that includes government authorities to members of civil society, irrespective of their economic and social status, especially the people whose lands are being considered for carrying out developmental activities. This will help to maintain a balance among the market, the government, and the people and their often competing socio-economical and ecological needs.

REFERENCES

McCully, P. (1996), *"Silenced Rivers. The Ecology and Politics of Large Dams"*, Zed Books, London.

Fernandes, Walter (1998), "Development Induced Displacement in Eastern India," in S.C. Dube (ed). *Antiquity to Modernity in Tribal India, Volume I: Continuity and Change Among Indian Tribes*, Inter-India Publications, New Delhi.

Fernandes, Walter and Mohammed Asif (1997), *Development-Induced Displacement in Orissa 1951-1995*, Indian Social Institute, New Delhi.

Cernea, Michael M (2000), "Risks, Safeguards and Reconstruction: A Model for Population Displacement and Resettlement", *Economic and Political Weekly*, October 7, 2000, p. 3659.

5 Way of Life for Sustainable Development

Mary Princess Lavanya

ABSTRACT

The term Spirituality has been used and misused in many situations that confuse the common meaning, and now appears to have as many definitions as persons defining it. Spirituality is nothing but a way of life or living. Spirituality has somewhat broader parameters, which include the search for a sense of meaning and purpose, concepts and images of God and ideas that include existential, paranormal, and experiential dimensions. The elders of the youth must be sensitive to their needs and problems and channelize their energy rightly towards the development of our Nation through sustainable development. Youngsters by being spiritual can transform the world by following the values, thus the change can be a sustainable one.

Introduction

Way of life is what spirituality is all about. Spirituality is a broad concept that goes beyond religious or cultural boundaries. It has been used and misused in many situations that confuse the common meaning, and now appears to have as many definitions as persons defining it. Spirituality is nothing but a way of life or living. It is more than a religion. Religion and spirituality are terms that are often used interchangeably, although they carry distinct connotations (Hill and Pargament, 2003). Religion evokes adjectives such as institutional, formal, outward, doctrinal, and authoritarian (Hill and Pargament, 2003). Definitions of religion focus on the process by which spiritual impulses are channeled into various social and political structures (Decker, 1993) or the way individuals organize their beliefs in order to regulate and make sense of the universe (Taylor, 2001). Religion formalizes and structures our spiritual beliefs into a cohesive system with specific rules and doctrines (Brady, Guy, Poelstra, and Brokaw, 1999).

Spirituality has somewhat broader parameters, which include the search for a sense of meaning and purpose (Parlotz, 2002), concepts and images of God (Wilson and Moran, 1998), and ideas that include existential, paranormal, and experiential dimensions (Taylor, 2001). It is individualistic, subjective, and emotional (Hill and Pargament, 2003). Over a lifetime, a person develops beliefs based on his/her world-view of how things work, and this can also be considered spirituality. Spirituality has less to do with the worship of one particular God and more to do with our perceived relationship and understanding of those forces considered higher than ourselves. Instead, it is a set of wishful characteristics of a future system. Humanity and religion have long been intertwined. Though its reach and impact has varied over the centuries, religion continues to be a significant force across most cultures in the world. Studies have found religion to be an important predictor of physical and mental health across many societies (Tarakeshwar, Stanton, and Pargament, 2003).

Hill and Pargament assert that religion and spirituality contain more integrated themes than separate ones. They state that polarizing these concepts to a place where religion is considered inflexible and dogmatic while spirituality is considered freeing and enlightening does a disservice to both ideals. Religion and spirituality contain overarching frameworks which intertwine them. Both originate from the need to acknowledge and uphold those things considered sacred. Both are considered means by which human beings strive to understand, cope with and perhaps transcend their daily lives (Hill and Pargament, 2003). An underlying sense of trust is integral to many areas of life. It influences one's sense of self, one's relationships with others, and an individual's concept of spirituality. When this trust collides with an event that is atypical, overwhelming, and possibly life-threatening the ability to rely on a spiritual belief system may be destroyed (Wilson and Moran, 1998).

The term spirituality is used in many different ways. Schneiders (1989) sees it as referring to:

1. A fundamental dimension of the human being;
2. The lived experience which actualizes that dimension; and
3. The academic discipline which studies that experience.

Helminiak (1996) lists the usages to include: human spiritual nature; concern for transcendence; lived reality; academic discipline; spiritualism and parapsychology. People cannot understand spirituality without some personal experience of it, and as such, experience is self-implicating. Reed (1991) sidestepped a clear definition of spirituality stating that it is integral to health as an ever-present resource. O'Brien (2003) described spirituality as complete involvement in life, noted by awareness and attention to the metaphysical, a transcendent and unifying principle in the universe. Frankl (1984) described spirituality as being able to hold onto one's spiritual commitments while interpreting suffering within a context of deeper meaning. Marcoen (1994) generally defined spirituality as a transcendent relationship with something greater than the self. He recognizes two types of spirituality, noting that this relationship may be validly interpreted from either a religious viewpoint or an agnostic experience.

Definitions

The word spiritual comes from the Latin root spiritus that originally meant "breath" and is one of many words like psyche (Greek), atman (Sanskrit) and ruach (Hebrew) associating breath with life. One of the many definitions of spirit in the Merriam-Webster Dictionary (1974) is the life giving, vital, animating force of human beings and also the vigor, courage, and ardor that infuses life with energy. The Merriam-Webster Dictionary (1974) further defines spirit as the essential quality, character or nature, or special attitude of the mind. Spirit is also defined as the incorporeal essence of the person, the soul, a supernatural entity, or a ghost. Distilled alcoholic liquors are referred to as spirits, perhaps because their volatility is reminiscent of the elusive and transcendent.

Characteristics of Spirituality

With respect for the groundwork laid by others, four characteristics may be presented as essentially necessary for spirituality, with the caveat that none alone is sufficient. These characteristics are that spirituality requires faith or acceptance of a belief system, that it involves a personal search for meaning and purpose, that it encompasses an awareness of connection or relatedness to others, and that it is self-transcendent.

1. Belief System

Spirituality must include a belief system, or at least the willingness to believe. Marcoen (1994) stated, "The spirituality of a person is never entirely self-made. It originates from an exchange process with the culture in which the person is embedded" (p. 535). All people have some basic belief they hold to be true, even if it is only that they exist. In general, people also have beliefs regarding the nature of the world they live in as rational and ordered or chaotic. Religions have carefully reasoned belief frameworks that require faith, and scientific disciplines have theoretical frameworks that incorporate assumptions. Both guide thought and action and drive the search for knowledge and understanding.

2. The Search for Purpose

The second characteristic of spirituality is the search or quest for meaning or purpose in life. This is the quintessential existential question, and a common aspect of many formalized belief systems is a core or central mystery revealed to the faithful through ritual, meditation, or prayer. Organized religions clearly articulate the need to seek enlightenment, salvation, or righteousness and the primary task of existentialism is to take responsibility for finding meaning. Meaning and purpose in life is often connected to vocation or mission in which a person feels called to a particular fate or destiny. There is commonly a shift from material values to more altruistic or idealistic values.

3. Harmonious interconnectedness

(Hungelmann et al., 1996) has been used in definitions of spirituality and is the third necessary characteristic. The recognition and acceptance of a connection or relationship among self, others, the world, and ultimate other is often achieved through the reflective self-examination and growth that can occur in the search for meaning. A harmonious connection is sometimes expressed as awe or reverence in a nonreligious context. Life is not dichotomized into sacred and secular, but there is a sense of wonder and appreciation that even the ordinary can be special. This does not mean unlimited optimism. "The spiritual person is solemnly conscious of the tragic realities of human existence" (Elkins et al., 1988, p. 11).

4. Self-Transcendence

The fourth characteristic of spirituality is self-transcendence. Transcendence is a characteristic specifically mentioned or implied in other definitions of spirituality in the nursing literature (Labun, 1988). Transcendence is the belief that extension beyond the self is possible, that there is more. Almost always this unseen dimension is perceived to be good or harmonious. Transcendence also refers to the experience of that which is outside the usual aspects of human perception or the metaphysical. Elkins et al. (1988) found transcendent experiences similar to Maslow's (1969) peak experiences in which personal power is drawn from contact with this unseen dimension. Frankl (1966) stated that self-transcendence is one of the two defining human phenomena. He defined self-transcendence as "a constitutive characteristic of being human that it always points, and is directed, to something other than the self" (p. 97). Transcendence is evident in Christian, Buddhist, and shamanistic theology and is implied in the Jewish tradition by the desire for righteousness or holiness. Psychologists concerned with developmental theories such as Maslow (1969) and Erikson (1986) have said that ego and body transcendence marks late adulthood. One is less focused on the failing physical body and personal interests, placing greater value on life achievements and relationships with others. Transcendence may be the cornerstone of a sense of well-being. Consciousness or awareness of the world is also an element related to self-transcendence.

Way of Life with Values

Values are standards or principles considered important in life which bring quality and meaning to life giving a person his identity and character. Values act as guidelines for better life and tell one what one should and should not do. Values that should be practiced in real life can be categorized into two. They are:

1. Values from within (spiritual);
2. Values for a living (practical).

From a historic-social perspective, "wise and good" people have been defined throughout the ages as those who conformed to social norms, beliefs and values. Conformity has and always will be valued because humans are creatures of habit and prefer routines and rituals; the less change the better, with "don't rock the boat" as the theme of every organization around the globe. Especially in modern times when stress is defined as any kind of change, good or bad, tranquility or distress respectively, and millions of dollars and Euros are spent annually on exercise programmes and training sessions with various techniques and programmes to reduce stress levels of the human race. Values are the standards of behavior in day-to-day activities and guiding principles in critical life situations. Values are ideal virtues and qualities that are primary doctrines that shape the world's outlook.

In the 21st Century values education is the only tool that could bring order, security and assured development in the chaotic world. It is a programme of planned educational action and a methodical effort deliberately framed to bring transformation in the society. It starts at home and continued in schools. It begins with childhood and should be present throughout one's life. The family system in India has a long tradition of teaching values effortlessly. But westernization, urbanization, globalization and the fast changing roles of parents have necessitated institutional intervention through schools, colleges, religious organizations and departments of governments to meet the rising needs of the modern society. These activities focus on the development of children and young adults by concentrating on core values like compassion, humility, unity, simplicity. In today's world human values are either discarded or distorted. Only when the basic ideologies are restored, world will be a better place to live in. 'In order to preserve, maintain and advance the position of our country in the world, it is imperative that there should be a comprehensive programme for imparting values through education.

Sustainable Development

Sustainable development is a pattern of resource use that aims to meet human needs while preserving the environment so that these needs can be met not only in the present, but in the indefinite future. The term was used by the Brundt land Commission which coined what has become the most often-quoted definition of sustainable development as development that "meets the needs of the present without compromising the ability of future generations to meet their own needs." The field of sustainable development can be conceptually broken into three constituent parts:

1. environmentalsustainability;
2. economic sustainability; and
3. sociopolitical sustainability.

According to Hasna, sustainability is a process which tells of a development of all aspects of human life affecting sustenance. It means resolving the conflict between the various competing goals, and involves the simultaneous pursuit of economic prosperity, environmental quality and social equity famously known as three dimensions (triple bottom line) with is the resultant vector being technology, hence it is a continually evolving process; the 'journey' (the process of achieving sustainability) is of course vitally important, but only as a means of getting to the destination (the desired future state). However, the 'destination' of sustainability is not a fixed place in the normal sense that we understand destination.

Spirituality and Values

Spirituality has been described as broader than religion, "a personal, individual value system about the way people approach life" (Laukhof & Werner, 1998, p. 62), varying from person to person and changing throughout life, a personal quest for meaning and purpose. Labun (1988) connected spirituality with love, faith, hope, and trust, all of which are interpersonal relationships. Hunglemann et al. (1996) defined it as "a sense of harmonious interconnectedness between self, others/nature, and Ultimate Other which exists throughout and beyond time and space" (p.263). Haase, Britt, Coward, Leidy, and Penn (1992) did a simultaneous concept analysis of spiritual perspective, hope, acceptance, and self-transcendence. They identified three critical attributes for spirituality as connectedness, belief, and creative energy. Their explanation of connectedness to others, nature, the universe, or God is influenced by Hiatt (1986), as is the characterization of belief as a perspective that refers to something more than the self. Hunglemann et al. (1996) and Reed (1991) called this quality self-transcendence.

Values and Development

Values are a powerful instrument to spur development. They are goals or standards that set the direction and mobilize the collective cultural energies of the society for great accomplishment. They prompt us to strive for the maximum that is conceivable, rather than the minimum that is achievable. Values form the basis for the tremendous developmental achievements of the past two hundred years, such as the Japanese commitment to teamwork and consensus, the American devotion to enterprise and innovation, the

German dedication to quality, and the Dutch commitment to partnership with other people, rather than exploitation. Development is retarded by the slow pace at which new values are acquired, which normally requires a change of generation. But values can also be consciously transmitted through education in order to abridge the time needed for transition. The efforts over the last ten years to implement the value of environmental security illustrate the range of knowledge, information, attitudes, institutions, systems, and skills needed to achieve any high value in life. The recommendations presented in this report are intended to form a basis for identifying and providing the values, attitudes, organizations and skills needed to achieve peace and prosperity at the dawn of the third millennium.

Over the last two centuries in countries around the world development has strengthened expansive values that encourage greater freedom, tolerance, individual initiative, self-confidence and self-respect, dynamism, risk-taking, efficiency, punctuality, organization, communication and cooperation, open-mindedness and respect for new ideas, innovation and creativity. At the same time development has weakened values that support respect for tradition and hierarchy, seniority and authority, self-effacement and humility, patience and perseverance, generosity and self-sacrifice. The nineteenth century tolerated values based on the exploitation by people over people through slavery, colonialism and war, and the domination of nature by man. The guiding values for the coming century are freedom and respect for the individual, social equity, tolerance of human diversity and harmony with the environment.

Spirituality and Religions

Zen Buddhism is a lifestyle that emphasizes detachment from the world. A person's life is devoted to seeking enlightenment rather than adherence to dogma, and as all are one in the universe, none can be, in the end, above any other. The path to enlightenment is not a step-wise progress through a formal set of belief statements or the practice of ritual behaviors. Christianity, Judaism, Hinduism, and some animistic belief systems incorporate ultimate others, more advanced in understanding and greater in power than the person, and have structured worship practices with a carefully reasoned justification for core beliefs. The Eastern worldview is comparatively atheistic.

Earth is considered as Mother in all religions. Earth has trees of care, earthquakes of sentiment, and seas of love. It stands for enlightenment seekers. This is what Earth actually has done to Buddha, Moses, Mohammed, and Jesus. In a deeper meaning, it reconnects me to God with a strong bond that no one would ever break—attachment to Mother Earth.

Indeed, spiritual growth is attained through connection to nature. Noticeably, different spiritual leaders fled the metropolitan life to ecological sites. They were reborn in an earthly panorama with natural tools. In fact, they delivered their teachings to later generations through nature. If these heavenly scenes could talk, they would speak for the great value of Earth.

Conclusion

In planning for values and good objectives, the teacher and student or the guru and disciple will have to coordinate and work together. Such cooperation was enshrined ages ago, which is possible now and for the ages to come. 'Arise, awake and stop not till the goal is reached' must be our watchword. When there is a pure mind and will power nothing is impossible to achieve. If we make our thoughts, words and deeds sacred, there can be no better way of coming out of evil, ill-will and dependency. The Vedic prayer: "Asatoma Satgamaya, Tamasoma Jyotirgamaya, Mrutyorma Amrutamgamaya". This prayer means that, 'Lead me from unreal to the Real, darkness to Light, death to Immortality', this gives us the greatest self-confidence in performing our duties. It serves as a constant reminder to each one about one's own goal. Sustainable development is possible only through multi dimensional approach. The elders of the youth must be sensitive to their needs and problems and channelize their energy rightly towards the development of our Nation through sustainable development. Youngsters by being spiritual can transform the world by following the values, thus the change can be a sustainable one.

REFERENCES

Brady, J.L., Guy, J.D., Poelstra, P.L., & Brokaw, B.F. (1999). Vicarious Traumatization, Spirituality, and the Treatment of Sexual Abuse Survivors: A National Survey of Women Psychotherapists. Professional Psychology: Research and Practice, 30, 386-393.

Burkhardt, M.A.,& Nagai-Jacobson, M. G. (2002). Spirituality: Living our Connectedness. Albany, NY: Delmar Thomson Learning.

Decker, L.R. (1993). The Role of Trauma in Spiritual Development. Journal of Humanistic Psychology, 33, 33-46.

Elkins, D.N., Hedstrom, L.J., Hughes, L.L., Leaf, J.A., & Saunders, C. (1988). Towards a Humanistic Phenomenological Spirituality: Definition, Description and Measurement. Journal of Humanistic Psychology, 28, 5-18.

Erikson, E.H. (1986). Vital Involvement in Old Age. New York: Norton Press.

Frankl, V.E. (1984). Man's Search for Meaning. NewYork: Washington Square Press.

Frankl,V. E. (1966). Self-transcendence as a Human Phenomenon. Journal of Humanistic Psychology, 6, 97-106.

Haase, J.E., Britt, T., Coward, D.D., Leidy, N.K., & Penn, P.E. (1992). Simultaneous Concept Analysis of Spiritual Perspective, Hope, Acceptance and Self-transcendence. Image: Journal of Nursing Scholarship, 24(2), 141-147.

Hiatt, J.F. (1986). Spirituality, Medicine and Healing. Southern Medical Journal, 79, 736-743.

Hill, P.C., & Pargament, K.I. (2003). Advances in the Conceptualization an Measurement of Religion and Spirituality. American Psychologist, 58, 64-74.

Hunglemann, J., Kenkel-Rossi, E., Klassen, L., & Stollenwerk, R. (1996). Focus on Spiritual well-being: Harmonious Interconnectedness of Body-mind-spirit: Use of the Jarel Spiritual well-being Scale. Geriatric Nursing, 17, 262-266.

Labun, E. (1988). Spiritual Care: An Element in Nursing Care Planning. Journal of Advanced Nursing, 13, 314-320. Lane, J. A. (1987). The Care of the Human Spirit. Journal of Professional Nursing, 3, 332-337.

Laukhof, G., & Werner, H. (1998). Spirituality: The Missing Link. Journal of Neuroscience Nursing, 30(1), 60-67. Marcoen, A. (1994). Spirituality and Personal well-being in Old Age. Ageing and Society, 14, 521-536.

Maslow, A.H. (1969). Various Meanings of Transcendence. Journal of Transpersonal Psychology, 1, 56-66. Merriam Webster Dictionary. (1974). New York: Pocket Books.

O'Brien, M. E. (2003). Spirituality in Nursing: Standing on Holy Ground (2nd ed.). Sudbury, MA: Jones and Bartlett.

Reed, P. (1991). Toward a Nursing Theory of Self-transcendence: Deductive Reformulation Using Developmental Theories. Advances in Nursing Science, 13(4), 65-77.

Tarakeshwar, N., Stanton, J., & Pargament, K.I. (2003). Religion: An overlooked Dimension in Cross-cultural Psychology. Journal of Cross-Cultural Psychology 34, 377-394.

Taylor, A.J.W. (2001). Spirituality and Personal Values: Neglected Components of Trauma Treatment. Traumatology, 7, 111-119.

Wilson, J.P., & Moran, T.A. (1998). Psychological Trauma: Posttraumatic Stress Disorder and Spirituality. Journal of Psychology and Theology, 26, 168-178.

A Case Study on Income Inequality and Poverty Among Tiwa Tribe of Morigaon District of Assam

Pankaj Saikia and **Mriganka Saikia**

ABSTRACT

Both the central and state planning authorities have framed and implemented various policies for improvement of standards of living of Scheduled Castes (SC) and Scheduled Tribes (ST) who have historically been most backward classes. We believe that the development process for any society/community is ultimately evaluated through its impact on quality of life and human well-being. Here we focus on the economic status of STs using some standard measures of income inequality and poverty. Almost all types of deprivations initiate from lack of access to income necessary to maintain a minimum acceptable standard of living.

Introduction

One of the major objectives of the government, reflected in various plan documents, has been to promote *economic growth with social justice* with a view to making the society more egalitarian. Both the central and state planning authorities have framed and implemented various policies for improvement of standards of living of Scheduled Castes (SC) and Scheduled Tribes (ST) who have historically been most backward classes. In order to evaluate the impact of national and state level development programmes, it is important that we obtain an accurate picture of standards of living of these less privileged social and ethnic groups. We believe that the development process for any society/community is ultimately evaluated through its impact on quality of life and human well-being. Here we focus on the economic status of STs using some standard measures of income inequality and poverty.

Conceivably, almost all types of deprivations initiate from lack of access to income necessary to maintain a minimum acceptable standard of living. UNDP would call this inadequate economic empowerment. However the national and state average HDI, income inequality and poverty index figures mask much of the variations in empowerment across states and social groups. It is thus critical to observe the income inequality and poverty indices separately for STs and non-STs to recognise the merits and limitations of planned development programmes aimed at improving the levels of living of the STs.

Apparently, household income is only an indispensable indicator of material well-being. An adequate household income is necessary though not sufficient to guarantee a reasonable quality of life. Higher the household income greater is the possibility of leading a decent life, implying a higher level of well-being. That is why a comparative analysis of earned income of households across communities is likely to unfold a few aspects of quality of life in relative terms. The present study looks at the relative positions poverty and inequality of blocks of Morigaon district of Assam.

Review of Literature

Chakrabarty (2008) in his research paper made an attempt to estimate poverty parameters among SCs /STs in All India level. Findings show that Sen. Index and FGT index suggest that intensity of poverty is more among the SCs and STs than among others. *Das* (2012) searched on social change and development of women among the major tribal groups of the state. In respect of interstate variation, the pace of socio-economic change which was the highest among the Tiwas and the lowest among the Bodos during 1971-1991 got completely reversed, and as such the Bodos experienced the highest and the Tiwas witnessed the lowest degree of change during 1991-2001and so it is important to find out the basic reasons behind such reversed variation. *Ghosh and Malik* (2009) in their paper have made an attempt to find the condition of tribal health in Ranibandh block of West Bengal. Tribal development is a vast and complex issue, which is multidimensional. Some of the important aspects of tribal development are health, education and economic development which are responsible for large scale poverty and inequality. *Haughton, Jonathan and Khander* (2010) define inequality as a broader concept than poverty because it encompasses over the entire population and not only focus on the poor. The study simultaneously explained the commonly used inequality measures, such as, Decile Dispersion Ratio, Gini Coefficient, Generalized Entropy Measures and Atkinson's Inequality Measures. They also explained the measures of Pro-Poor Growth and Decomposition of Income Inequality. *Swamy* (2010) in his paper clearly showed with facts that the literacy rate among ST population in comparison with that of the general population indicates a growing gap between literacy rates of these communities. The study points out that the major factor accounting for low educational achievements and low aspirations on the part of tribe folk is their poor social and economic condition .They live in unhealthy environment, do low-paid physical labour, and own very little land. The study finds that educational system must suit with the rural and agricultural base-towards a knowledge skills-based economy one of the important schemes for ameliorate poverty among tribal people.

Objective

The objective of this study is to investigate the poverty and income inequality among the people residing in the six blocks of the district.

Among the measures of inequality we include Gini coefficient or Gini measure, Theil's entropy measure and the squared coefficient of variation. Among the poverty indices we have considered the head count ratio, Sen's index and Foster-Greer-Thorbeck index.

Methodology

Data Sources

There are 6 development blocks in Morigaon District i.e. Bhurbondha, Mayong, Kapili, Lahorighat, Dolongghat, Baropujiwa. Total No. of STs according to data available from Tiwa Autonomous Council, 7072 in Moirabari, 13,695 in Dolonghat, 25175 in Mayong, 15609 in Lahorighat, 14207 in Kapili, 35395 in Bhurbandha and 268 in Batadrava development Block. In the Morigaon district, where the bulk of the Tiwas are concentrated, they constitute 76.6 per cent of the total tribal population of the district. For the proposed study, both the primary and secondary data / information shall be used. The primary data shall be purposefully collected by the researcher in a set of well-designed questionnaire from the sample respondents. In Morigaon district, the tiwa people is concentrated in across the blocks. Out of seven blocks, in this study we took six major Tiwa concentrated blocks. To study about poverty and inequality of Tiwa people, a multi-staged purposive sampling procedure will be followed to select sampling units. In this study data collected from both primary as well as secondary sources have been made use of while information collected from development officials, office of Tiwa Autonomous Council, data from the relevant literature published and unpublished, official records and files, census reports etc. While selecting the villages from blocks, we give emphasis on variability or diversity of data, such as, tribal population size of the village, availability of electricity, access to pure drinking water, distance to town, transport and communication, pattern of occupation, etc. These factors influence poverty, inequality and quality of life. After having selected the sample villages and the number of sample households, we drew random samples from each village. In the first step, we enumerated the households of each selected village with their names. In second step, the names of the households were arranged in an ascending lexicographic order assigning a serial number 1 to N_i. Here, N_i is the total number of households in the ith village (i=1, 2, 3....12). Then, uniformly distributed random numbers lying between 1 and N_i were generated for each village. A total of 202 households were surveyed taking 20 per cent households from villages.

Tools for Analysis of the data

Among the measures of inequality we include Gini coefficient or Gini measure, Theil's entropy measure and the squared coefficient of variation and among the poverty indices we have considered the head count ratio, Sen's index and Foster-Greer-Thorbeck index.

Measures of Inequality

Income inequalities in the seven selected blocks are calculated using three alternative measures of inequality, viz, Gini coefficient, Theil's entropy measure and the squared coefficient of variation. They satisfy the three desirable properties of a measure of inequality, viz., each measure is scale independent, population size independent and each follows the all important Pigou-Dalton condition – the inequality measure should rise if income transfer occurs from a poorer to a richer person, relative ranking remaining the same.

This study uses the geometric definition or the trapezoidal rule for grouped income data to compute the Gini coefficient. It, can be derived from the general formula for grouped data given by,

$$G = \frac{1}{2} \sum_{i=1}^{n} \sum_{j=1}^{n} p_i \, p_j \left| \frac{y'_i}{p_i} - \frac{y'_j}{p_j} \right|$$

Where y'_i is the income share of the ith income class only (not cumulative), p_i is the cumulative population proportion up to the ith income class, i.e., proportion of persons with highest income of the ith class or less and n is the number of income classes. From formula which uses the sum of weighted mutual differences, we can derive the trapezoidal rule (Kakwani, 1980) following some manipulation as under.

$$G = 1 - \sum_{i=1}^{n} p_i \; (Q_i + Q_{i-1})$$

Where, Q_i is the cumulative income share up to the ith income class, definition of p_i being the same. To compute G, the data need to be arranged in ascending order of income classes. There are several alternative forms of computing G (Sen, 1973; Rao, 1981), but all these measures are equivalent to the geometric definition (Anand, 1980). By considering differences of all possible pairs of income proportions, the Gini coefficient avoids the total concentration on differences with respect to the mean, which the variance

(*V*) and coefficient of variation (C) cannot. In avoiding the ad hoc *squaring* procedure of C and *V*, the Gini coefficient is a more direct measure of inequality taking note of differences between every income pair.

The term *entropy* is borrowed from thermodynamics. Entropy, in thermodynamics, implies increasing disorder. But here *entropy* is used to imply reduction in inequality rather than its converse. Theil goes on to define entropy as the expected information content in a particular situation. It implies the weighted average of information content of a situation where the weights are the respective probabilities. But apart from borrowing the term, Theil's entropy measure of inequality has hardly anything to do with the principles of thermodynamics. If $H(x)$ denotes entropy, $h_i(x_i)$ the information content in the ith situation and x_i the probability that the ith situation will occur, then

$$H(x) = \sum_{i=1}^{n} x_i \; h_i \; (x_i)$$

It has been assumed that $h_i(x_i) = \log \frac{1}{x_i}$. In other words, the more unlikely the event, the greater must be the information content in the situation. It implies that lower is the probability that the ith event will occur the higher the information content of the situation. Considering the ideal situation where probabilities of occurrence of all events are the same, i.e $x_i = \frac{1}{n}$, Theil's measure is expressed as

$$T = \log n - H(x)$$

$$= \sum_{i=1}^{n} x_i \; \log \; n \; x_i$$

Obviously, $\sum_{i=1}^{n} x_i = 1$. But for grouped income data, the following form is used to compute *T*.

$$T = \left\{ \sum_{i=1}^{n} \left(\frac{Y_i}{Y} \right) T_i \right\} + \left\{ \sum_{i=1}^{n} \left(\frac{Y_i}{Y} \right) \log \; (Y_i / Y) \; (n_i / n) \right\}$$

where Y_i denotes the mean income of the ith class, *Y* the mean of the entire population and T_i's are to be calculated for each class separately. The first term reflects the within group inequality, while the second term captures the between groups inequality. However, most studies use Theil's index to compute only the second term in.

The most rudimentary measure of inequality – variance, satisfies the Pigou-Dalton condition. But to get a clearer picture of relative variation we consider the squared coefficient of variation. It is simply $C^2 = \frac{V}{\mu^2}$, where V denotes the squared variance of grouped income data and μ is the mean income of the population. However, a major drawback of C^2 is that it attaches equal weights to income transfers from any level to all other income levels.

Both the coefficient of variation and the Gini coefficient satisfy the Pigou-Dalton condition, which requires that an income transfer from a richer person to a poorer person must reduce the value of the inequality measure. The coefficient of variation is equally sensitive at all income levels. But the sensitivity of Gini coefficient depends not on the size of income levels but on the number of people in between them. Sen (1973) provides a remarkable interpretation of the ungrouped variant of the Gini coefficient as presented in. He writes: "In any pair-wise comparison the man with the lower income can be thought to be suffering from some depression on finding his income to be lower. Let this depression be proportional to the difference in income. The sum total of all such depressions in all possible pair-wise comparisons takes us to the Gini coefficient".

Measures of Poverty

Among the standard measures of poverty we consider the Head Count Ratio (*H*), Sen's Poverty Index and the Foster-Greer-Thorbeck Index (FGT). We present a brief overview of these measures.

Let $y = (y_i, y_2, \ldots, y_n)$ be a vector of incomes of n households arranged in increasing order, $z > 0$ the predetermined poverty line, $g_i = z - y_i$ the income shortfall of the ith household and q the number of poor households (having income less than or equal to z). It follows then that $H = \frac{q}{n}$ is the well-known head count ratio, which simply is the proportion of poor households. The Income-Gap ratio is $I = \frac{1}{qz} \sum_{1=1}^{q} g_i$. It merely expresses the total income gap (shortfall) of the poor as a proportion of the maximum total income of the poor. Sen's Poverty Index (1981) is given by $P = H\{I + (1 - I)G_p\}$, where G_p is the Gini coefficient among the poor. Sen's index, which is a ranked relative deprivation, satisfies both the monotonicity and weak-transfer axioms. According to Sen (*op cit*), these two axioms must be satisfied by any reasonable measure of poverty.

The monotonicity axiom states that other things unchanged a reduction in income of a household below the poverty line must raise the poverty measure. The weak transfer axiom says that a pure transfer of income to a poor household below the poverty line from a richer household, without making either cross the poverty line must reduce the poverty measure. Clearly, *H* violates both these axioms. *I*, on the other hand, satisfies the monotonicity axiom but violates the weak transfer axiom. But being a function of Gini coefficient among the poor, *P* is not additively decomposable across population sub groups.

Following Sen (*op cit*), *FGT* index for ungrouped data expresses poverty as a normalized weighted sum of income shortfalls of the poor. For ungrouped data *FGT* index is written as $FGT = \frac{1}{n\ z^2}\sum_{i=1}^{q} g_i^2$. In contrast to *P*, which adopts a rank order weighted scheme, *FGT* takes the weights as the shortfalls themselves (Foster, Greer and Thorbeck, 1984). *FGT* index satisfies both the monotonicity and weak transfer axioms. In addition, it is additively decomposable over population subgroups. *FGT* index is associated with the squared coefficient of variation of income distribution among the poor. If the squared coefficient of variation among the poor is computed as

$$C_p^2 = \sum_{i=1}^{q}\left(\bar{y}_p - y_i\right)^2 / (q\,\bar{y}_p^{\,2})$$ is the mean income of the poor, then

the *FGT* index can be expressed as

$$FGT = H\,[I^2 + (1 - I)^2\, C_p^2]$$

Since the head count ratio merely gives the percentage of the population below the poverty line and fails to show the intensity of their poverty, we here used both Sen and Foster-Greer-Thorbeck indices as both quantify the *intensity* of poverty among the poor. Stated differently, they denote the degree or the extent of poverty.

Results and Discussion

In Table 6.1 we present mean income per person (nominal per capita) in the entire sample as also the mean income as well as normalized mean income of the poor separately, across the selected blocks. It is clear from Table 6.1 that the poorer blocks like Dolongghat, Mayong and Baropujiwa have a more egalitarian distribution of income.

Per capita income of STs is lower in all blocks than that of Non-ST in the district. But the difference is significantly higher in blocks bhubondha, kapli ,lahorighat than that of other blocks.

We now consider a block and community-wise ranking in terms of per capita income. In terms of per capita income of STs, Mayong is at the top and Baropujiwa at the bottom. Among the non-STs Kapili tops the list in per capita income, Lahorighat is at the bottom. Further, normalised per capita incomes of the *poor* inter-block variations are observed. For instance, in Bhurbondha, a typical poor ST can afford to purchase only 76 per cent of the minimum basket of goods and services necessary to keep him exactly on the line of poverty. The same figure is just 57 per cent in Dolongghat and as low as 54 per cent in Baropujiwa. In fact, the poor as a class are doing better in Bhurbondha than in most other blocks. A typical poor non-STs in can however buy 61 per cent of the minimum basket. Perhaps this shows substantial inequality between a typical poor non-STs and a ST with regard to standard of living or quality of life. In block and community-wise ranking, STs in Baropujiwa enjoying just 54 per cent of the poverty income are at the bottom of the ladder, while non-STs in Bhurbondha with 76 per cent of the poverty income is ahead of others.

Table 6.1: Estimated Mean Income

Blocks	Nominal Mean Income of the Sample (Rs. per person per annum)		Normalised Mean Income of the Poor +	
	ST	Non-ST	ST	Non-ST
Bhurbondha	3384	5652	0.76	0.72
Mayong	3715	3982	0.61	0.62
Kapili	3663	6377	0.62	0.62
Lahorighat	3560	6716	0.72	0.73
Dolongghat	2588	3544	0.57	0.61
Baropujiwa	2266	3457	0.54	0.65

Source: Computed Value.

Table 6.2: Estimated Income Inequality

Blocks	Gini Coefficient		Theil's Entropy Measure		C^2	
	ST	Non-ST	ST	Non-ST	ST	Non-ST
Bhurbondha	0.3037	0.4328	0.1564	0.3322	0.3251	0.7477
Mayong	0.4492	0.3832	0.3564	0.2583	0.9337	0.5789
Kapili	0.4648	0.4663	0.4522	0.3887	1.3890	0.8466
Lahorighat	0.4279	0.4214	0.3261	0.3226	0.8558	0.6445
Dolongghat	0.3995	0.4265	0.2771	0.3113	0.6528	0.7331
Baropujiwa	0.3334	0.3493	0.1899	0.2159	0.4595	0.4979

Source: Computed Value.

Table 6.2 presents the income inequality measures. The non-STs exhibit more unequal distribution of income than STs in most blocks. Actually, those belonging to STs have a lower per capita income; while among non-STs there are rich as well as poor households leading to a greater income inequality. Among STs, income distribution is more unequal among STs of Mayong, Kapili and Baropujiwa.

The three different measures of poverty, computed from survey data, are presented in Table 3. The table shows that the incidence of poverty among STs is a good deal higher compared to others. Thus, every alternate person among STs is a poor, while every third person, not belonging to STs, is poor. By head count, the poorest state is Dolongghat where roughly 65 per cent of STs are poor. By head count, poverty among STs is most severe in Baropujiwa and least in Bhurbondha. The gap between STs and others is strikingly high in the states of Lahorighat, Kapili, Mayong. So, it can safely be inferred from the comparisons of head count ratio, that incidence of poverty among STSs is far greater vis-à-vis non-STs.

From Sen index, it is clearly observed that the intensity of poverty among STs is severe compared to that among non-STs. Intensity of poverty in Bhurbondha is minimum across by Sen index; the intensity is highest in Dolongghat. The intensity of poverty among STs - Baropujiwa has the lowest rank preceded by Dolongghat and Kapili. FGT index of poverty gives almost the same ranking of blocks as observed by using Sen index.

The general impression is that the lower the ranking of a state in terms of *incidence* of poverty, the lower is also its ranking in terms of *intensity* of poverty. That is, the three measures of poverty are closely related in the sense that the greater the *incidence* of poverty, the greater is its *intensity*.

Table 6.3: Estimated Poverty Parameters

Blocks	Head Count Ratio		Sen Index		FGT Index	
	ST	Non-ST	ST	Non-ST	ST	Non-ST
Bhurbondha	0.2888	0.2217	0.0899	0.0875	0.0221	0.0223
Mayong	0.4878	0.3389	0.2643	0.1889	0.1100	0.0698
Kapili	0.5345	0.2989	0.2778	0.1578	0.1040	0.0576
Lahorighat	0.5277	0.2621	0.2100	0.0989	0.0621	0.0279
Dolongghat	0.6544	0.4889	0.3489	0.2783	0.1529	0.1112
Baropujiwa	0.7393	0.4882	0.4101	0.2273	0.1698	0.0678

Source: Computed Value.

Summary and Conclusion

This study focuses on the relative positions of STs *vis-à-vis* the rest of the population in terms poverty and income inequality. Some standard measures of poverty (head count ratio, Sen and FGT indices) and income inequality (Gini, Theil's entropy measure and the squared coefficient of variation) have been employed. Among these, those blocks, which house more than 75 per cent of Tiwa population, have been selected for this study. We sum up our results below. Per capita income in is clearly higher for non-STs compared to that of STs. But among the poor, mean income does not vary much across communities.

Every alternate person of STs is poor while every third person not belonging to STs is poor. Poverty is severe among the groups in the district of Doongghat, Baropujiwa, and Mayong. The *incidence* and *intensity* of poverty are much higher among those belonging to the STs than that among others. The gap in terms of head count ratio between STs and non- STs is distinctly high in the states of Lahorighat, Kapili and Mayong. The estimated indices show that the incidence and intensity of poverty are strongly positively correlated. This observation is based on household sample data from only a few blocks, purposely selected to measure the incidence of poverty and its intensity among STs as against non-STs.

REFERENCES

Anand, S. (1980), *Inequality and Poverty in Malaysia: Measurement and Decomposition,* Oxford University Press, London.

Chakrabarty, G. (2008), "Quality of life of Scheduled Castes and Scheduled Tribes in Rural India" in S. Muhammad Ayub Buzdar and Aktar Ali (eds.), " Parents Attitude toward Daughters Education in Tribal Area of Dera Ghaji Khan (Pakistan)", *Turkish Online Journal of Qualitative Inquiry* , 2 (1).

Chakrabarty, G. and P.K. Ghosh (2000), *Human Development Profile of Scheduled Castes and Scheduled Tribes in Rural India: A Bench Mark Survey,* NCAER, New Delhi.

Das, M (2012), *Tribal Women of Assam - A Social Geographical Perspectives,* EBH Publishers, Guwahati.

Foster, J., J. Greer and E. Thorbeck (1984), 'A Class of Decomposable Poverty Measures.' *Econometrica,* Vol. 52, No. 3, pp. 751-65.

Haughton, J and S R Khander (2010), *Handbook on Poverty and Inequality,* Rawat Publications. New Delhi.

Kakwani, N. (1980), *Income Inequality and Poverty –Methods of Estimation and Policy Applications,* Oxford University Press.

Kurien, C.T. (1982), 'Economic Conditions of Scheduled Castes', *Yojana,* October 16-31, pp. 13-18.

Nayak, V. and S. Prasad (1984), 'On Levels of Living of Scheduled Castes and Scheduled.

Tribes', *Economic and Political Weekly,* July 28, pp. 1205-1213.

Rao, V.K.R.V. (1981), 'Measurement of Poverty', *Economic and Political Weekly,* Vol. XVI, No. 35, Aug 29, pp. 1433-36.

S. Ghosh and S. Malik (2009), "Assessment and Administration of Health in a Tribal Community of India". *The Internet Journal of Biological Anthropology,* 3(2).

Saggar, M. and I. Pan (1994), 'SCs and STs in Eastern India, Inequality and Poverty Estimates', *Economic and Political Weekly,* March 5, pp. 567-574.

Sen, A.K. (1973), *On Economic Inequality,* Oxford Clarendon Press.

Sen, A. K. (1981), *Poverty and Famines: An Essay on Entitlement and Deprivation,* Oxford University Press, New York.

Shariff, A (1999), *India Human Development Report,* NCAER, Oxford University Press, New Delhi.

Swamy, N.R (2010), "Tribal Education as a Tool for Rural Transformation: A Case Study of Paniyas in Wayanad Kerela", *Kurukshetra* .59(1):15-20.

7

Significence of Rural Non-farm Sector in the Development of Rural Assam *A Case Study of Dhemaji District*

Dr. P. Sailajananda Saikia

ABSTRACT

The significant role played by the rural non-farm sector (RNFS) in the over-all development of rural economies is now well-recognized. Although the debate on agriculture-induced diversification as the cornerstone of the development of rural non-farm sector continues to attract a great deal of attention, many recent studies on urban-linkages of rural non-farm growth clearly point to the role of rural non-farm sector as an important link between industry and agriculture. This study is a modest attempt to understand the unfolding dynamics of the rural non-farm sector in Assam, in relation to its importance in the employment generation strategies. Given the high dependencies on agriculture and forest based activities, a near complete absence of non-household manufacturing and excessive dependence on government jobs as a source of employment in the service sector, the role of rural non-farm sector needs to be the cornerstone of any strategy for income and livelihood diversification in the state. An attempt has been made in this paper to look into the role of non-farm sector in the development of rural areas. Dhemaji being one of the most underdeveloped districts in the state where there is no industry, the role of rural non-farm sector plays a critical role in income and employment generation in the district.

Keywords: Rural non-farm sector; Income; Employment; Dhemaji district.

Introduction

The Indian economy grew at an impressive rate in the last decade and demographic pressure also slowed.[1] Yet, the incidence of unemployment towards the end of the 2011 was more than seven per cent. The situation is especially disconcerting in the rural sector. Employment in rural sector, which is associated mostly with agriculture, has stagnated during the 90s (Jha 2006). Considering the increased pressure on land there exists limited scope for increasing employment in agriculture so that employment in the non-farm sector becomes an important option.

Studies also suggest that with the process of development, the share of non-farm income and employment in the total income and employment of the rural households increases in the developing countries.[2] A combination of farm and non-farm income at the household level provides resilience against adverse situations in either of the sectors, though agriculture is known for more frequent adversity. There are also evidences to show that productivity and profitability in the non-farm sector is generally higher than in the farm sector; as are the average wages and working conditions that obtain in the non-farm sector (Fisher et al. 1998). A greater reliance on the non-farm sector would therefore provide a demand-pull to rural economy and also ensure welfare for rural workers.

The significant role played by the rural non-farm sector (RNFS) in the over-all development of rural economies is now well-recognized. Although the debate on agriculture-induced diversification as the cornerstone of the development of rural non-farm sector continues to attract a great deal of attention, many recent studies on urban-linkages of rural non-farm growth clearly point to the role of rural non-farm sector as an important link between industry and agriculture. In terms of employment generation, the role of RNFS in absorbing the labour, particularly in the context of stagnant growth of employment in formal manufacturing sector, can hardly be overstressed. However, given the heterogeneity and diversity within the non-farm sector itself, there is a need to study the growth performance as well as labour absorption capacity of the sector in specific regional and sectorial contexts.

There have been very few studies on the role and dynamics of Rural Non-Farm Employment (RNFE) in the development of North-Eastern states of India. Given the paucity of data and the wide ranging diversity of livelihood strategies within the region there is a clear need to understand the growth, composition and determinants of RNFE in different parts of the region giving due emphasis to locale specificities as well as macro-level linkages. Standard ideas on growth linkages and implications of the growth process for the employment and earning potentials for the rural masses have been found to be inadequate in explaining the development of this region. The specificities of the north eastern region lies in its enormous diversity, in terms of resource endowments, population composition, ecological and social preconditions and the historical encounter with modernity. Such is the magnitude of this diversity that many scholars have objected to the blanket term 'north east' on the grounds that it conceals the diversity within the region.

In this context, this study is a modest attempt to understand the unfolding dynamics of the rural non-farm sector in Assam in general and Dhemaji district in particular, in relation to its importance in the employment generation strategies. Given the high dependencies on agriculture and forest based activities, a near complete absence of non-household manufacturing and excessive dependence on government jobs as a source of employment in the service sector, the role of rural non-farm sector needs to be the cornerstone of any strategy for income and livelihood diversification in the state. It is important to note that the different patterns of RNFE growth have different implications for rural households. It calls for different types of policy interventions. In partially commercialized, agrarian economies, typically characterized by absence or under-formation of input and product markets, high transaction costs and low levels of technology, the goal of diversification within and beyond the farm sector becomes crucial for poverty eradication and securing basic survival needs of the poor.

Objectives

The study tries to look at the nature of the rural non-farm economy in Dhemaji District of Assam, utilizing both primary and secondary data. The primary objectives of the study are:

1. To find out the extent, composition and growth of rural nonfarm employment in Dhemaji district in Assam, during 2005-10.
2. To study the determinants of RNFE at the district as well as the household levels.
3. To understand the role and significance of non-farm sector activities in the overall livelihood diversification strategy of rural households.
4. To bring out policy prescriptions to help employment diversification in rural Dhemaji district, Assam.

Scope and Methodology

The main focus of the study is on the significance and the determinants of RNFE in Dhemaji district of Assam. In particular the attempt has been to look into the nature of the rural non-farm economy evolving in the state, as well as its linkages with micro-level strategies for livelihood diversification in this predominantly tribal state. As already mentioned, the study is based on both primary as well as secondary information.

Firstly, a village analysis of the pattern of workforce restructuring in Assam has been undertaken from the Population Census data for the period 2005-10. Other secondary sources data from NSSO[3], Economic Census and sector specific reports of Government of Assam has also been utilized to understand the extent, types and quality of employment in the rural non-farm sector. After identifying the key sectors of the rural non-farm economy and the relative position of districts in terms of share of RNFE in rural workforce a primary survey has been conducted to find out the household level determinants of participation in RNFE.

The basic purpose of the primary survey was to find out the household characteristics determining entry into the non-farm economy. The division of household working days between agricultural and non-agricultural activities was another focus of the primary survey. Such a survey was considered necessary because at very low levels of commercialisation, and declining environmental quality, farm households tends to opt for a diversification of their livelihood options on a flexible and short term basis rather than a permanent and durable shift towards a non-agricultural occupation – a fact which is often not captured satisfactorily by macro-studies.

The methodology adopted for selection of samples for the primary survey was based on the following considerations. An important aspect of the economy of Dhemaji district of Assam is that it is mainly a flood affected area and based on agriculture economy, with very low levels of infrastructural development and a remarkably low population density. Apart from the considerable inter-sub division variations in the extent of workers engaged in the non-farm sector, a significant dimension of the RNFE in the state is its spatial concentration in few rural locations which are either near urban centres or are well connected. Thus, to find out the household level determinants of participation in the rural non-farm economy, a multi-stage sampling method was followed. In the first stage, sub divisions with relatively high share of workers in the non-farm sector were selected. In the next stage, three villages from each of the sub divisions were selected on the basis of distance from the urban centres, so as to represent the different types of growth of the rural non-farm sector. One of the villages in each of the districts is nearer to the urban centre, one is relatively far off and one is an intermediate village. After the selection of the study villages, households were selected randomly from amongst the households residing in the villages. The size of the sample household selected from each village was 50-60 per cent of the total households in the village. Simple statistical and econometric techniques were used to analyse the secondary and primary data.

Introduction to the Study Area

Dhemaji district of Assam is located in the North-eastern part of Brahmaputra river basin between North Latitude 27°15′ to 28° 00′ and East Longitude 94°05′ to 95°30′ covering an area of 3,237 sq.km. The district has been sub-divided into two civil sub-division (CSD), which contains four circles and five blocks.

Population of the district is 688077 (as per 2011 census) having total rural and urban populations as 639605 and 48472 respectively with density of 213 per sq.km. As per the land used pattern, the net cropped area is 1,06,634 ha cultivable land is 1,24,81 ha, cultivable fallow land is 18,976 ha and the area occupied by water bodies is 24,050 ha.

The district receives heavy rainfall during May to July with an average annual rainfall of 3,435 mm under the influence of southwest monsoon. In general temperature varies from 10° to 37°C and during winter, temperature goes down to as low as 2° to 5°C. Humidity is very high throughout the year being 70 per cent during winter and rises up to 90 per cent during rainy season.

Physiographically, the district is more or less flat and the area can be divided into high-level plain of Brahmaputra river (between altitudes 107 m & 122 m AMSL) and flat flood plain area (between altitudes 89 m & 96 m AMSL). Numbers of perennial streams flow through the district from north to south and join the Brahmaputra River. Thus the River Brahmaputra is effluent in nature. The major streams that drain the area are Kumotia, Gai, Kanibil, Sisi, Simen, Dikari and Royang.

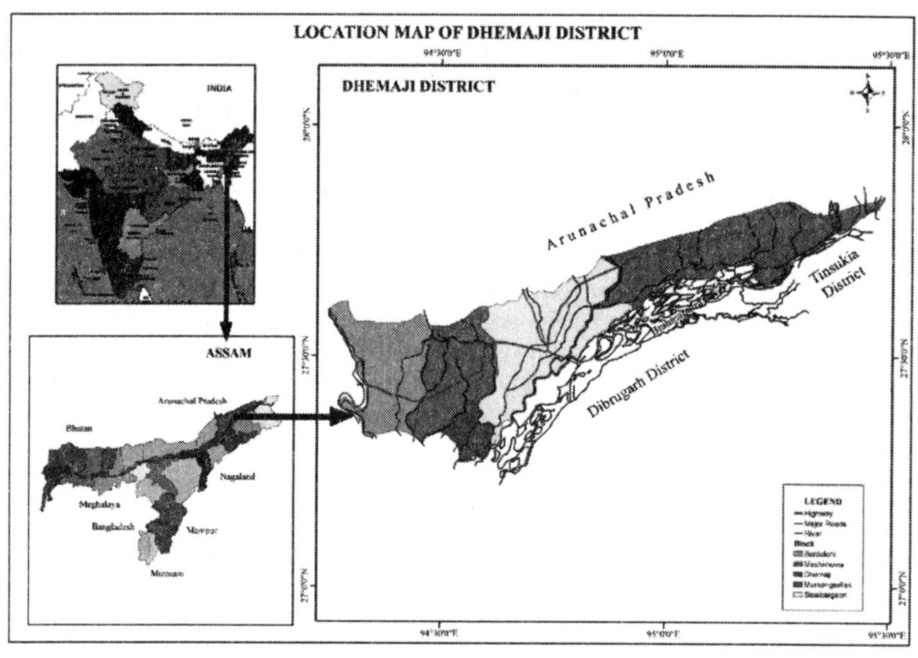

Map of Dhemaji District

The Rural Non-Farm Economy: Definition, Dynamics and Determinants

The importance of Rural Non-Farm Sector (RNFS) in providing employment and earnings to a substantial section of the rural population has been clearly brought out by many studies (Liedholm and Kilby, 1986; Shand, 1986; Visaria and Basant, 1994). The RNFS is no longer viewed as a 'passive side route' to provide employment for some; rather its centrality in the overall strategy of rural transformation is well recognized now. It is quite clear that in peasant economies, characterized by heavy demographic pressure on land, small and fragmented holdings, iniquitous land distribution structures etc., agriculture alone cannot solve the problems of rural unemployment and underemployment (Chadha, 1993a). Given the low employment elasticity in the increasingly capital-intensive manufacturing sector, and problems of urban congestion, the necessity for providing employment within the rural sector itself is being increasingly realized.

Modern agricultural growth is based on strong backward and forward linkages with industry and other non-agricultural activities some of which may partly be located in the rural areas themselves (Mellor, 1976). The prospect of non-farm sector growth also critically depends on the nature and pace of agricultural growth at least because of three different reasons viz. expansion of demand for non-farm goods and services, growth of rural enterprises supplying agricultural inputs. Rising agricultural productivity and wages in agriculture, by raising the opportunity cost of labour in the non-farm sector, restructures the later by a shift from low-return, labour-intensive activities into more skilled, higher investment, high return activities (Hazell and Haggblade, 1991:515). Similarly, a healthy growth of the rural non-farm sector can contribute substantially towards a more productive and diversified agricultural growth. The advantages associated with rural non- farm sector, according to a number of studies, include utilization of local talent and local 'slack' resources, which cannot be easily shifted or utilized elsewhere; reduction in migration to urban, industrial centres i.e. 'localization of employment'; narrowing down of rural-urban gaps i.e. easing urban congestion; generally less capital-intensive and more labour absorbing growth pattern; lesser degree of inequality in rural income distribution (Bhalla and Chadha,1983:95-101); higher earnings and reduction in poverty levels (Chadha,1994); higher participation of women in non-farm activities etc.(Unni,1991; Misra, 2000).

The Rural Non-Farm Sector: Conceptual Issues

The rural non-farm economy (RNFE) is generally defined as comprising all those non-agricultural activities, which generate income to rural households (including income in kind and remittances), either through waged work or in self-employment. In other words, it includes all economic activities in rural areas except agriculture, hunting and fishing (Lanjouw and Lanjouw, 1995; 2001). Since it is defined negatively, as non-agriculture, it incorporates a wide range of activities including manufacturing, petty trading, services, as well as transfer payments and remittances from temporary or seasonal migration to rural areas (Davis and Pearce, 2001).

The meaning of 'rural' in RNFE is critical in understanding its nature, importance and viability (Lanjouw and Lanjouw, 1995). There are some important difficulties in defining the RNFE in a spatial perspective.[4] In fact, the RNFE can be classified on many dimensions: on-farm/off farm, wage/ self-employment, agriculturally related/ otherwise. Davis (2003) notes that an ideal classification of the RNFE should capture some or all of the following distinctions:

1. links to farming or the food-chain,– since agricultural linkages are often key determinants of the RNFE's potential for employment and income generation;
2. market linkages: local markets or distant markets – since the latter have the scope to create employment and earnings independent of the rural economy; and,
3. relative earnings and scale effects: Those which are sufficiently large, productive and capitalized to generate incomes above returns obtainable in agriculture, and those that offer marginal gains – since the capacity of the RNFE to foster growth depends on the former, while the latter can maintain the households above the poverty line (Davis, 2003)[5].

While diversification per se can refer to increasing mix or multiplicity of activities, regardless of the sector, RNFE refers to the shift away from traditional agricultural sector to non-agriculture activities. Again, there is a need to distinguish between different levels of diversification of a household or individual economy, though the two may be interrelated to some extent (Start, 2001). The RNFE may be characterized by at least three categories: the activities undertaken, employment and the use of labour time; and incomes generated. All these three categories, to some extent, overlap, but have distinct advantages and limitations. Income classifications have the advantage that they include sources that do not derive from activity and employment, such as transfers and rents, while data on employment, brings out a number of important dimensions such as, self-employment versus waged employment, full time versus part time, year-round versus seasonal, local versus distant etc.

The Role of RNFE in Rural Livelihoods

Generally, the significance of the RNFE as a source of employment is assessed on the basis of secondary data. However, the role of this sector in rural livelihoods can be understood not only in terms of its share in employment, but also in terms of proportions of income, allocation of time and its relationship with household level vulnerabilities, risk-coping and risk-dispersing mechanisms as well as its significance in the overall livelihood diversification strategies. The secondary sources of information, more often than not, are found to be inadequate to judge all these diverse linkages of the rural non-farm economy with the livelihood issues in rural areas.

Nevertheless, large scale household level surveys carried out by various agencies do point out that the RNFE plays an important role in terms of its share in household's income, time use and diversification strategies. Hazell and Hagblade (1991), for example, on the basis of NCAER data, found the share of RNFE in income of rural households in India to be around 25-35 per cent, as against its share of 20-25 per cent in employment. They argue that the higher income than employment share implies either higher returns to labour in non-farm employment or extensive part-time and seasonal non-farm activity which are not captured in the employment statistics. According to Walker and Ryan (1990) the share of non-farm income in total income of rural households in India has increased from 20 to 27 per cent between 1971-72 to 1981-82, while the share of agricultural income declined from 60 to 53 per cent during the same period as per NCAER[6] data. Around 70 per cent of the increase in real household income during the period could be attributed to the rise in non-farm incomes. Fisher et al (1997) have argued that non-farm employment is particularly important to some evidence to suggest that the growth of RNFE might lead to increase in inequality (Coppard, 2001).

Determinants of RNFE

Rural non-farm livelihoods depend upon the rural population having the capacity or opportunity to take part in the RNFE. The RNFE generally incorporates both diversification under distress i.e. distress- push or diversification in response to better opportunities, i.e. demand pull. Given the enormous diversity that characterizes the RNFE, different categories of households, facing different sets of constraints and opportunities opt for different types of rural non-farm activities. Reardon et al. (1998) suggest that when relative returns are higher to the RNFE than to agriculture, and returns to agriculture are relatively more risky, pull factors are at work. Conversely, when farm output is inadequate and opportunities for consumption smoothing, such as credit and crop insurance, are missing, or when input markets are absent or fail and the household needs cash to pay for farm inputs, push factors are at work. Under such conditions, wages or incomes are likely to be lower in the rural non-farm economy. Among the key push factors pointed out in the literature are demographic pressure, scarcity of cultivable land, deforestation and decline in natural resource base, decline in agricultural productivity, lack of access to various inputs, absence or incompleteness of rural financial markets, transient shocks and catastrophic events. Pull factors on the other hand include higher earnings, higher returns to investment, comparatively lower risks, generation of 'cash' income, and socio-cultural factors like appeal of urbanized life-styles (Davis and Pearce, 2000).

In many developing countries, the seasonal character of the RNFE is inclined to decrease with increased diversification and to show a trend towards more constancy. There often exists a positive correlation of RNFE activities with higher income levels of rural families, higher potential for diversification of income sources and higher productivity in agricultural activities. However, the interdependence between cause and effect is complex and has to be analyzed with reference to the specificities of each case, before patterns and clusters can be identified.

Recent research has also shown a positive correlation between a higher diversification of non-farm activities and income and the level of education, quality of and access to infrastructure, quality, objectives and organization of services, opportunities created by local, regional and national government policies, and access to credit and financial services (Davis, 2001; Davis and Pearce, 2000).

Various studies provide evidence of growth of non-farm sector in India and show that it is dependent upon agricultural development, infrastructure, urbanization, rural incomes, population pressure, land man ratio, commercialization of agriculture and so on. The prospect of rural non-farm growth is largely determined by the linkages of such activities with the rest of the economy. In the following discussion we have presented the causal determinants of the growth of the RNFE in terms of some broad inter-sectoral linkages.

A number of studies in India suggest that growth of agriculture is likely to stimulate the growth and development of the rural non-farm sector (Hazell and Haggblade, 1991; Bhalla, 1990, 1993; Papola, 1987; Shukla, 1991, 1992; Unni, 1991, 1994). The role of agriculture as a driving force for the diversification of the rural economy has been widely noticed in the literature. In an influential formulation, Mellor (1976) has argued that as a result of the green revolution technologies and subsequent increase in agricultural productivity and earnings in the farm sector, demand-led growth of both farm and non-farm sector would take place, thus stimulating a 'virtuous cycle' of growth of food production and employment. Agricultural development and commercialization are expected to enhance the scope for expansion of the RNFE through various channels such as: supply of raw materials, greater demand for inputs and allied services, increased demand for consumption goods and generation of surplus for investment. The various linkages between the agricultural and non-agricultural sectors of the rural economy include, capital flows (investment of agricultural surpluses in non-agricultural activities), labour flows (the counter cyclical involvement of agricultural labour in non-agricultural activities according to the seasonal character of labour demand in agriculture), production linkages (supply of agricultural inputs like fertilizers, equipments and building materials etc. to the farmers), forward linkages (agro-processing), consumption linkages (demand for housing, consumer durables and other non-food items as a result of rising agricultural incomes) etc. (Visaria and Basant, 1994b: 20-25).

Rural Non-Farm Employment in Assam: Size and Composition

The Rural Non-Farm sector has a tremendous scope for development in the state. In a recently conducted survey, NABARD[7] has identified 10 sectors for development which includes sectorial schemes for the development which includes sectors like agriculture, fishery, rural retail trade, sericulture and silk textile, fibre production, construction, small plantation product, handloom, handicraft mainly cane, bamboo and wood products. These activities are developed for creation of additional employment in the rural areas.

Assam, from a low level of economic diversification during the pre-independence period, has shown a relatively rapid expansion of the non-farm sector, particularly since the seventies. The share of non-farm employment in rural employment in the state has gone up from only 21.41 per cent in 1993-94 to 32.32 per cent in 1999-00. From the census data[8], it can be inferred that rural employment in non-household manufacturing, construction, trade and commerce, and transport, storage and communications have expanded during 1971-1991, while the relative share of household manufacturing and other services has shown a decline. Employment in transport, storage and communications has recorded the highest growth rate during this period, followed by mining and quarrying and non-household manufacturing.

Table 7.1: Rural Non-Farm Labour Force in North East India

State	1993-94			1999-00		
	R_M	R_F	R_P	R_M	R_F	R_P
Arunachal Pradesh	20.93	3.84	13.61	24.38	4.89	16.58
Assam	22.36	17.65	21.41	35.35	20.60	32.32
Manipur	33.49	39.56	35.88	22.05	30.43	24.70
Megahlaya	17.46	9.48	14.01	14.03	12.72	13.45
Mizoram	13.65	6.73	11.22	15.99	12.53	14.49
Nagaland	32.13	10.81	25.55	29.47	8.07	20.34
Sikkim	43.02	32.97	40.86	43.16	29.93	39.25
Tripura	51.56	45.48	50.52	54.72	50.93	54.29
All North East	25.32	18.82	23.76	34.86	19.97	31.34
All India	25.90	13.8	21.60	28.60	13.70	23.70

Source: NSS 50th and 55th rounds, extracted from household level data on CDROM).

Notes: R_M= Rural Males, R_F = Rural Females, R_P= Rural Persons

Determinants of Participation in Rural Nonfarm Activities

The low level of economic development in Assam as well as the highly uneven nature of this development process has resulted in a situation where relatively high degree of diversification of the workforce in the few urban and well-developed areas coincide with substantially low levels of diversification in some of the remote parts of the state. The situation of Dhemaji district in terms of infrastructure is not well developed and most of the areas are flood affected, many villages are there which are yet to be connected with roads, and where very little diversification has taken place. At the same time rural households have increasingly started to diversify their earnings portfolio in response to new opportunities being provided by various government initiatives as well as the market forces. After the restrictions on commercial felling of trees, many of the households have started looking for alternative sources of livelihood, both within and outside agriculture. The purpose of the following analysis is to look into the degree, nature and determinants of participation of rural households in various nonfarm activities in the relatively well-communicated villages of Assam.

Characteristics of Sample Households

The village wise distribution of the selected sample households has been presented in Table 7.2. The samples were selected from six different villages of Dhemaji district.

Table 7.2: Village-wise Distribution of Sample Households

Sl.No.	District	Name of the Village	Number of Households	Percentage
1.	Dhemaji	Akajan	36	12.5
2.		Kulajan	102	35.4
3.		Demow	31	10.8
4.		Sille	19	6.6
5.		Sirepani	39	13.5
6.		Telam	61	21.2
	Total		288	100.0

The proportion of ST population in the district is high compare to other districts in the state. The ST population is 47.29 per cent and the population density in the district is 176 per sq. km. The distribution of ST and others (which includes SC, OBC and General) households presents an important aspect of the economic reality of the region. In the case of Dhemaji district of Assam, all the indigenous persons are regarded as ST and Others are includes SC,OBC, MOBC and Generals. The share of non-indigenous population in a particular area affects the diversification process to a considerable extent, as many of the migrants come to work in the nonfarm sector.

Table 7.3: Average Family Size and Mean Number of Workers per Family

Sl. No.	Name of the Village	Average Family Size	Mean No. of Workers per Family	Percentage of Workers to Total Family Members
1.	Akajan	5.39	3.03	56.19
2.	Kulajan	5.66	3.05	53.90
3.	Demow	4.58	2.94	64.08
4.	Sille	4.32	2.84	65.85
5.	Sirepani	5.31	3.49	65.70
6.	Telam	4.51	2.89	64.00
	Total	5.13	3.05	59.38

Agrarian Structure in Study Villages

The agrarian structure is an important determinant of the labour-use options and decisions of the households. However, one fundamental problem studying agrarian relations in Dhemaji district of Assam is the non availability of reliable information on the amount of land owned by the households. Traditionally, in most parts of the state, agricultural land was collectively owned. However, there has been rapid privatization of land ownership in recent decades.

Table 7.4: Distribution of Households according to Land Ownership Categories in Study Villages

Sl. No.	Land Ownership Category (acres)	Name of the Villages						
		Akajan	Kulajan	Demow	Sille	Sirepani	Telam	Total
1.	Landless	16 (44.4)	49 (48.0)	2 (6.5)	8 (42.1)	1 (2.6)	21 (34.4)	97 (33.7)
2.	Marginal (0.1-2.5)	20 (55.6)	50 (49.0)	0	9 (47.4)	22 (56.4)	21 (34.4)	122 (42.4)
3.	Small (2.5-5.0)	0	3 (2.9)	3 (9.7)	0	13 (33.3)	16 (26.2)	35 (12.2)
4.	Medium (5.0-10.0)	0	0	12 (38.7)	2 (10.5)	3 (7.7)	3 (4.9)	20 (6.9)
5.	Large (More than 10)	0	0	14 (45.2)	0	0	0	14 (4.9)
	Total	36	102	31	19	39	61	288

Table 7.5: Occupational Distributions of Households in the Study Villages

Sl. No.	Occupation	Name of the Villages						
		Akajan	Kulajan	Demow	Sille	Sirepani	Telam	Total
1.	Cultivation	14 (38.9)	18 (17.6)	28 (90.3)	1 (5.3)	26 (66.7)	38 (62.3)	125 (43.4)
2.	Agricultural Labour	0	0	0	0	0	4 (6.6)	4 (1.4)
3.	Casual Nonfarm Labour	10 (27.8)	45 (44.1)	0	11 (57.9)	1 (2.6)	0	67 (23.3)
4.	Government Service	6 (16.7)	2 (2.0)	2 (6.5)	1 (5.3)	8 (20.5)	15 (24.6)	34 (11.8)
5.	Trade and Business	3 (8.3)	25 (24.5)	1 (3.2)	5 (26.3)	2 (5.1)	3 (4.9)	39 (13.5)
6.	Forest related Activities	0	9 (8.8)	0	1 (5.3)	0	1 (1.6)	11 (3.8)
7.	Other	3 (8.3)	3 (3.0)	0	0	2 (5.1)	0	8 (2.7)
	Total	36	102	31	19	39	61	288

Non-Farm Occupations

The relative importance of farm and non-farm occupations in the study villages has been presented in Table 7.5. This classification is based on the primary occupation of the households. The sharp inter-village difference in the share of non-farm occupations is worth noticing. In Dhemaji district, the proportion of households depending upon non-farm sources varies from 73.5 in Kulajan to only 9.7 in Demow, 33.3 in Seripani, 89.5 per cent in Sille. In total, 51 per cent of households depend upon non-farm households, while the rest depend upon farm-based occupation[9]. Before proceeding further, it is important to clarify that these figures are much larger than the average figures for Assam. This is so because, deliberately we have chosen the districts having higher share of rural non-farm workers and, secondly, because within the selected districts we have purposively chosen villages nearer to urban areas. However, the results very clearly bring out the localized and highly concentrated expansion of the rural non-farm economy in the state.

So far as the share of ST and Others households in non-farm occupations is concerned, the status is considerable satisfactory. As the district doesn't have any industrial establishment the role of RNRS is comparatively high. In terms of landownership categories, predictably enough, a higher percentage of non-land owning households earn their livelihood from the non-farm occupations. However, when we investigate the share of migrants and non-migrants in farm and non-farm occupations it is found that migrants have a remarkably higher share in non-farm occupations (86.0 per cent) than that of the non-migrants. The proportion of households depending upon non-farm occupations shows a secular decline with rise in land ownership (Table 7.6). However, given the land market imperfections and rigidities, this result needs to be interpreted carefully. It might have resulted from the fact that many of the non-farm sector workers, who are migrants from outside the state, simply do not have the rights to own land in Assam. But, in Table 7.6. Where the relative importance of farm and non-farm occupations have been presented with respect to the ST households, it is found that the inverse relation between landownership and participation in non-farm occupations still holds good.

In terms of educational categories, among the households having illiterate heads, 48.5 per cent work in the non-farm sector. Among the households having heads with more than 12 years of schooling, as high as 80 per cent are in the non-farm occupations. Although the relationship is far from straight forward, by and large, households having heads with a higher educational standard, have a higher proportion dependent upon non-farm occupations (Table 7.7). Again, of all the households surveyed, around 58 per cent have heads who are illiterates, but the share of such households among the non-farm households is only marginally lower than that of those in farm occupations. On the other extreme, among the households depending upon non-farm occupations, a relatively higher percentage has heads who have studied beyond class 7. This phenomenon is obviously linked to the heterogeneity within the non-farm sector. Such trends are also pronounced in the case of the ST households. In table 7.6., for example, it is shown that among the ST households, out of 113households having illiterates as household heads, 33.6 per cent are in non-farm occupations, but the share of non-farm occupations goes upto 68 per cent when we consider households with heads having more than 12 years of schooling.

Table 7.6: Share of Households Depending upon Non-farm Occupations in Study Villages

Sl. No.	Name of the Village	No of Households Depending Upon		
		Farm Occupation	Non-farm Occupation	Total
1.	Akajan	14 (38.9)	22 (61.1)	36 (100.0)
2.	Kulajan	27 (26.5)	75 (73.5)	102 (100.0)
3.	Demow	28 (90.3)	3 (9.7)	31 (100.0)
4.	Sille	2 (10.5)	17 (89.5)	19 (100.0)
5.	Sirepani	26 (66.7)	13 (33.3)	39 (100.0)
6.	Telam	43 (70.5)	18 (29.5)	61 (100.0)
	Total	140 (48.6)	148 (51.4)	288 (100.0)

Table 7.7: Educational Qualifications of Households Heads and Participation in Non-farm Occupations

Sl. No.	Educational Qualification of Household Heads	No of Households Depending Upon		
		Farm Occupations	Non-farm Occupations	Total
1.	Illiterate	86 (51.5)	81 (48.5)	167 (100.0)
2.	Up To Primary	33 (51.6)	31 (48.4)	64 (100.0)
3.	Up to Middle	9 (40.9)	13 (59.1)	22 (100.0)
4.	Up to Secondary	8 (34.8)	15 (65.2)	23 (100.0)
5.	Up to Higher Secondary	3 (42.9)	4 (57.1)	7 (100.0)
6.	Beyond Higher Secondary (20.0)	1 (80.0)	4 (100.0)	5
	Total	140 (48.6)	148 (51.4)	288 (100.0)

Distribution of Working Days across Different Activities Another problem with assessing the significance of non-farm activities through the relative importance of various primary occupations is that it does not take into account the participation of households in various non-farm activities as subsidiary activities for a comparatively small period of time. Earlier studies show that many of the tribal households in rural occupations have not yet shifted to non-farm occupations, but have been gradually participating in non-farm occupations like wage labour in road construction and petty trading in vegetables and fruits for a few weeks in a year. In order to capture this dimension of the labour use of the surveyed households, we have presented the distribution of total family working days across various activities in Table 7.8. It is important to note that though traditional manufacturing, cottage industries and handicrafts were not reported either as primary or secondary occupations, labour disposition patterns bring out its limited importance in few of the study villages. The overall share of non-farm activities is higher than that in terms of occupational classification of households. The share of forest related activities is also higher, primarily because of the nature of forest dependency in the state. Because of climatic, living style and cultural factors, local, tribal households generally spend some time in the collection of forest resources.

Similarly, there is some increase in the share of animal husbandry, which again is taken up generally as a subsidiary activity in villages nearer to urban areas.

Table 7.8: Distribution of Total Family Working Days across Different Activities

Name of the Village	Agriculture	Share of Total Family Working Days in						
		Animal Husbandry	Forest	Non farm Wage Labour	Govt. Service	Trade/ Business	Cottage Industry	Others
Akajan	25.12	0.0	10.37	21.03	18.25	20.24	4.98	0.0
Kulajan	28.72	1.35	16.27	28.81	3.37	19.30	1.62	0.57
Demow	65.81	2.66	7.23	0.00	18.10	3.75	0.80	1.65
Sille	19.43	4.81	1.22	48.31	9.73	16.51	0.0	0.0
Sirepani	58.33	5.07	6.03	7.21	21.98	0.82	0.0	0.56
Telam	65.81	3.23	4.89	1.11	25.59	7.55	0.21	0.67
Total	42.83	2.62	9.33	16.64	14.87	11.93	1.15	0.62

Table 7.9 bring out the share of all non-farm working days in total family working days in the study villages. As expected there are wide inter-village differences in terms of the relative importance of the nonfarm activities. The share of all non-farm activities ranges from only 43 per cent in Demow to nearly 80 per cent in Sille. However, when we exclude the time spent in

forest related activities, to take into account its overlapping nature with farm operations in the state, the overall share of non-farm activities comes down from 57 per cent to 48 per cent. In villages such as Akajan and Kulajan the share comes down significantly, whereas in Sapper Camp it affects the share of non-farm activities marginally.

Table 7.9: Share of Non-farm Working Days in Total Family Working Days

Name of the Villages	Percentage of Non-farm Working Days to Total Working Days
Akajan	64.51
Kulajan	55.01
Demow	26.96
Sille	79.35
Sirepani	35.64
Telam	38.37
Total	47.84

Multiplicity of Livelihoods and Non-farm Activities

One of the significant aspects of the livelihoods in many risk-prone economies is the multiplicity of livelihoods. As an attempt to disperse risk and avoid unexpected short falls in earnings, production or consumption levels household tend to diversify their sources of livelihoods. In doing so, they typically diversify their portfolio of earnings and tend to participate in a number of different activities simultaneously or sequentially. A rigid framework focusing upon the primary occupations alone tend to neglect the significance of such risk dispersion strategies of the households. Multiplicity of sources of livelihoods not only provides the households to diversify their sources of earnings; it also helps them in effectively utilizing some of their slack resources, such as labour of household members in off-peak seasons and beyond normal working hours.

Concluding Observations

The process of rural economic transformation is intrinsically linked with the expansion of non-farm activities within the rural economy. However, the rural non-farm sector is generally characterized by an extraordinary degree of diversity, in terms of its composition, levels of earnings, types of skill required as well as backward and forward linkages with other sectors of the economy, including agriculture. The very fact that the rural non-farm sector comprises of both high-end occupations, with better earnings and higher skill intensity as well as low-end jobs with abysmally low levels of earnings, has led to a debate regarding the casual mechanisms underlying its expansion. The variations in the level as well as composition of the non-farm sector in different developing economies as well as regional settings has necessitated the study of its growth in terms of localized growth linkages, with a greater emphasis on local specificities. In this back drop, the present study tried to capture some aspects of the nature and significance of the rural non-farm sector in one of the least studied states of India, namely Assam.

A selective review of the recent literature on the topic reveals that there is far greater appreciation of the role and significance of this sector in the overall growth process in general and in employment generation in particular, both within the academia as well as in the policy making bodies. The possibility of simultaneous existence of both push and pull factors in expanding the size of the rural non-farm sector has been well recognized, as empirical evidences suggest that this generally incorporates both diversification under distress i.e. distress-push or diversification in response to better opportunities, i.e. demand-pull. Again, depending upon the local conditions, the growth of the sector could be fuelled either through strong urban linkages or through the multiplier effects of a robust agricultural growth, or through a mix on both these sets of linkages. Spatial characteristics of the rural economy tend to influence the nature as well as degree of growth in the nonfarm activities. A large number of studies have also tried to find the determinants of the growth of the non-farm sector, both at the levels of various spatial units as well as at the levels of individuals and households.

Assam has its own historical and geographical specificities, which has a strong bearing upon its development process. The economy has grown at a very high rate since the nineteen seventies and starting from a very low level of economic and infrastructural development, it has attained a moderate level of economic development in terms of many development indicators. In comparison with many other states of India, however, the development performance of the state has not been spectacular. State intervention in general and generous central assistance in particular has been instrumental in shaping the pace and the nature of economic development of the state. Although agriculture has grown at a very high rate, the growth of secondary sector has been especially tardy in the state. The structural transformation of the Assam economy has resulted in increasing diversification of the workforce, emergence of a modern non-farm economy, rapid urbanisation and gradual integration with the regional and national economy, but the most important aspect of the process is that, while the share of tertiary sector in the NSDP has increased. The share of the primary sector has decreased from around 70 per cent during the same period. The key aspect of the changing sectoral composition of the state is that the expansion of service sector has been almost entirely driven by government-sector activities.

Apart from the relatively slow growth of NSDP during this decade, the dependence of the state on service sector in general and public administration in particular increased substantially. As such industrialisation never really had a firm footing in the state's economy, Although agriculture has been growing over the years, it is primarily expansion of area under cultivation, rather than improvements in yield rates, which have contributed to its growth. Correspondingly, there has been phenomenal expansion of the tertiary sector employment and somewhat sluggish expansion of employment in the secondary sector. Within the secondary sector employment, construction had a higher share than that of manufacturing. All these have created a kind of growth in the rural non-farm sector that is highly uneven across space and which, again has strong links with expansion of the service sector.

The share of non-farm employment in rural employment in the state has gone up Analysing the census data, it was noticed that rural employment in non-household manufacturing, construction, trade and commerce, and transport, storage and communications have expanded during this period. Employment in transport, storage and communications has recorded the highest growth rate during this period, followed by mining and quarrying and non- household manufacturing.

The second most important source of employment in the rural non-farm sector comes from the construction sector. A substantial portion of employment opportunities can be attributed to stronger inter-sectoral linkages in the rural areas as a result of rising productivity, increasing marketisation and commercialization of the agro-economy. However, given the low levels of commercialization and productivity in agriculture, it is unlikely that the non-farm economy has been exclusively driven by the growth impetus in the farm economy. Inter-sectoral production linkages are remarkably low in the state. However, rising farm incomes might have resulted in greater demand for non-farm products and services in the rural areas through consumption linkages. To find out the determinants of non-farm growth at a disaggregated level, we used the village level data on non-farm employment, from 1991 -01 census.

To investigate the determinants of participation of rural households invarious non-farm activities in the relatively well-communicated villages of Assam, a sample survey of 288 households was carried out in six villages, located in Dhemaji districts of the state. It was found that, in these relatively well-communicated villages, 51 per cent of households depend upon non-farm occupations, while the rest depend upon farm based occupation. When the share of these non-traditional non-farm occupations, such as government service, trade and business and casual non-farm labour are taken into account, it is found that in total, 51 per cent of households depend upon such occupations, implying the relative insignificance of the traditional non-farm sectors like animal husbandry, household manufacturing etc. Sharp inter-village differences were noticed in terms of the significance of non-farm occupations, which ranged from 9.7 per cent to 89.5 per cent. These wide differences in the relative importance of various occupational groups in the study villages capture an important dimension of the unevenness and spatial variations in the level and pattern of diversification in rural Assam. So far as the share of ST and non-ST households in non-farm occupations is concerned, it is found that the former have considerably lower participation in the non-farm occupations, than the later. In terms of landownership categories, predictably enough, a higher percentage of non-land owning households earn their livelihood from the non-farm occupations. The proportion of households depending upon non-farm occupations shows a secular decline with rise in landownership. We also tried to assess the relevance of the non-farm sector through the distribution of working days in a year across various activities. Since a considerable proportion of surveyed households were found to be engaged in multiple activities, the mean number of livelihoods per households was also computed for different categories of households. It was found that the mean number of households in case of those who have non-farm occupations as their primary source is higher than that of those having farm-based occupations. But there are considerable differences across the villages.

Among the households who depend on the non-farm sector, the household level determinants of participation in highly remunerative non-farm occupations include the education of the head of the household. Size of the operational holdings and landlessness has a negative influence on entry to such high-earnings occupations. Interestingly, the results suggest that the ST status, which was found to be significant in previous models, is not significant in determining the household's entry into better-paid non-farm occupations. In the third model we have tried to identify the factors, which influence the entry of the households to casual non-farm labour market. The regression has been estimated for households who are in the non-farm sector. Quite expectedly, landlessness emerges as the strongest explanatory variable, influencing the decision of the household to enter the rural casual labour market in the non-farm economy. The ST status is negatively linked with participation in this activity. Thus, within the non-farm economy, the ST households in Assam are more likely to be in the other non-farm occupations, while migrant households are more likely to work in the wage labour market with considerably lower earnings. The econometric investigation, at least partially, explains the heterogeneous nature and local peculiarities of the rural non-farm economy in the state.

NOTES

1 Though the rate of Growth of the Economy Varies Depending on the Choice of Base Year and Other Factors, most of the Study Finds Growth in the Economy during the Decades of 1990s at around 6 per cent.

2 Though Proportion of Household inco me Separately Available from the Agriculture and Non-agriculture Sector Varies Across Regions, the Studies have generally Found that Non-farm Activities on an Average Contribute Between 25 and 35 per cent of the Total Household Income in Rural India.

3 NSSO- National Sample Survey Organization.

4 Barrett and Reardon (2000) note that 'an Activity can be "Local" with Two Sub-categories (*a*) at Home (or the more ambiguous term "on-farm"), (*b*) Local away-from-home, with sub-categories of (*i*) Country side or strictly rural. (*ii*) Nearby Rural Town; and (*iii*) Intermediate city'. These Distinctions are Important Particularly with Reference to the Extent of Dependency of Households on the Local Economy. (Quoted in Davis, 2001). In a similar vein, while Discussing the Problems of Interpreting the NSS Data on Employment to Understand RNFE in India, Chadha Draws Attention to the Important Difference Between 'Non-farm Employment for Rural Households' and the Rural Non-farm Sector as such (Chadha, 1993b: 297).

5 Start (2001) includes the following Dimensions of the RNFE to Understand its Nature: (*i*) Degree of Linkage to Agriculture and Other Sectors, (*ii*) The Relations of Production (which, according to him, at the Rural Economy Level Refers to the Structure or Scale of Production; and at the Household Level Refers to whether the Worker is Employed or Self-employed), (*iii*) the Level of Technology, Capitalization or 'Modernisation', which often has a Direct Bearing on (iv) the Levels of Productivity and Associated returns.

6 NCAER- National Council of Applied Economic Research.

7 NABARD- National Bank for Agriculture and Rural Development.

8 During 1990-91 to 1995-96 the Share of Manufacturing in NDP at Current Prices Declined from 5.11 per cent to 3.27 per cent, while that of Public Administration Increased from 13.52 per cent to 14.15 per cent (Bezbaruah and Dutta, 2001).

9 It is Interesting to note that Although there is a Rich Tradition of Traditional Handicrafts in Assam, given the Low Levels of Division of Labour and Specialization in the Traditional Economy, the Traditional Non-farm Activities such as Household Manufacturing and Community and Personal Services, by and Large, were not Pursued as Primary Occupations. As such, due to the very Nature of the Tribal Economy, there is hardly any Occupational Group that can be included in the Category of Personal and Community Services, except for the Traditional Priests and healers and those Working in the Village Institutions. Non-farm Occupations such as Personal and Community Services and Traditional Handicrafts, more or less, Imply Continuity with the Traditional Economy of the Villages. The Dynamism Associated with the Non-farm Economy may be Associated with some of the Modern Non-farm Activities, rather than with all the Activities Outside the Farm Economy. Thus the real extent, to which the Traditional Economy has been Transformed in terms of Occupational Diversification, cannot be meaningfully derived from the above-mentioned figures on aggregate non-farm activities. It is interesting to note that there is hardly any change in the Share of Non-farm Occupations as a Result of this Reclassification. Thus almost the entire spectrum of non-farm activities found in rural Assam, are non-traditional.

REFERENCES

Anderson, D. and M.W.Leiserson (1980), 'Rural Non-farm Employment in Developing Countries, 'Economic Development and CulturalChange, Vol. 28, No. 2.

Basant, R and B.L.Kumar (1989), 'Rural Non-agricultural Activities in India: A Review of Available Evidence', Social Scientist, Vol. 17, Ng. 1-2.

Basu, D.N. and S.P. Kashyap (1992), 'Rural Non-agricultural Employment in India: Role of Development Process and Rural-UrbanEmployment Linkages', Economic and Political Weekly, Vol. 27, No. 51-52.

Bhalla, Sheila (1993), 'Patterns of Employment Generations in India',The Indian Journal of Labour Economics,Vol. 36, No. 4.

Bhaumik, S.K. (2002) 'Employment Diversification in Rural India: A Statelevel Analysis', The Indian Journal of Labour Economics,Vol. 45, No. 4.

Chadha, G.K. (1993a) 'Editor's Introduction', Special issue on Non-farm Sector, The Indian Journal of Labour Economics,Vol. 36, No. 3.

Chadha,G.K. (2002) 'Rural Non-farm Employment in India: What does Recent Experience Teach Us ?', The Indian Journal of Labour Economics,Vol. 45, No. 4.

Davis, Junior R. (2001) 'Conceptual Issues in Analysing the Rural Nonfarm Economy in Transition Economies', NRI Report No. 2635, Natural Resource Institute, Kent.<http;/ /www.nri.org/work/rnfl_transition.htm>.

Davis, Junior R. (2003) 'The Rural Non-farm Economy, Livelihoods and their Diversification: Issues and Options', NRI Report No. 2753, Natural Resource Institute, Kent.

Dev, S. Mahendra (2002) 'Pro-poor Growth in India: What do we know about the Employment Effects of Growth 1980-2000?', Working Paper No. 161, Overseas Development Institute.

Dev, S. Mahendra and Robert E. Evension (2003) 'Rural Development in India: Agriculture, Non-farm and Migration', Working Paper No. 187, Stanford Centre for International Development, StanfordUniversity, Stanford.

Harris, B. (1987) 'Regional Growth Linkages from Agriculture and Resource Flows in Non-farm Economy', Economic and Political Weekly, Vol. 22, No. 1-2.

Kumar, Alok (1993), 'Rural Non-Farm Employment: A Static and Dynamic Study of Inter-State Variations', The Indian Journal of Labour Economics, Vol. 36. No. 3.

Lanjouw, Jean O. and Peter Lanjouw (1995) Rural Non-farm Employment: A Survey, Policy Research Working Paper No. 1463, The World Bank.

Lanjouw, Jean O. and Peter Lanjouw (2001) 'The Rural Non-farm Sector: Issues and Evidences from Developing Countries', Agricultural Economics, Vol. 26: 1-23.

Mishra, Deepak K. (2005) 'Transnational Cooperation and Livelihood Security in North East India', Journal of Politics, Vol. 12, pp. 96-136.

Vaidyanathan, A.(1986), 'Regional Variations in Rural Non-agricultural Employment: An Exploratory Hypothesis', Economic and Political Weekly,Vol. 21.

Economic Inequality, Poverty and Food Security in the World

Mrs. Shivani Mohan and Shambhavi Mishra

ABSTRACT

Economic Inequality' means the unequal distribution of income and financial assets in the population. Most research on Inequality has focused on the distribution of income but asset Inequality is a distinct form of economic Inequality that also deserves attention. The relationship between Inequality and the development process has long been of interest, and both directions of causality have been extensively investigated. A substantial literature in economics and social sciences has investigated the relationship between income Inequality and economic growth, and a variety of social phenomena. There are several channels through which economic Inequality influences these phenomena.

Economic Inequality

"Inequality is not just bad for social justice; it is also bad for economic efficiency"[1]

"We are now living in a new Gilded Age, as extravagant as the original," says the Nobel Prize–winning Princeton economist and New York Times columnist Paul Krugman.[2]

In the days of Krugman's youth, *"The economic disparities you were conscious of were quite muted."*

'Economic Inequality' means the unequal distribution of income and financial assets in the population. Most research on Inequality has focused on the distribution of income but asset Inequality is a distinct form of economic Inequality that also deserves attention (Orton and Rowlingson, 2007). It is important to be clear from the outset that Inequality in this report does not deal directly with other dimensions of Inequality such as gender or ethnicity.[3]

In a classic contribution, Dalton (1920) argued that any measure of economic Inequality must be concerned with economic welfare to be of relevance. The particular measure that he chose followed directly from the utilitarian framework, and he based it on a comparison between actual levels of aggregate utility and the level of total utility that would obtain if income were equally divided. Since he took a strictly concave utility function, i.e., with diminishing marginal utility of income, and the same function for all, the maximization of aggregate welfare required an equal division.[4]

The relationship between Inequality and the development process has long been of interest, and both directions of causality have been extensively investigated. The idea that the structural transformation that takes place as an economy develops may lead first to rising and then to falling Inequality – known as the Kuznets (1955) hypothesis – was once hugely influential. The view that Inequality may, conversely, affect the rate and nature of economic growth has an equally distinguished pedigree, dating back at least to Kaldor (1956). In the 1990s, a burgeoning theoretical literature suggested a number of mechanisms through which wealth Inequality might be detrimental to economic growth: when combined with credit constraints and increasing returns.[5]

Income Inequality is of fundamental interest not only to economists, but also to other social scientists. A substantial literature in economics and social sciences has investigated the relationship between income Inequality and economic growth, and a variety of social phenomena. There are several channels through which economic Inequality influences these phenomena. The studies on the relationship between economic Inequality and economic growth have reinvigorated gradually since the past twenty years. One of the most basic principles of democracy is the notion that every citizen's preferences should count equally in the realm of politics and government. *"A key characteristic of a democracy is the continued responsiveness of the government to the preferences of its citizens, considered as political equals."*[6] But there are a variety of good reasons to believe that citizens are not considered as political equals by policy-makers in real political systems. Wealthier and better-educated citizens are more likely than the poor and less educated to have well-formulated and well-informed preferences. For example, Persson, and Tabellini (1994) shows that there is significantly negative relationship between Inequality and growth in democratic countries.[7] On the contrary, Barro (1999)[8] argues that it is possible that thepredicted negative effect of Inequality on growth can arise even if there are no transfers in equilibrium. This is because the rich may prevent redistributive policies through lobbying and buying of votes of legislators. But then a higher level of economic Inequality would require more of these activities to prevent redistribution of income through the political process. Barro (2000) concludes that there is a negative relationship for poor countries, but a positive relationship for rich countries. With the finding that Inequality in China and India comes along with their economic growth, Quah (2001)[9] raises that Inequality can increase or decrease economic growth. The increasingly unequal distribution of income – and the even more unequal distribution of wealth – is problematic for a democratic system to the extent that economic Inequality engenders political Inequality.

If we're concerned about economic Inequality, income Inequality isn't the only way, or even the best way to me assures it. The most credible definition of economic Inequality refers to the gap in overall material well-being. By that definition, it is clear that we are far from answer of dangerous invidious inequalities. With all due attention to the Lamborghinis, Net Jets, and cavernous mansions flaunted by today's super wealthy, the real, lived difference between today's rich and poor does not approach the shocking contrast of garish opulence and bare foot misery that marked the real Gilded Age.

A nation's level of income Inequality, in isolation, tells us very little. It would be analytically convenient fall possible causes of income Inequality were morally undesirable, and equally so. The general lesson, then, is that the level of economic Inequality is a reliable indicator of neither individual well-being nor social justice. A society's least-privileged class can fare very well in a highly unequal society (such as in the United States) and fare dismally in a highly equal society (such as Ethiopia). Either a high or low level of economic Inequality may be consistent with justice—with people getting what they are due as free and morally equal members of society—or it may be a side effect of injustice. In the case of injustice, the important thing is not the side effect—some level of Inequality—but its primary causes: the injustices where they have occurred.[10]

Harvard economist Louis Kaplow observes: A country with low Inequality may have implemented effective policies aimed at the poor or may have destroyed the incentives and wealth of the upper classes, to the detriment of the poor. If one reported social welfare measures instead, one would know more. Focusing on Inequality rather than welfare obscures the situation.[11] It's important to emphasize the point that the level of income Inequality within a country may or may not be a by-product of wrongdoing or injustice, depending on the mechanisms that have produced it. The low informational content of measurements like the Gini coefficient is powerfully illustrated by a path-breaking new study by Branko Milanovic, Peter H. Lindert, and Jeffrey G.Williamson.[12]

The authors notes that the higher a population's mean income, the higher the possible income Inequality. The idea, in a nutshell, is that a generally wealthy population is a sweeter target for plunder by the ruling political class—the people with access to the coercive instruments of government—than is a generally poor population. The social consequences of increasing Inequality under conditions of economic growth may not entail as much relative impoverishment or perceived injustice as the recorded Gini might suggest (emphasis added).[13]

The search for explanations for economic Inequality has led to consider more complex and specific mechanisms beyond aggregate income distribution. First, functional income distribution leads to inequalities in factor incomes.[14] Second, growing differences within wages may increase inequalities among employees. Third, inequalities in family revenues are the result of the combination of incomes from different sources and of family structures. Fourth, the redistributive effects of taxation, social incomes – pensions and subsidies - and access to public services provided outside the market shape inequalities among families in terms of net incomes and standard of living.

More recent studies have involved economic Inequality and economic growth with social environment spill overs[15]; human capital investment and neighbourhood effects[16]; social unrest and conflict[17]and political economy.[18]

Economic Inequality has many dimensions. Differences exist between people in their individual earnings, and this has been the main concern of labour economics. These differences do not however necessarily lead to Inequality of household incomes, where we have to add the earnings of different household members, add income from capital and from transfers, and subtract taxes to arrive at disposable income. Rising dispersion of earnings may be offset by less Inequality of capital income, or by progressive taxation. During the "Golden Age" of the 1950s, the earnings gap widened in a number of countries, including the US, but this did not lead to a rise in the Inequality of household incomes. But should we be looking at household consumption rather than household income? Inequality in consumption may indeed appear a more natural concern. On the other hand, people may only be able to sustain their consumption by going into debt. This consideration points to the need to measure household net worth, or the difference between its assets and its liabilities.[19]

Inequality or economic Inequality once again, therefore, is expected to be existent for a long run. But Inequality forcibly augmented by artificial elements should be eliminated beyond doubt in order for a better economic environment and sustainable social institutions.

There is little evidence that high levels of income Inequality lead down a slippery slope to the destruction of democracy and rule by the rich. The unequal political voice of the poor can be addressed only through policies that actually work to fight Poverty and improve education. Income Inequality is a dangerous distraction from the real problems: Poverty, lack of economic opportunity, and systemic injustice.

Borders define the physical scope of legal and economic institutions. Differences in the quality of institutions explain, among other things, the large degree of economic Inequality. Political boundaries defined by histories of colonial aggression, war, and dumb luck do not define the natural and inevitable domain of moral evaluation.

Poverty

"Our vision and our responsibility are to end extreme Poverty in all its forms in the context of sustainable development and to have in place the building blocks of sustained prosperity for all."[20]

Poverty has been described as a situation of "pronounced deprivation in wellbeing" and being poor as "to be hungry, to lack shelter and clothing, to be sick and not cared for, to be illiterate and not schooled...Poor people are particularly vulnerable to adverse events outside their control. They are often treated badly by institutions of the state and society and excluded from voice and power in those institutions." [21]

Monrovia Communiqué of the High-Level Panel quotes that *"Our vision and our responsibility is to end extreme Poverty in all its forms in the context of sustainable development and to have in place the building blocks of sustained prosperity for all. The gains in Poverty eradication should be irreversible. This is a global, people-centred and planet-sensitive agenda to address the universal challenges of the 21st century: promoting sustainable development, supporting job-creating growth, protecting the environment and providing peace, security, justice, freedom and equity at all levels."*[22]

The members of the Secretary-General's High-Level Panel of Eminent Persons on the Post-2015 Development Agenda, were asked for recommendations that would *"help respond to the global challenges of the 21st century, building on the Millennium Development Goals (MDGs) and with a view to ending Poverty"*.[23]

Ending extreme Poverty is just the beginning, not the end. It is vital, but our vision must be broader: to start countries on the path of sustainable development – building on the foundations established by the 2012 UN Conference on Sustainable Development in Rio de Janeiro,[24] and meeting a challenge that no country, developed or developing, has met so far.

Developing a single, sustainable development agenda is critical. Without ending Poverty, we cannot build prosperity; too many people get left behind. Without building prosperity, we cannot tackle environmental challenges; we need to mobilise massive investments in new technologies to reduce the footprint of unsustainable production and consumption patterns.[25] The causes of Poverty, exclusion and Inequality are innumerable. It must connect people in rural and urban areas to the modern economy through quality infrastructure – electricity, irrigation, roads, ports, and telecommunications. It must provide quality health care and education for all. It must establish and enforce clear rules, without discrimination, so that women can inherit and own property and run a business, communities can control local environmental resources, and farmers and urban slum-dwellers have secure property rights. It must give people the assurance of personal safety. It must make it easy for them to follow their dreams and start a business.

Developing countries, including ones with major pockets of Poverty, are cooperating among themselves, and jointly with developed countries and international institutions, in South-South and Triangular cooperation these activities have become highly valued.[26]

Today's adolescents and youth are 1.8 billion strong and one quarter of the world's population. Young people face many obstacles, ranging from discrimination, marginalisation, and Poverty, to violence. They find it hard to find a first job, so we believe a jobs target with a specific indicator for youth employment, should be included in the next goal framework.[27]

By 2030 the world would have 1.2 billion fewer people hungry and in extreme Poverty.[28] The combination of goals, targets, and indicators under the MDGs was a powerful instrument for mobilising resources and motivating action. For this reason, we recommend that the post-2015 agenda should also feature a limited number of highpriority goals and targets, with a clear time horizon and supported by measurable indicators.

With this in mind, the Panel recommends that targets in the post-2015 agenda should be set for 2030.25 Longer time frames would lack urgency and might seem implausible, given the volatility of today's world, while shorter ones would not allow the truly transformative changes that are needed to take effect.[29]

The Panel recommends that the post-2015 goals, while keeping those living in extreme Poverty, and the promises made to them, at the heart of the agenda, should raise the level of ambition for 2030 to reach all the neediest and most vulnerable. They should call for improving the quality of services. They should capture the priorities for sustainable development. And they should connect to one another in an integrated way.Of course, given vastly different capabilities, histories, starting points and circumstances, every country cannot be asked to reach the same absolute target. All countries would be expected to contribute to achieving all targets, but how much, and at what speed, will differ. Ideally, nations would use inclusive processes to make these decisions and then develop strategies, plans, policies, laws, or budgets to implement them.[30]

The panel envisions a world in 2030 where a renewed global partnership, building on the solid foundations of the Millennium Declaration and the Rio principles and outcomes, has transformed the world through a universal, people-centred and planet-sensitive development agenda achieved with the shared commitment and accountability of all.

They further quote that *"We have a historic opportunity to do what no other generation has ever done before: to eradicate extreme Poverty by 2030 and end Poverty in many of its other forms. But we will not be able to do this if we neglect other imperatives of the sustainable development agenda today – the desire to build prosperity in all countries, the need to slow or reverse environmental degradation and man-made contributions to global warming, the urgent need to end conflict and violence while building effective and accountable institutions for all. Tackling these social, economic and environmental issues at the same time, while bringing to bear the energy and resources of everyone concerned with development – governments at all levels, international organisations, civil society, businesses, foundations, academics and people in all walks of life – is our singular challenge."*

It can be said that *"The human rights approach underlines the multidimensional nature of Poverty, describing Poverty in terms of a range of interrelated and mutually reinforcing deprivations, and drawing attention to the stigma, discrimination, insecurity and social exclusion associated with Poverty"*[31]

Food Security

Food Security is a complex issue and its definition has evolved over time. The question of Food Security has a number of dimensions that go beyond production, availability and demand for food. The initial focus on Food Security as a global concern was on the volume and stability of food supplies. In the 1974 World Food Summit, Food Security was defined as *"availability at all times of adequate world food supplies of basic foodstuffs to sustain a steady expansion of food consumption and to offset fluctuations in production and prices"*. In 1983, FAO expanded its concept to include vulnerable people securing access to available supplies, stating that Food Security meant *"ensuring that all people at all times have both physical and economic access to the basic food that they need."* Later, the 1996 World Food Summit redefined Food Security to take demand, vulnerability and nutritional aspects into account. At the summit, countries agreed that *"Food Security exists when all people, at all times, have physical and economic access to sufficient, safe and nutritious food to meet their dietary needs and food preferences for an active and healthy lifestyle"*. In 2002, an FAO Expert Consultation on Food Security gave a working definition of Food Security: Food Security exists when all people, at all times, have physical, social and economic access to sufficient, safe and nutritious food which meets their dietary needs and food preferences for an active and healthy life. Household Food Security is the application of this concept to the family level, with individuals within households as the focus of concern[32] provided by different organisations such as the World Bank, FAO and UNDP's Human Development Report. In general, Food Security is defined as economic access to food along with food production and food availability. Food availability alone, therefore, does not ensure Food Security; access to food is equally important. Since then, several definitions have been provided by different organisations such as the World Bank, FAO and UNDP's Human Development

Report. In general, Food Security is defined as economic access to food along with food production and food availability. Food availability alone, therefore, does not ensure Food Security; access to food is equally important.[33] As is well known, FAO (2002)[34] that exists when all people, at all times, have physical, social and economic access to sufficient, safe and nutritious food that meets their dietary needs and food preferences for an active and healthy life". As per USDA[35] nutritional target of roughly 2,100 calories per day per person.

It is at times assumed that the relationship between economic growth and health is unidirectional with improving economic conditions leading to better health. In reality, and as confirmed by recent research, the reverse is equally true and health is an 'economic engine.' That is, better health which is an important end in itself leads to and may, in certain cases, be a necessary prerequisite for economic development. Hence besides being an end in itself, the economic role of health and nutrition thus provides an additional and compelling rationale for public policy to support well targeted nutrition improving interventions in ways directly analogous to the support given for increasing other forms of capital investments.[36]

Relation Between Poverty, Inequality and food Security

While global trends point to Poverty reduction, wide gaps persist between and within countries. In the poorest countries, extreme Poverty, food insecurity, Inequality, high death rates and high birth rates are linked in a vicious cycle. Reducing Poverty by investing in health and education, especially for women and girls, can break this cycle.[37]

The extent, to which agricultural growth contributes to Poverty reduction, depends, however, on the degree of Inequality in a country[38] and on the share of agriculture in the economy and in employment. Most agricultural growth, over the long term, stems from technical change.[39]

Important risks associated with the development of biofuels relate to worsening income distribution and a deterioration of women's status. The distributional impact of developing biofuel crops will depend on initial conditions and on government policies. The consensus with regard to the impact of cash crops on Inequality appears to lean towards greater Inequality.[40]

With regard to Inequality of access, it was assumed that in the coming years the countries will achieve a relatively small reduction in the coefficient of variability of food consumption, as a result of the probable reduction of extreme Poverty. Progress towards this goal would mean a relatively greater increase in food consumption by the poorest sectors of the population, as compared with the middle- and high-income sectors. The FAO suggests that the present range of values of the coefficient of variability of food consumption could go down from values of between 0.21 and 0.36 to a range between 0.20 and 0.31 by 2015. On this basis, and bearing in mind the persistence of Inequality in the region and the slow progress being made in the reduction of absolute Poverty, a uniform 5 per cent reduction in this coefficient was projected. The rates of undernutrition projected to 2015 also took into account a change in the minimum energy requirements. A 1.3 per cent increase was assumed in this respect, since the FAO estimated that population ageing would raise the requirements by 2.6 per cent by 2030.[41]

The question of smallholders and in particular women's access to and control over land should be regarded a key concern for economic and legal equality but also with the view to sustainable development, Food Security and Poverty reduction. - Land tenure, is at the heart of many problems as it is difficult for poor women and men farmers and peasants to sustain themselves with limited and insecure access to land. The impact is felt most gravely by women, who face particular social and cultural barriers to their access to and control over land. Unless more effective government legislation on land tenure security and agricultural investment is developed and enforced, rural communities around the world will continue to be vulnerable to land grabbing and food insecurity. Land grabbing by external investors is more likely to take place in contexts where vulnerable communities do not have secure land tenure and where there is weak or unimplemented land legislation, coupled with discriminatory traditional practices.

The negative impacts of large-scale land acquisitions should be mitigated by incorporating the Voluntary Guidelines on governance of land tenure into national legislation, making provisions sensitive to each country's circumstances but nonetheless upholding the main principles, especially on gender equality.

Women play a critical role in agriculture in developing countries contributing to ensuring Food Security and nutrition. Women are farmers, unpaid workers on family farms, paid or unpaid agricultural labourers on other farms and agricultural enterprises, food processors and vendors, home gardeners, cooks, and carers for children, sick and the elderly.[42]

Rural skills development, including extension services and promoting technological change in rural areas, is also vital for enhancing Food Security and protecting the environment. More and better technical vocational education and training (TVET) oriented to both on-farm and off-farm activities and aligned with market-based outcomes and market demand, is vital to enhance rural productivity and competitiveness.[43]

Apart from insufficient availability of food, child malnutrition is usually also affected by other factors related with extreme Poverty, such as lack of access to drinking water and sanitation, which is reflected in infectious diseases and diarrhoea which, in turn, result in rapid loss of weight. In most of the countries of the region, however, the most usual expression of hunger and Povertyamong children is chronic under nutrition (moderate to serious deficits in height for age, or retarded growth). These deficiencies are serious because they represent the accumulated effect of lack of adequate food and nutrition during the most critical years of a child's development, so that their ill effects are largely irreversible. They are one of the main mechanisms for the intergenerational transmission of Poverty and Inequality.[44]

Effect on Africa and Asia

Africa

During the world economic crisis, Africa's economies continued to expand, and growth forecasts remained positive. However, the progress of social indicators such as health, education, and participation has been limited. Inequality and ineffective policies are often blamed for the poor links between economic growth and human development, but data shows that these links are less robust than is often assumed. A pattern of inclusive growth is essential to Poverty reduction in sub-Saharan Africa. The design and implementation of policies and institutions conducive to inclusive growth require a better understanding of the relationships linking growth, Inequality, and Poverty.The growing number of success stories across Africa indicates that broader social and economic progress is realistically attainable for most Africans. However, the need to ensure that the continent's economic growth also creates jobs and helps rescue millions from Poverty is of utmost importance. But this outcome is predicated on the adoption and implementation of pro-poor policies and correct strategies for economic development. The debate over growth and development and reduction of Poverty is topical in Africa, as well as elsewhere in the world.[45]

Inequality affects many different aspects of life, both between countries and within rural and urban areas of countries. Money and income are the most glaring. Worst affected by the growing Inequality gap are sub-Saharan Africa and the countries of the former USSR – here the percentage of people surviving on less than a dollar a day rose from 6.1 per cent in 1990 to 20.3 per cent in 1999.

The Gini index measures equality in income and consumption in a society. The lower the number,the more equal the society. 0 is perfect equality,100 perfect Inequality. Hungary is the most equal society according to this measure, followed by Japan, Belgium and Sweden. Brazil, Nicaragua, South Africa and Namibia (0.67) are among the most unequal. In many countries, though not all, Inequality began increasing during the debt crisis of the early 1980s.[46] Debt repayments and structural adjustment policies have had a devastating impact on health and education systems.In most countries of sub-Saharan Africa primary school enrolment declined throughout the 1990s. As health and water services were privatized they become inaccessible to the very poor.

Poverty, gender and Food Security are interrelated. Effective policy targeting Poverty must address "the inequalities in power, incomes and asset bases that generally underpin malnutrition and lack of basic services," which are inherently gendered.[47] Women experience food insecurity in ways that highlight their marginalization and vulnerability: limited power in their households and communities translates into lower nutritional levels for girls and women.[48]

Agriculture is also fundamental to economic development in sub-Saharan Africa, where 417 million rural people live in countries with agriculture-based economies.[49] Studies have observed that gross domestic product (GDP) growth that originates in agriculture is approximately four times more effective in reducing Poverty than GDP growth that originates outside the sector.[50] Currently, 30 to 40 per cent of the continent's total GDP and approximately 60 per cent of its total export earnings are directly linked to agriculture.

Across Africa, the urban poor spend a large portion of their income on food; urban Poverty is a problem of Food Security and vice-versa. Inadequate nutrition directly contributes to multiple health problems and lower brain and physical development, severely impacting an individual's ability to move out of Poverty. Further, Poverty is gendered: men and women experience Poverty differently, and much of women's Poverty is invisible when attention is not targeted on how gendered power relations distribute wealth and resources inside households and communities.[51]

Therefore, the attainment of gender equality, especially through equal access to resources, and the empowerment of rural women engaged in agriculture are critical elements of reducing Poverty, reducing hunger through Food Security and attaining meaningful inclusive economic growth and sustainable development in sub-Saharan Africa.[52]

Challenges of creating a meaningful policy response to urban Food Security exist throughout Africa. Women are also key providers of food, household income and other resources linked to nutrition, playing an essential and often dominant role in the provision of the "three pillars" of Food Security: food availability, food access and availability of the non-food resources critical for nutritional security (child care, health care, clean water and sanitation).[53] Policies targeted to enhance these roles — and that address the social, cultural and economic constraints women face — are needed to respond to the high numbers of malnourished and food-insecure individuals.

During the last two decades, the HIV/AIDS epidemic has greatly increased vulnerability in rural areas, particularly in Africa. The impact of HIV/AIDS is manifold and includes reduced income, productivity, Food Security, lower nutritional status and increased discrimination. Some of the effects of the condition are intergenerational and can therefore increase vulnerability in the long term. In particular, HIV/AIDS, directly or indirectly, has life-threatening consequences for children when they themselves are infected or have lost one or both parents due to AIDS. Children affected and infected by HIV/AIDS have less access to education and health services and are more exposed to discrimination and to the worst forms of child labour.[54]

Asia

As of 2012, Asia remains the most populous continent, with 4.1 billion people—over 60 per cent of the world's 7.0 billion total. Moreover, the United Nations estimates show the global population increasing by more than 2 billion people between 2012 and 2050—with Asia accounting for more than half of that increase. Coupled with Asia's economic growth and increasing affluence, consumption patterns are shifting from cereal grains toward more costly proteins and vegetables.[55]

New forms of South-South Cooperation led by emerging growth poles such as Brazil and China are redefining international development cooperation. Impressive domestic results of Brazil and China in boosting growth and tackling domestic Poverty—including through the role of agriculture—give them certain credibility with developing country partners who are seeking the same success.[56] Inequality is more acute in those circumstances in which Poverty is combined with other exclusionary practices based, for example, on physical disability, sexual orientation, ethnicity or race.[57] The impact on Inequality will depend on the crop and technology employed, with a scale-neutral technology favouring equal distribution of benefits.[58]

Although Asia is economically vibrant and is considered the engine of global economic growth, the number of undernourished people has been rising—from 526 million in 1995–1997 to 567 million in 2006–2008.[59]

In developing countries, where many poor people already face difficulties securing their daily food supplies, a spike in prices could catalyze greater hardship and social instability. In developing Asia—home to about two-thirds of the world's poor—food price inflation in the late 2000s was a significant blow to the region's progress in Poverty reduction. According to Asian Development Bank estimates, if food prices had stayed the same, about 112 million more people could have been saved from Poverty every year (based on the $1.25/day Poverty line). Price volatility also helps to push people into the Poverty trap. Food prices have been far more volatile than non-food prices in developing Asia during 2000–2010, particularly in Pakistan.

Trends in Inequality within countries, in contrast, are less clear. There is some evidence that income Inequality, especially in transition countries and some large developing countries (India, Indonesia, and China), has worsened since the 1980s, even though in the case of China, both the number and percentage of poor fell.[60] However, if instead of measuring Inequality based on incomes, the Human Development Indicator is utilized, there appears to be some convergence in standards of living, with the gap declining both proportionately and absolutely between 1950 and 1995 (Crafts 2000).[61]

Promoting rural development can contribute substantially to Poverty reduction and Food Security. A majority of the region's poor live in rural areas and this often poses a dilemma for national policymakers when choosing policies to stabilize food prices and/or protect the agricultural sector. For example, protectionism to sustain high food prices is a popular tool to support farm income. But such policies do not always yield the desired result if farmers are themselves poor. Sustained low agricultural productivity brought about by limited global competition reduces food production and small-scale farmers may end up not being able to produce enough food for their own demand, let alone the market's. High food prices can also reduce the farmer's own purchasing power, crowding out spending on seeds and fertilizers, thus further reducing food production.

Policy Measures

Without a change in prices, Povertyreduction will depend on two factors: average income (or expenditure) and its distribution. An increase in average income without a change in distribution reduces Poverty, while an increase in income Inequality without a change in average income increases Poverty. However, any change in food and non-food prices also alters purchasing power, influencing the percentage of people living below the Poverty threshold. Increases in food and non-food prices will reduce people's real income, which in turn increases Poverty. Shares of food and non-food consumption vary across income groups—the poor spend a relatively large share of their income on food consumption—thus, a change in food versus non-food prices will also have implications for the distribution of real income. In this context, a change in Poverty can be decomposed intothree factors:

- An income effect encompassing changes in average income or expenditure and its distribution;
- A food price effect; and
- A non-food price effect for a detailed description of the methodology).

The pure income effect measures the impact of changes in people's nominal income on Poverty, assuming food and non-food prices remain the same. The food and non-food price effects measure the impact of changes in these prices on Poverty, assuming nominal incomes do not change. Given this decomposition method, the combined effect of the three components will result in the net impact on Poverty reduction.[62]

Three key policy recommendations emerge from this report:

- Improvedata and capacity as the basis for evidence-based decision making;

- Foster growth that enhances Food Security at national and household levels; and
- Significantly enhance the efficiency and retool the allocation of public spending. Successful design and implementation of these strategies will require visionary leadership, sound laws and institutions, politicians who are accountable and listen to the voices of the people, and civil society that is patient and accepts the tenets of democracy. Public spending on agriculture, education, health, infrastructure; and social protection are most critical for achieving Poverty reduction and Food Security.[63]

Fostering growth that improves household-level Food Security must become a key priority, especially in countries with high levels of Poverty. Agricultural growth may play a role in enhancing macro-level Food Security either through growth in agricultural exports or food production for the domestic market.

Specific policy options can include:

- Prioritizing Poverty Reduction Expenditures
- Extending tax exemptions and zero tax rates for basic products
- Policies conducive to employment creation
- Include social expenditures in fiscal stimulus packages in times of crisis[64]

A growth strategy that builds on manufacturing-led growth for improving Food Security as suggested by the findings of this report will require building a strong, competitive, and relevant vocational education system. From a demand perspective, the alternative to a general education—vocational training—must be made worthwhile and competitive. Governments should employ national media to dispel the current negative perception of a vocational education and career. Within a national plan, the government should portray both education systems—general and vocational—as complementary in their national development goals.[65]

Power relations are at the centre of development. The interests of the political arena and how these translate to policy determine all successful attempts at significant Poverty reduction. Poverty reduction requires effective and accountable states, institutionalization of rights, sustained public engagement, expansion of the bargaining power of the poor and those who represent them, and pacts that are structured around issues of employment, welfare and growth.[66]

Most countries that have successfully reduced Poverty adopted heterodox policies that reflected their national conditions, rather than fully embracing market-conforming prescriptions. Countries and peoples must be allowed the policy space to adopt different models of development where aspects of livelihood and Food Security, land reform, cultural rights, gender equity, social policy and associative democracy figure prominently. Education, occupation, gender of household head, and family size are found to be the most important factors that affect income-Poverty as well as consumption-Poverty (food insecurity).[67]

Conclusion

Poverty and Inequality are part of the same problem. High levels of Inequality make it difficult to reduce Poverty even when economies are growing; and poor countries are generally more unequal than rich ones. Inequality manifests itself in relation to wealth and income status, health and education outcomes, gender and ethnicity, as well as access to employment and social services.[68]

Food Security has deteriorated in most countries in the region as a result of the global food price crises in 2007/08 and 2010/11.[69] Contemporary Poverty reduction strategies have paid insufficient attention to the lessons of history. They have increasingly focused on "targeting the poor", to the neglect of key institutional, policy and political dimensions that may be both causes of Poverty and Inequality, and obstacles to their reduction. Evidence from countries that successfully reduced Poverty over relatively short time frames shows that progress occurred principally through state-directed strategies combining economic development objectives with active social policies in ways that are mutually supportive. It also shows how Poverty outcomes are shaped by complex interconnections of ideas, institutions, policies and practices across the social, economic and political spheres.[70] Food Security presents a serious challenge for the region because of high dependency on food imports, diminished capacity for generating foreign exchange to finance food imports, rising food demand driven by continued high population growth, and limited potential for agricultural growth because of severe water constraints and water resource management issues.[71]

Employment-centred strategies and programmes should lead to increased purchasing power, as well as enhanced social empowerment and bargaining power, thereby contributing to Food Security and Poverty reduction. These virtuous dynamics also require a rights-based approach, in which the interdependency of the right to food and the right to work is strongly advocated for.[72]

Most countries that have successfully reduced Poverty adopted heterodox policies that reflected their national conditions, rather than fully embracing market-conforming prescriptions. Countries and peoples must be allowed the policy space to adopt different models of development where aspects of livelihood and Food Security, land reform, cultural rights, gender equity, social policy and associative democracy figure prominently.[73]

Thus, it can be concluded that nothing can be done in a single day. What is needed is a combined and continuous effort on the part of the International

Organisations, Governments of different countries, the Non-Governmental Organisations, both at international and national level, and most importantly the "People", without those help, determination and support, the problems of Poverty and Inequality cannot be dealt with.

NOTES

1 Anup Shah,Poverty Around The World, Global Issues (12 November, 2011), http://www.globalissues.org/article/4/Poverty-around-the-world.

2 Paul Krugman, *For Richer*, New York Times Magazine (October 20, 2002), http://query.nytimes.com/gst/fullpage.html?res=9505EFD9113AF933A15753C1A9649C8B63.

3 These and other Non-economic Dimensions of Inequality have recently Formed Part of an *'Equalities Review'* Chaired by Trevor Phillips, see http://www.theequalitiesreview.org.uk/.

4 Amartya Sen, *On Economic Inequality*, Clarendon Press ,Oxford (1997) , http://graduateeconomist.files.wordpress.com/2012/07/published-1997-on-economic-Inequality-by-amartya-sen.pdf.

5 Paolo Brunori and Francisco H. G. Ferreira, *Inequality of Opportunity, Income Inequality and Economic Mobility: Some International Comparisons*, The Institute for the Study of Labour (January 2013), http://ftp.iza.org/dp7155.pdf.

6 Robert Dahl (1971, 1).

7 Milanovic (1994) Argues that Inequality in Richer Countries Decrease because those Countries can be Aware to Build up a Fairer Social Environment.

8 Robert Joseph Barro is an American Classical Macro-economist and the Paul M. Warburg Professor of Economics at Harvard University.

9 Danny Quah (born in Malaysia) is Professor of Economics and Kuwait Professor at the London School of Economics and Political Science and Tan Chin Tuan Visiting Professor at the National University of Singapore. He Served Previously as Council Member on Malaysia's National Economic Advisory Council and as Consultant for the Bank of England, the World Bank, and the Monetary Authority of Singapore.

10 Will Wilkinson, *Thinking Clearly about Economic Inequality*, Policy Analysis (14 July, 2009), http://www.cato.org/sites/cato.org/files/pubs/pdf/pa640.pdf.

11 Louis Kaplow, *Why Measure Inequality?*, The Journal of Economic Inequality 3 (2005): 65-79.

12 Branko Milanovic, Peter H.Lindert, and Jeffrey G. Williamson, *Measuring Ancient Inequality*, World Bank Policy Research Paper4412, November 2007.

13 Branko Milanovic, Peter H. Lindert, and Jeffrey G.Williamson, *Measuring Ancient Inequality*, Vox, (7 December, 2007), http://www.voxeu.org/index.php?q=node/772.

14 Atkinson and Bourguignon, 2000; Franzini and Pianta, 2009.

15 Durlauf, 1994.

16 Durlauf, 1996.

17 Alesina and Perotti, 1996

18 Chang, 1998.

19 The *Human Development Report*, http://hdr.undp.org/en/reports/global/hdr2011/papers/HDRP_2011_06.pdf.

20 *Meeting of the High Level Panel of Eminent Persons on the Post-2015 Development Agenda in Monrovia,Liberia,* Monrovia Communiqué of the High Level Panel (1 February, 2013), http://www.post2015hlp.org/wp-content/uploads/2013/02/Monrovia-Communique-1-February-2013.pdf.

21 IBRD, 2000-2001: 15.

22 Monrovia Communiqué of the High-Level Panel, 1 February, 2013.

23 The High-level Panel of Eminent Persons will be Convened by the UN Secretary-General to Advise him on a Bold and at the same Time Practical Development Agenda beyond 2015.

24 The Future We Want, United Nations, A/RES/66/288*, 11 September 2012.

25 *A New Global Partnership: Eradicate Poverty and Transform Economies through Sustainable Development,* United Nations Publications (30 May 2013), http://www.un.org/sg/management/pdf/HLP_P2015_Report.pdf.

26 South-South Cooperation is Guided by the "Principles of Respect for National Sovereignty, National Ownership and Independence, Equality, Non-conditionality, Non-interference in Domestic Affairs and Mutual Benefit." High-level United Nations Conference on South-South Cooperation, Nairobi, Kenya (2009).

27 Young People are Defined here as those Aged 15 to 24.

28 World Bank, PovcalNet (as of 2010): http://iresearch.worldbank.org/PovcalNet/index.htm?1.

29 Local and Regional Authorities are Already Working with a Horizon of 2030 (Manifesto for the City of 2030) Balancing a Long-term Vision with the Fast Changing Nature of the World Today.

30 Similar National Target Setting was Used after the Jomtien Summit on Education (1990) and the World Summit on Children in New York (1990).

31 Office of the United Nations High Commissioner for Human Rights, *Principles and Guidelines for Human Rights Approach to Poverty Reduction Strategies,* United Nations (June 2012), http://www.ohchr.org/Documents/Publications/PovertyStrategiesen.pdf.

32 FAO 2002 Ch.2.

33 Surabhi Mittal and Deepti Seethi, *Food Security in South Asia: Issues and Opportunities,* Indian Council for Research on International Economic Relations (September 2009), http://www.icrier.org/pdf/WorkingPaper240.pdf.

34 The State of Food Insecurity in the World 2001, FAO.

35 International Food Security Assessment, 2011-21, USDA.

36 *Report of the Expert Committee on National Food Security Bill,* http://eac.gov.in/reports/rep_NFSB.pdf.

37 *Poverty And Inequality: Breaking The Cycle,* 7 Billion Actions, (July, 2011), http://www.7billionactions.org/uploads/browser/files/7b_factsheets_Poverty_and_Inequality_v5.pdf.

38 Timmer, 2002.

39 Timmer, 1988.

40 Maxwell and Fernando, 1989.

41 FAO, 2002a.

42 *Synthesis Report on the Global Thematic Consultation on Addressing Inequalities,*UNICEF and UN Women with Support from the Governments of Denmark and Ghana *(13th March 2013),* http://www.worldwewant2015.org/node/299198.

[43] *Promotion of Rural Employment for Poverty Reduction*, International Labour Conference (2008), http://www.ilo.org/wcmsp5/groups/public/@ed_norm/@relconf/documents/meetingdocument/wcms_091721.pdf.

[44] Ernesto Espíndola, *Poverty, hunger and Food Security in Central America and Panama* , United Nations Publication,(May 2005), http://www.eclac.org/publicaciones/xml/1/21981/sps_88_ing.pdf.

[45] Institute for African Development Spring Symposium 2013, *Growth, Poverty, and Inequality: Confronting the Challenges of a Better Life for All in Africa*, Cornell Institute for African Development (19-20April, 2013), http://iad.einaudi.cornell.edu/system/files/Program%20Brochure%202013%20with%20cover%20-%20web.pdf.

[46] Information Sheet on Debt, Aid and the Environment.

[47] Satterthwaite, 2003: 182.

[48] DeRose, Das and Millman, 2000: 520.

[49] World Bank, 2008.

[50] Ibid.

[51] Andrea M. Brown, Uganda's National Urban Policy: *The Emerging Response to Poverty, Food Security and Gender in Urban Uganda*, Africa Initiative (May, 2013), http://www.cigionline.org/sites/default/files/AI_PB_6.pdf.

[52] http://www.ipc-undp.org/pub/IPCPovertyInFocus24.pdf.

[53] Quisumbing, 1995.

[54] *LO: HIV/AIDS and work: Global estimates, Impact on Children and Youth, and Response* (Geneva, 2006).

[55] *Food Security and Poverty Key Challenges and Policy Issues*, Asian Development Bank (April 2012), http://reliefweb.int/sites/reliefweb.int/files/resources/food-security-Poverty.pdf.

[56] *Poverty in Focus: The Role of South-South Cooperation in Inclusive and Sustainable Agricultural Development*,International Policy Centre for Inclusive Growth: UNDP, http://www.ipc-undp.org/pub/IPCPovertyInFocus24.pdf.

[57] Ibid.

[58] *Impacts on Poverty and Food Security*, The Food and Agricultural Organisation (2008), ftp://ftp.fao.org/docrep/fao/011/i0100e/i0100e06.pdf.

[59] FAO 2011.

[60] Sharma, Morley, and Diaz-Bonilla, 2001.

[61] It should be noted that this Convergence may Result in Part from the Components of the HDI and the Way it is Calculated: There is a Natural Limit to the Expected Lifetime; there is a Statistical Limit to the Percentage of Literacy, and Income per capita (which in principle is unbounded), it is in fact Truncated in the HDI at some Level Considered "Sufficient" for Human Development; Income Levels above that are not included in the index.

[62] This Decomposition Provides three Counterfactuals: (*i*) the Food Price Component Measures the Impact of Food Price Increases on Poverty when Non-food Prices and People's Incomes had not Changed, (*ii*) the Non-food Price Component Measures the Impact of Non-food Price Increases when Food Prices and People's Income had not Changed, and (*iii*) the Income Component Measures the Impact of an Increase in People's Incomes on Poverty when Food and Non-food Prices had not Changed. Therefore, the Sum of the Three Components Provides their net Impact on Poverty.

63 Clemens Breisinger, *Beyond the Arab: Awakening Food Policy Sustainable Solutions for ending Hunger and Poverty*, International Food Policy Research Institute (February 2012), http://www.ifpri.org/sites/default/files/publications/pr25.pdf.

64 *Income in Equality and the Condition of Chronic Poverty*, United Nations, http://www.undp.org/content/dam/undp/library/Poverty%20Reduction/Inclusive%20development/Towards%20Human%20Resilience/Towards_SustainingMDGProgress_Ch6.pdf.

65 Ibid.

66 *Combating Poverty&Inequality: Structural Change, Social Policy and Politics*, Social and Economic Policy:UNICEF Policy and Practice (May 2011), http://www.unicef.org/socialpolicy/files/May2011_ChildPovertyInsights_EN.pdf.

67 Keshav Lall Mahajan, *Relationship between Income-Poverty and Food insecurity in Rural Far-western Mid-hills of Nepal*, International Association of Agricultural Economists Conference, Beijing, China (2009), http://ageconsearch.umn.edu/bitstream/51462/2/Relationship%20between%20Income-Poverty%20and%20Food%20insecurity%20in%20Rural%20Far-western%20Mid-hills%20of%20Nepal.pdf.

68 *Combating Poverty&Inequality: Structural Change, Social Policy and Politics*, Social and Economic Policy: UNICEF Policy and Practice (May 2011), http://www.unicef.org/socialpolicy/files/May2011_ChildPovertyInsights_EN.pdf.

69 Breisinger, Collion, et al. 2011; IMF 2011b.

70 *Combating Poverty and Inequality*, United Nations Research Institute for Social Development (February 2013) ,http://www.unrisd.org/80256B3C005BCCF9/(httpAuxPages)/C7515ADB78142BADC1257B08004CA838/$file/01%20-%20Combating%20Poverty%20and%20Inequality.pdf.

71 World Bank, FAO, and IFAD 2009; IFAD 2011; Breisinger et al. 2010; Ecker et al. 2010.

72 In Particular, the Right to Food Guideline 8, Discusses the Obligation of the State to Respect and Protect the Rights of Individuals Regarding Access to Natural Resources, and Facilitate Sustainable, Non-discriminatory and Secure Access to such Resources, if need be by undertaking Land Reform. The Guidelines make Recommendations on Labour, Land, Water, Genetic Resources, Sustainability and Services.

73 Combating Poverty and Inequality: Policy Brief of the Executive Committee of Economic and Social Affairs, United Nations (2010), http://www.un.org/en/development/other/ecesa/documents/policy_briefs/ecesa_pb_1.pdf.

9

The Country Specific Strategies of Empowering the Marginalized Sections of Society

Dr. Abhishek Tripathi

ABSTRACT

Within the emerging processes of development, vast sections of the society especially, the ethnic minorities, women and children, the migrants and slum dwellers, peasants and workers, tribes and indigenous people, the low and the backward castes, the socio-historically vulnerable sections, the aged and such other groups of the society have remained socially, economically and politically marginalized. They are unable to prevent the livelihood insecurity, ill health, political disempowerment, regular drudgery, physical displacement and migration, social segregation and alienation and loss of cultural identity of these groups.

Introduction

The contemporary world has been widely characterized by the restructuring of the economic order, ever increasing interactivity between the local and global communities through the information and communication technologies and mass media and explicit reformulation of the discourses of social development. Within these emerging processes however, vast sections of the society especially , the ethnic minorities, women and children , the migrants and slum dwellers, peasants and workers, tribes and indigenous people, the low and the backward castes, the socio-historically vulnerable sections, the aged and such other groups of the society have remained socially, economically and politically marginalized. The existing strategies for social development by the state, and the increasing activism by the civil society to espouse the cause of marginalized often fall short of their goal. They are unable to prevent the livelihood insecurity, ill health, political disempowerment, regular drudgery, physical displacement and migration, social segregation and alienation and loss of cultural identity of these groups. In the wake of globalization a vast section of these people have further become decontextualised and paradoxically posited in relation to their interface with the dominant processes of development. The accumulated indignation and deprivations of the marginalized are frequently manifested in many parts of the world by their large scale participation in the grassroots collective mobilization and in the organized social movements of diverse forms, with multiple meanings and strategies to redefine the existing order of life. Significantly enough the state and the civil society initiatives to selectively co-opt and integrate collective mobilization, and the ideas generated out of it to the social development discourse has been an order of the day.

Objectives

The main objectives of empowering the different types of marginalized sections of society like as- women's and children, ethnic minorities the migrants and slum dwellers, peasant and workers, tribes and indigenous people and the low and the backward castes as follows:

- First and the most important objectives is to bring them on the social forefront.
- Another objective is that there development and progress will lead to a natural development of society and our country as well.
- By empowering them we will able to diminish and the canonistic mentality of the other class of the people.
- There empowerment will also lead to there enlacements and they will cons us, about there rights which have been provided to them by constitution of India.

Marginalization

Marginalization is the social process of becoming or being made Marginal. Marginalization involves people being degrees of power. Marginalization has the potential to result in severe material deprivation, and in its most extreme form can exterminate groups. Material deprivation is the most common result of marginalization when looking at how unfairly material resources (such as food and shelter) are dispersed in society. Along with material deprivation, marginalized individuals are also excluded from services, programmes, and policies.

Indian constitution recognizes socially marginalized communities based on the Caste they belong to. On the basis of caste, Scheduled Castes (SC), Scheduled Tribes (ST), Other Backward Classes (OBC) and the Religious Minorities and also Women are marginalized in the field of so many sectors. According to census of India 2001, the total population of SC account for 16.2 per cent of Indian population. ST account for 8.1 per cent of the total. Though there is no official head count for OBCs the National Surveys suggest that the population of OBCs from 41 per cent of the population. Marginalization can be understood within three levels: individual, community, and global structural/policies. These are follows:

- Levels of Marginalization

The levels of marginalization are as following:

1. Individual
2. Community
3. Global and Structural/Policies

1. Individual

Marginalization at the individual level results in an individual's exclusion from meaningful participation in society. An example of marginalization at the individual level is the exclusion of single mothers from the welfare system prior to the welfare reform of the 1900's. The welfare system is based on the concept of the universal worker; entitlement to welfare is based on one's contribution to society in the form of employment. A single mother's contribution to society is not based on employment resulting in the mother's ineligibility of social assistance for many decades. In modern society, caring work is devalued and motherhood is seen as a barrier to employment. Single mothers are marginalized for their significant role in the socializing of children and due to view that an individual can only contribute meaningfully to society through employment. As a result single mothers continue to suffer from material deprivation, as well their children.

2. Community

Many communities experience marginalization, with particular focus in this section on Aboriginal communities and women. Marginalization of Aboriginal communities is a product of colonization. As a result of colonialism,Aboriginal communities lost their land, were forced into destitute areas, lost their sources of income, and were excluded from the labour market. Additionally, Aboriginal communities lost their culture and values through forced assimilation and lost their rights in society. Today various communities continue to be marginalized from society due to the developments of practices, policies and programmes that " met the needs of white people and not the needs of the marginalized groups themselves", and it also connects marginalization to minority communities when describing the concept of whiteness as maintaining and enforcing dominant and discourse.

3. Global and Structural/Policies

Globalization, immigration, social welfare and policy are broader social structures that have the potential to contribute negatively to one's access to resources and services, resulting in marginalization of individuals and groups. Globalization impacts the lives of individuals and groups in many capacities with the influx of capitalism, information technology, company outsourcing/ job insecurity ,and the widening gap between the rich and the poor.

Companies are outsourcing, jobs are lost, the cost of living continues to rise, and land is being expropriated by large companies. Material goods are made in large abundances and sold at cheaper costs, while in India for example, the poverty line is lowered in order to mask the number of individuals who are actually living in result of globalization. Globalization and structural forces aggravate poverty and continue to push individuals to the margin in society, while governments and large corporations do not address the issues.

Empowerment of Marginalized Sections of Society

Empowerment envelops developing and building capacities of individuals, communities to make them part of the main stream society. Empowerment, however is not simply a mechanical process of sharing, distribution or redistribution of power. Rather, it involves far wider changes in social and economic institutional arrangements, political ideologies, traditional practices and even in the mindset of the marginalized people through conscientisation.

Strategies

In the wake of globalization, a paradigm shift in the development strategy of the state, proliferation of grassroots mobilizations and the emergence of a new collective identity among marginalized groups, the concepts of social development and empowerment have acquired new connotations. Bringing together original contributions from scholars and potential obstacles in the way of social development and empowerment of the marginalized in the current scenario.

The strategies made by the government regarding the progress of marginal sections of society are given below:

- To save the rights of women's, the Constitution of India have been provided the Right of Equality, right against Exploitation, Right to Freedom under the fundamental rights. There are so many Acts like as Hindu Marriage Act,1955 and Special Marriage Act,1954, Hindu Adoptions and Maintenance Act, 1956, Suppression of Immoral Traffic in Women and Girls Act, 1956, The Hindu Minority and Guardianship Act,1956, The Hindu Succession Act, 1956, The Christian Matrimonial Cause Bill,1960,The Maternity Benefit Act, 1961, The Dowry Prohibition Act, 1961, The Factory Act,1948; The Factories (Amendment) Act,1976;Mines Act,1952; and Plantation Labour Act,1951, Medical Termination of Pregnancy ACT, 1971, The Adoption of Children's Bills,1972, Marriage Law (Amendment)Act, 1976, Marriage Law Amendment Bill,1981 etc, to save the right of women's;
- To save the rights of Children the Constitution of India have been provided the Right against Exploitation under Article 23 & 24 and the Constitution also provide the Right of Education under Article 21A;

- To save the rights of Minorities by Constitution;
- The government have provided the reservation for SC/ST, OBC in different fields like education, employment etc;
- It is also prescribed in the Constitution of India many schemes, programmes and plans like MNAREGA, etc have made for the welfare of marginalized sections of society;
- There are many different types of Acts and Laws like SC/ST Acts, Child labour Prohibitated Act, Minimum wages Act etc for the marginalized section of society which are protect them his right.

Conclusion

The main expects describe in the paper include Educational Empowerment, Economical Empowerment, Social and Political empowerment of marginalization section of society; through Laws and gender justice and human right. The government are trying to improve there condition but the status of these section are not so much improve. It is also can be said that we should ensure the basic minimum needs of the marginalized people like water, food , education, etc. If we want to make progress of country we must given equal place and opportunity to the marginalized section because they are also the part of our nation.

REFERENCES

Census of India, 2001.

Www. google.com

UNDP data 1990 and 2001, 2002

Bina Agarwal, "Are we not Peasants Too? Land Rights and Women's Claims in India" (2002).

T.K. Roy, Sumati Kulkarni, Y. Vaidehi "Social Inequalities in Health and Nutrition in Selected States" EPW February 14, 2004.

Eco Tourism and Tribal Development
Some Empirical Evidences

Dr. Nanjunda and S. Jyothi Lakshmi

ABSTRACT

Eco tourism now a day's become widely recognized way of avenue to improving socio economic status of the tribal people. Eco tourism even though causes impact little bit on equilibrium of ecology in many ways it helps for the generation of local lively hood resources for the tribal groups. It is found that tourism initiatives may be creating around few thousands new jobs in three to five years (both direct and indirect) in Karnataka. Govt of Karnataka has taken a lot of measure to develop the ecotourism spots in the state. The basic rationale of this paper is to find out how ecotourism may be a vital avenue for financial inclusion reducing tribal poverty of marginalized sections of the people. This paper is based on the field work conducted in different parts of Coorg districts of Karnataka State south India which is famous for its greenery and natural beauty. This study shows how ecotourism plays vital role in financial inclusion of marginalized section of the tribal society.

Introduction

Experts felt that eco tourism must benefit tribal populations socio economic development to give them incentives to protect the natural resources. Strategies must be economically feasible if private investors are to bear the projects. The speedy growth of the tourism sector is a sign of the region's thriving and diversified economies. This growth would be useful for the states inclusive growth. This inclusive growth will be helpful in reducing inequality and poverty among tribes."Based on performances of other National Heritage Areas, designation of Coorg Districts of Karnataka may be predictable to reinforce the regional economy through increased tourism, job creation, and stimulation of public and private partnerships for new investment opportunities. With sufficient planning and management, augmented heritage and nature tourism will, in turn, assist preserve the unique character of the region. A priority will be to ensure that these kinds of tourism do not demolish the very resources that attract visitors in the first place".

Development of the tourism sector can help the local tribal economy in a number of ways. The most important impact is the creation of employment for the tribes. Employment will be shaped in the hotels, restaurants and other kinds of lodgings as well as in the tour operating sector. More importantly, employment will also be created through indirect channels in a variety of sectors including local market for handicrafts, etc. Apart from employment creation, the sector can also increase the demand for the local fruits, vegetables and milk, etc. produced in the villages around tourist spots, for the consumption of the tourists. The development of this sector also provides tax revenues to the government in terms of user charges, etc., and this can be used for the development of the area. More prominently, a thriving tourism industry links up the hill areas with the rest of the country and brings down the social and economic isolation of the tribal people. (Sabyasachi, 2003).

Objectives

1. To study about the current socio economic status of the tribal people started various economic activities near ecotourism spots.
2. To revel perception of local venders (businessman) about economic development through eco tourism.

Research Design and Methodology

Primary data has been collected through survey method with a pre tested interview schedule, focus group discussion and participant observations. Secondary data about the programmes and their coverage etc. has also been collected through published sources.

(a) **Study area**

This study has been conducted in Coorg Districts of Karnataka India

(b) **Sample Design:** Primary data has been collected through a survey of 5O tribal families who are running various economic activities at different ecotourism spots.

Research Components

The proposed research study consists of Three major components:

(a) Survey

A total of 50 tribal families had been selected for the study who are running various business activities near different eco tourism spot.

(b) Community norms Study

In this component we had conducted separate focus groups interviews with the members other than the samples of the study including formal and informal community leaders, local influential persons, media personnel, religious leaders etc.

(c) Interview and Consultation

Government functionaries were interviewed regarding Govt. policies for the promotion of eco tourism.

Collection of Data

Primary data will be collected at different levels with different questionnaires.

1. At the household level - 50
2. Govt. and NGO people -10

Analysis of Data

The qualitative data has been analyzed using *NUD*IST* database software and the quantitative data will be analyzed using SPSS software

Result and Discussion

Table 10.1

Sl. No.	Issues	Number	
		Number	Count
1.	Green mountains/sun rise spots/river side/old temples	21	21%
2.	Ancient monuments/wild life sanctuaries	13	13%
3.	Trekking, and waterfalls/rafting	9	9%
4.	Museums/Forts/Palace	4	4%
5.	Nature therapy, home stay centers	3	3%
	Total	50.00	50.00
	X^2=115.106; P< .000		

Different Ecotourism Spots and Percentage of Business Activities

This tables shows more than 21 per cent of them have started their business near Green mountains/sun rise spots/ river side/old temples. 13 per cent of them have started their economic activities near Ancient monuments/wild life sanctuaries. While 9 per cent of them have running business near Trekking, waterfalls museums/forts/palace. Next 3 per cent of them started business near Nature therapy, home stay.

Table 10.2: Different Types of Eco-Tourism based Economic Activities of the Studied Tribes

Issues	Number	Count
Running small moveable shops (eatable items/snacks)	31	31%
As a local guide/photographer/assistant	7	7%
Selling ornaments, local handicrafts	4	4%
Tour operating business	6	6%
Amusements	2	2%
Total	50	50.00
$X^2 = 130.116$; P<.000		

It is found that 31 per cent of the respondents have been engaged in running small moveable shops. 7 per cent of the respondent are working as local guides photographer or local assistance to the visitors. 6 per cent of them are or running tour operators. 2 per cent of them or working in amusements.

Table 10.3: Monthly Income of the Tribal Families after Eco-tourism Business

Monthly Income Families (%)	Number	Count
10000 and above	11	11%
8,000	19	19%
6,000	10	10%
4,000	6	6%
Above three thousand	4	4%
Total	50	50.00
X^2=114.105; P< .000		

Table 10.3 increased monthly income of the respondents after starting new economic activities. The total monthly income of 11 per cent of respondents has been increased more than 10000/- rupees as a net profit. 19 per cent of the respondents are earning more than 8000 rupees of net profits. 10 per cent of them are getting more than 6000 rupees per month. 6 per cent of them are getting more than 5000/- of net profit. This shows that economic activities near eco tourism spots have worked much for them.

Table 10.4 is intend to show Businessmen's Opinion of about improvement of their economic status. 27 per cent of them felt total income has improved a lot.9 per cent of them said income improved Modestly.7 per cent of them felt it is improved By and large.4 per cent of them said income level is not complete improved where as 4 per cent of them said income is not improved at all. Totally ecotourism has played a vital role in improving economic status of the tribal respondents.

Table 10.4: Tribes Opinion on Eco-tourism and Economic Status

Opinion	Number	
	Number	Count
Total income improved a lot and situation improved at family level	27	27%
Income improved modestly	9	9%
By and large it is economic status improved	6	6%
Slightly Improved	4	4%
Not improved	4	4%
Total	50	50.00
X^2=152.116; P<.000		

Discussion and Conclusion

This study has clear shows that there are wide prospective for eco tourism in Coorg dist . Data ravels about how income of the family involved in the various to eco tourism m rural migration can b e considerably checked out. Ecotourism fetches them a moderate alternative source and financial incentives that encourage local people to protect their environment. This study has also proved that total income of he faly has risen after starting different types of business near tours places. Study has also proved that because of eco tourism local handi crafts will get wide marketing. Local NGOs feels eco tourism not only saves local environment but also increase state revenue. state govt needs to provide all fundamental facility to these tourism spots first . majorly of the spots in Coorg is even not known tot eh out side world so far. Govt has to start new more Tourism Cities & Theme Parks to concentrate Real Time Governance & Institutions for Coördinated Action.

It is found that Coorg is suitable for increasingly trendy idea of eco-tourism, which provides a thrilling adventure for those fascinated in participating. Essentially eco-tourism offers people the opportunity to seek out scenic yet hard to access areas such as rain forests or mountains, and this delicate biosphere area has abundance of these features. Eco-tourism is after all welcomed here as it would be the best recurring income generating activity for the local people. Community felt eco-tourism in in coorg districts may be helpful to develop the income and social status of the local people either in many ways. Also experts feel the revenue generated from these means that resources can be useful for the protection of natural resources and help the local people. It is well known truth that this form of eco trip has become very trendy for people concerned in eco conservation. Eco-tourism in Coorg will offer visitors with stimulating trips to places such as Cauvery Nisarga Dhama, Abbifalls, Nagarhole National Park, Brahmagiri Reserve Forests and other fragile biodiversity places (in Coorg district) , whilst ensuring that the eco-system is not disturbed in anyway.

Eco-tourism in Coorg can hopefully ensure will generate enough income for the development. Then district will have own resource to conserve natureCurrent study has found that scope for eco tourism for low-income groups, is constructive both in the short term and in the long term. Study has proved a considerable investment in terms of time and money, holidays can increase significant benefits socio economic development of the many local people. Further, it has also decorated innovative aspects of the social impacts of tourism, and has exposed the probable new social policy for effective socio economic development and accomplishment of existing interventions. We need to attract private investment through public private participation

The Coorg economy is ideally situated to take:

1. Leisure tourism in the hill stations
2. Religious tourism
3. Adventure tourism

Benefit of this situation and scale up its tourism sector. The two inputs that are essential for the development of this tourism sector, i.e., natural and human capital, are plentifully available in the state. Thus, it has the potential to match the rise in tourism demand with an increase in supply of tourism services. though industrial and mainly services-related activity naturally flourishes in areas that are already developed in terms of infrastructure, urbanization, etc, tourism can be developed in comparatively underdeveloped areas, provided they have something of interest to the tourist. Thus, in comparison to industry and these other services sectors, the tourism sector is mainly suitable for promoting inclusive growth. Coorg is predominantly well gifted in this respect and can develop different kinds of tourism activities. Eco-tourism provides the Urban Dweller an opportunity to experience various facets of Coorgs bountiful nature and wildlife. This has resulted in wider participation in conservation efforts from travelers who have experienced what nature has to offer.

This study has clear shows that there are wide prospective for eco tourism in Coorg districts. Data ravels about how income of the family involved in the various eco -tourism activities. Also tribal migration can be considerably checked out. Ecotourism fetches them a moderate alternative source and financial incentives that encourage local people to protect their environment. This study has also proved that total income of the tribal family has risen after starting different types of business near tours places. Study has also proved that because of eco tourism tribal art and culture will get wide marketing. Local NGOs feels eco tourism not only saves local environment but also increase state revenue. Eco tourism for low-income groups like tribes, is constructive both in the short term and in the long term. Study has proved a considerable investment in terms of time and money in need to develop the eco spots. New infrastructure can increase significant benefits of socio economic development of the tribal people. Further strong tourism policy is need of the hour. We need to attract private investment through public private participation.

REFERENCES

Gonsalves, D.V. and D'Souza, J. (1998). Impact of Tourism Industry on Ground Water in Himalya. Ambio 26: 235-242.

Jena, Nalin. (1996). National Parks and Sanctuaries vs People's Rights – Some Issues of Concern, pages 276-291, In: Gopal Iyer, K. (Editor) Sustainable Development: Ecological and Socio-cultural Dimensions Vikas Publishing House, New Delhi.

Mehmentoglu, M (2005) A Case Study of Nature Base Tourists Specialists Versus Generalists, *Journal of Vacation Marketing*, 23: 357.

Kothari, A., Pande, P., Singh, S. and Variava, D. (1989). Management of National Parks and Sanctuaries in India: A Status Report. Indian Institute of Public Administration, New Delhi.

Gender and Poverty in India
A Case Study of Urban Coimbatore

Dr. G. Vanithamani

ABSTRACT

A woman is more vulnerable to poverty than a man in this world, as she is the one directly involved in family and its economic affairs. When she faces crisis to meet minimum required needs for her children and family, she struggles and fights to any extent. This struggle and fight is called "Women Poverty". Women workers are not only concentrated in the unorganised economy, they are in the more insecure forms of unorganised employment, where earnings are the most unreliable and the most scanty. While in some instances, their income can be important in helping families move out of poverty; this is only true if there is more than one earner. Coimbatore city has a sufficient number of women workers working in unorganised sector. Moreover, this women workers is highly unskilled, involved in heavy physical work of different types for long hours with limited payment; lack of guaranteed wages; and lack of job security. As well, there were no facilities of various forms of leave, for sickness or maternity, for instance. These women workers working in unorganised sector are generally exploited. Workers were living below the minimum accepted standards without adequate shelter and toilet facilities.

The analysis easily estimated that the women working in unorganised sector were living a life far below from satisfaction. This study found that though the women workers contribute substantially to the growth of Coimbatore; these workers continue to labour under severe problems. They work more than men as they have to play a dual role both in and outside the home. Poverty, lack of access to education and inadequate health facilities are their major problems. Policy objectives must also identify the multiple barriers to economic security women face based on their race, customs, immigration status, sexuality, physical ability and health status. These approaches must promote the equal social and economic status of all women by growing their opportunities to sense of balance work and family life.

Introduction

A woman is more vulnerable to poverty than a man in this world, as she is the one directly involved in family and its economic affairs. When she faces crisis to meet minimum required needs for her children and family, she struggles and fights to any extent, she sacrifices self to feed children. This struggle and fight is called "Women Poverty". Women are an integral part of every economy. All round development and harmonious growth of a nation would be possible only when women are considered equal partners in progress with men. Empowerment of a woman is essential to harness the women labor in the main stream of economic development. Women workers are not only concentrated in the unorganized economy, they are in the more insecure forms of unorganized employment, where earnings are the most unreliable and the most scanty. While in some instances, their income can be important in helping families move out of poverty; this is only true if there is more than one earner. Lifting women out of poverty will depend, to a large extent, on a better understanding of how many poor there are, where they live, why they are poor, and what their precise circumstances are. According to an estimate by National Commission on Self-employed Women (1988a), of the total number of women workers in India, about 94 per cent of the workforces are in the informal or unorganised sector, whereas just six per cent are in the organized or formal sector. However, the condition of women in this sector is miserable as they work for extremely low wages, with a total lack of job security and social security benefits, and they are not protected by any government labor organizations or labor legislation. There are hardly any unions in this sector to act as watchdogs.

The feminist approach to poverty focuses on the gender implications and social costs of poverty. They include the growing involvement of women and children in the unorganised economy; differential treatment of girls and boys in households; pressure to get girls married off quickly; higher school drop-out rates for girls; less control over fertility; and recourse to prostitution. Studies on female poverty have given rise to policy recommendations that there be poverty-alleviation or employment-generation programmes designed specifically for women, or that households maintained by women alone be targeted for social programmes (United Nations, 1995, p. 41).

Concept of Poverty

Poverty can be defined as a situation when people are unable to satisfy the basic needs of life. The definition and methods of measuring poverty differs from country to country. According to the definition by Planning Commission of India, poverty line is drawn with an intake of 2400 calories in rural areas and 2100 calories in urban areas. If a person is unable to get that much minimum level of calories, then he/she is considered as being below poverty line. Poverty has traditionally been defined in terms of income or consumption. Thus it is "the inability to attain a minimum standard of living" (WDR, 1990). In India, as per capita incomes have increased, there has been a rise in the socially acceptable minimum standard of living and the Tendulkar Committee recalculated the poverty line to include a basic level of shelter, clothing and medical expenditure. The Indian government's recent poverty measure estimated that Rs.28 (US$0.56) per day, per person in urban areas and Rs.22.50 (US$0.44) in rural areas is sufficient to reach this new minimum standard, after correcting for inflation. These values are quite close to the Indian rupee's purchasing power parity compared to the US dollar. The new poverty estimates for 2011-12 will only add to the furor triggered by the Commission's affidavit in the Supreme Court in October in which the BPL cap was pegged at an expenditure of Rs. 32 and Rs. 26 by an individual in the urban and rural areas respectively at the going rate of inflation in 2010-11.

Empirical Analysis

The present study survey covered workers from six different types of work in Coimbatore Urban area. Six different types of workers are:

1. Women textile workers
2. Women petty retail traders
3. Women tailors
4. Sales women in textile shop
5. Women engineering workers
6. Women construction workers.

The survey was carried out at different intervals to explore various aspects of the lives of women working in the unorganised sector. The primary data was collected 20 samples from each category totally 120 female respondents were collected. While occasional reference will be made to secondary data, the focus is primarily based on fieldwork investigation.

Educational Qualification

The age of entry into a job is an indicator of the organized nature of an occupation. For the present study the working ages of women were between 15 and 60 years. Most were married, (85%). Ten per cent were unmarried and remaining per cent were widowed (once married). One of the important indicators of poverty is the level of literacy, because illiterate and unskilled women are engaged in low paid jobs like textile, construction, tailor (unorganised work). Table 11.1 shows the educational qualification of the sample respondents.

Table 11.1: Educational Qualification

Educational Level	Workers	Percentage
Illiterate	78	65.00
Primary	24	20.00
Middle	12	10.00
Secondary	6	5.00
Total	120	100.00

Most of the women laborers (65%) were illiterate. A fraction (20%) had schooling primary education i.e. Vth class, and of these 10 per cent in the sample had studies up to the eighth standard (Middle), while 5 per cent had passed the secondary Higher secondary education (Xth and XIIth class). The absence of literacy resulted in the employment of (unskilled) women in the unorganised sector.

Monthly Income of the Respondents

Women working in the study area are also susceptible to critical financial risks. Particularly vulnerable are the poorest of the poor. While analyzing the income level of women workers in the agriculture sector, it is worthwhile to highlight their present economic position. Economic position refers to the cash earning of the respondents. For workers engaged in the unorganised sector, minimum wages and statutory working hours are alien words. The wages are not determined by any wage law and there are no equal wage criteria. As stated earlier, the unorganised sector is not protected by government labor legislation. The wages are determined according to the quantum of work and vary from one employer to another.

Table 11.2: Monthly Income of the Respondents

Monthly Income (in Rs.)	Workers	Percentage
Up to 1000	30	25.00
1001-2000	36	30.00
2001-3000	30	25.00
Above 300C	24	20.00
Total	120	100.00

Of the total women workers in the study area, 25 per cent were earning their monthly income up to Rs. 1000, 30 per cent were earning between Rs. 1001-2000, around 25 per cent of the women workers were earning between

Rs. 2001-3000 and 20 per cent of the workers were earning above Rs. 3000. Hence, it is clear that a majority of the women workers had a monthly income ranging between Rs. 1001 and Rs. 2000.

Total Family Income

The real standard of living of the people depends upon the total earnings of the household. Total earnings of the family refer to the contributions by different members of the family to the total income. Table 11.3 provides this information.

Table 11.3: Total Family Income

Total Family Income (in Rs.)	Workers	Percentage
Below 2500	7	5.8
2501-5000	30	25.0
5001-7500	46	38.3
7501-10000	20	16.6
Above 10000	17	14.3
Total	120	100.0

A maximum of 38.3 per cent of the women workers had a family monthly income of between Rs. 5001-7500 and around 25 per cent was between Rs. 2501-5000. Next to this category, 16.6 per cent of the women workers had a family income of between Rs. 7501-10000. Above Rs. 10,000 was the total family income for the 14.3 per cent of the women workers and 5.8 per cent of the women worker's family income was below Rs. 2,500.

Debt Position

The gap between income and expenditure is generally bridged through borrowing. The purpose of borrowing is essential as it would reflect whether the households are borrowing for productive/unproductive/consumption purposes and it would reflect their socio-economic well being. The workers who were indebts were asked about the amount of loan and the results are shown in table 11.4.

Table 11.4: Debt Position

Classification	Workers	Percentage
Borrowed	75	62.5
No Borrowings	45	37.5
Total	120	100.0

It is pertinent to note here that debt as such was not a problem if it is put to productive use. In this study, 62.5 per cent of women workers obtained loans for meeting the current consumption needs which aggravates the burden of debt. As the workers could not manage these smaller amounts themselves, they have taken it as loans to fulfill their urgent requirements. It is evident from the table that around 37.5 per cent did not borrow money.

Monetary Value of the Assets

Financial independence is a requirement of gender equality. Thus one of the major indicators connected with the female poverty is the control of assets. Table 11.5 shows the classification and ownership of property of sample households.

Table 11.5: Monetary Value of the Assets

Asset Value (in Rs.)	Workers	Percentage
Below 25000	25	20.8
25001-50000	32	26.7
50001-75000	22	18.3
75001-100000	20	16.7
Above 100000	21	17.5
Total	120	100.0

Out of the total sample of 120, A maximum of 26.7 per cent of the women workers were having assets worth between Rs.25001-50000. Nearly 21 per cent of the women workers had assets ranging below Rs. 25001. Nearly 18 per cent of the women workers possessed assets ranging between Rs. 50001-75000 and above 1 lakh, respectively. Only 20.8 per cent of the workers had assets ranging below Rs. 25000. Hence, the asset holdings of the sample workers was very poor as only 20.8 per cent were in possession of a few assets having a money value upto Rs. 25,000, which means those women workers were assetless, because of insufficient earnings.

Decision Making power of Women

Participation in the decision-making process is also an indicator of power and control over the affairs of the family. Not only land, but family labor including women is often controlled by men. In spite of women's contribution toward family income, their position in the family hierarchy mostly remains subordinate. Table 11.6 shows the decision-making power of women in the surveyed households.

Table 11.6: Decision making Power of Women

Decision making Power in the Households	Reporting Households	Percentage
Husband	62	52.00
Father-in-law	25	21.00
Son	16	13.00
Wife	10	8.00
Mother-in-law	7	6.00
Total	120	100.00

This table reveals that 8 per cent of women were found making decisions and these women were divorced, widowed, or married to men who were addicted to alcohol or gambling. The remaining 92 per cent men were found making decisions, because of their feeling that the women are incapable of taking decisions due to illiteracy or low level of education among them or their confinement to the four walls of the houses.

Conclusion

Coimbatore city has adequate number of women workers working in unorganised sector. Moreover, this women workers is highly unskilled, involved in heavy physical work of different types for long hours with limited payment; lack of guaranteed wages; and lack of job security. As well, there were no amenities of various forms of leave, for sickness or maternity. These women workers working in unorganised sector are generally exploited. They are made to work for long hours and wages paid to them are not according to their work. This study attempt to know the extent of poverty exposed that lack of economic opportunities among women, educational deprivation, gender inequality in access to assets and decision-making produce cycles of poverty for Indian women. These workers were living below the minimum accepted standards without adequate shelter and toilet facilities. From the above analysis, it can be easily estimated that the women working in unorganised sector were living a life far below from satisfaction. This study found that though the women workers contribute substantially to the growth of Coimbatore; these workers continue to labour under severe problems. They work more than men as they have to play a dual role both in and outside the home.

Poverty, lack of access to education and inadequate health facilities are their major problems. The best policy solutions to address women's poverty must merge a variety of decent employment opportunities with a system of social services that support families. Policy objectives must also identify the multiple barriers to economic security women face based on their race, customs, immigration status, sexuality, physical ability, and health status. These approaches must promote the equal social and economic status of all women by growing their opportunities to sense of balance work and family life.

REFERENCES

Baden, Sally with Milward, Kirsty (1985) 'Gender and poverty', BRIDGE Report 30, BRIDGE, IDS, Brighton.

Elaine Zuckerman (2002), 'Poverty Reduction Strategy Papers and Gender', Background Paper for the Conference on Sustainable Poverty Reduction and PRSPs – Challenges for Developing Countries and Development Cooperation Berlin, May 13-16.

Himanshu (2010) 'Towards New Poverty Lines for India', Economic & Political Weekly, Vol xlv. No. 1.

Jackson and Cecile (1996) 'Rescuing Gender from the Poverty Trap', World Development.

Joyce Lyimo (2002) 'Gender and Rural Poverty in Tanzania: Case of Selected Villages in Morogoro Rural and Kilosa Districts', LADDER Working Paper No. 18.

Martha Chen et al (2005) 'Progress of the World's Women: Women, Work and Poverty', United Nation Development Fund for Women, New York.

Martin Ravallion (2008) 'A Global Perspective on Poverty in India', Economic & Political Weekly, October 25.

National Commission on Self-employed Women (1988a)

Pearce, D.M. (1978) 'The Feminization of Poverty: Women, Work and Welfare', Urban and Social Change Review, 28-36.

Power, J. (1993) 'The Report on Rural Women Living in Poverty' Rome: International Fund for Agricultural Development.

Rashmi Bhat (2002), 'Feminisation of Poverty and Empowerment of Women – An Indian Perspective & Experience', Townsville International Women's Conference – Australia.

Santosh Nandal (2005) 'Extent and Causes of Gender and Poverty in India: A Case Study of Rural Hayana', Journal of International Women's Studies Vol. 7 #2 November.

United Nations Development Programme (1995) 'Human Development Report 1995' New York: OUP.

Valentine M. Moghadam (2005) 'The 'Feminization of Poverty' and Women's Human Rights' Division of Human Rights, Social and Human Sciences Sector, UNESCO.

Zoe Oxaal and Sarah Cook (1998) 'Health and Poverty Gender Analysis', Report No. 46, Institute of Development Studies, Brighton.

Ancient Indian Wisdom Promoting Corporate Social Responsibility in India

Niteesh Kumar Upadhayay and Kuhumita Laha

ABSTRACT

Religion and philosophy play a significant role in the development of human values and behaviour which has a great impact on business and corporate management. Researches also suggest that the encouragement of religious principles in business can lead to benefits in the in terms of creativity, honesty and trust, personal fulfillment, and commitment, which will ultimately lead to increased corporate and business performance. CSR activities are sometimes forced or pushed by the religious sentiments and religious texts. One of the examples can be principle of Zakah in Islam etc. Importance of dharma is also an eternal part of all religions. According to it, persons following the path of dharma will remain close to god. Thus, ethical considerations and traditional values are one of the push factors for a company to get involved in CSR activities.

Keywords: Corpoarte Social Responsibility, Corporate Accountability, Ethical Business, Corporate Governance, Corporate Governance.

Introduction

The concept of social responsibility among the business communities is a phenomenon that can be traced back to the ancient Chinese, Egyptians and Sumerians. As a matter of fact, it has been discovered that these societies delineated rules for commerce to smooth the progress of trade and ensure that the wider goal of public interest was valued during the course of business transactions (Dutta and Bothra 2009, p. 248). Jesus taught that wealth encourages greed and selfishness and doesn't lead to true happiness (Christian Beliefs on Religion, Wealth and Poverty).

CSR is a western concept which finds its origin in 19th century. That was the time when the world had started discussing the topic of CSR. However, the essential features of it can be easily traced back to ancient religious texts also. One such example can be taken from Rig Veda. There is a particular verse (5-60.6), which says that affluent people in society should share their wealth with poor for social development. Although, we find no religious text ever using the word Corporate Social Responsibility or Corporation, the essence of this concept is very much ingrained in some of their verses. According to Christian theology, where "Man as Angel" could use business to serve a social purpose whereas "man as devil" could misuse corporate power and responsibility (Banerjee 2007, p. 15).

Corporate Social Responsibility means to step ahead of charity and requires that a company or a group of entities take into full account its impact on all stakeholders and the environment while making corporate decisions. Manu Smriti also leads us to one of the most important principle which says that- "A person should never seek to earn or secure wealth through pursuits which are forbidden or illegal or immoral [IV-15]" (Jois 2002, p.18). We find that ancient texts like Manu Smriti talks in detail about the nature of work to be done by persons, including business organizations and states that whatever is good for society is also good for the company in long run.

Manu Smriti also clears the dilemma that whether companies should involve themselves in CSR activities or not by stating in its text that: Some people declare that acquiring wealth alone will do well for any human society. There are others who declare that fulfillment of human desires and the acquirement of wealth is better and, after all individuals have to fulfill their desires and desires are never-ending. There are others who declare that *dharma* or righteous code of conduct is sufficient and, there are also others who say that acquisition of wealth alone is sufficient. But the correct one among them is the one who maintains the balance between earning wealth and the righteous code of conduct. Fulfillment of desires to earn wealth should be in conformation with *Dharma* and, wealth which contravenes *dharma* should be rejected [CH-II-224 and CH-IV-176] (Jois 2002, p. 18). Therefore, as per the above text, Manu Smirti states that companies should ensure that they are not just thoughtful about profit but they should also take care of the means used to earn that profit. Wealth earned by violations of principle of *drama* is not a good wealth and should be rejected. Thus, the above text signifies the importance of CSR in the working of any business organization.

We can also find consistent stress on the principle of CSR in Islam as well. In Quran and other Islamic texts we will not find the mention of the word like corporation or a corporate. Islam talks about responsibility in general and to be followed by every person following Islam including corporations. Islam lays down the code of ethics for business corporations and businesses peoples, Fair Trade, fulfilling covenants, and free competition are few important essentials to be followed by the corporations during business (Quran, 4:29). Below are few principles which deal with CSR in Islam.

Zakah (AL Zakah) is one of the five fundamental pillars of Islam, and its observance distinguishes true believers from mere nominal Muslims according to Quran (Quran, 2:43). According to the principle of *Zakah*, when a Muslim has enough to cover the essential needs for himself and his family over a year, he is in possession of the *Nisab* (Taman 2011, p.488). If he has assets more than what he is obliged to give, then he is obliged to pay *Zakah* on the excess. The importance that God has placed on *Zakah* in the Quran demonstrates how strongly Islam is associated with CSR. Even the corporations are also expected to pay *Zakah*. *Zakah* is due on the passage of every one lunar year. *Zakat* is obligatory after a time span of one lunar year passes with the money in the control of its owner. Then the owner needs to pay 2.5 per cent (or 1/40) of the money as Zakat (A lunar year is approximately 355 days). *AL Zakah* is almost similar to the concept of the mandatory CSR contribution but the only difference is of guiding force, for later the guiding force is of legal nature and for *AL Zakah* the guiding force is religious in nature.

If we go further, we also find that the CSR is also promoted by the concept of *Sadaqah*. According to Quran Sadaqah can be defined as small daily acts of charity. Allah encourages every Islamic follower to give *Sadaqah* and there is no amount fixed for *Sadaqah*. The money raised for *Al Zakah* and *Sadaqah* is used to feed poor, donate clothes and other activities. A large amount of money raised from *AL Zakah* is used to manage Madrasa which provide free education to millions of Students (Blanchard).

Moving to Hindu religious texts, if we refer to Vedic literatures, we find the notable mention of important terms like *'Sarva loka hitam'* which means 'well-being of stakeholders'. This shows the importance of stakeholders for any person including any artificial body like corporations.

Kautilya in Arthasastra also stated that happiness cannot be obtained by wealth and profit alone but only by doing things rightly and doing right things, i.e., *sukhasya mulam dharma* (Muniapan 2011). Kautilya also maintained that a leader (king) should have no self-interest, happiness and joy for himself. His satisfaction lies in the welfare (happiness) of his people. The same advice can also be found in *Shanti Parva* of the Mahabharata, wherein the public interest (welfare) is to be accorded precedence over the leader's interest (Muniapan 2008). So, if we look at business organisations as a leader or a king, then they are supposed to help others and should engage themselves in welfare of the society.

Muniapan and Dass in their study on Vedic CSR highlighted a similar development of CSR in the ancient India. Early conceptualisation of CSR was broadly based on religious virtues and values, such as honesty, love, truthfulness and trust (Muniapan 2011). Such values were found central in the golden rule constructed by Immanuel Kant's Categorical Imperative. It has also been argued that this golden rule can be applied to make companies accountable to stakeholders and society implicitly. This argument suggests that those who do not practice such values are deemed to be unethical (Muniapan 2011).

Thiruvalluvar in Tamil Nadu who wrote the Thirukkural around 2nd century B.C., dealt with the distinctiveness of socially accountable organizations. Thiruvalluvar says: the king who administers justice and protects his people will be considered of divine quality; He further says:

> *In the modern context of business, we would like to see organizational leaders setting such examples for the societal and global well being. Such leadership actions will not only promote CSR but also GSR (Global Social Responsibility) or USR (University Social Responsibility).*
>
> – Dr. Balakrishnan Muniapan

In nutshell, the Vedanta concept of *"dharma"* and *"karma"* provides an inside-out approach to CSR. According to old saying, one should save his wealth against future calamity and not to think "what fear has a rich man of calamity?" because when riches begin to forsake one even the accumulated stock dwindles away (Chanakya Niti-Sastra).

Corporate Social Responsibility in 20th Century

Due to the removal of trade barriers and restrictions on foreign investment, last few decades have seen a huge growth of FDI, especially in the developing countries. We have witnessed a great change in the number of the Transnational Corporation since 1970.when there were only 7,000 transnational corporations (TNCs). By 1994 there were 37,000 TNCs with over 200,000 globally stretched affiliates (Dias 2011, p. 495). Involvement of multinational companies in different countries added by the advances in technology and communication had also played an important role, in dramatically reducing the cost of investing in any part of world especially in developing countries which are known for cheap labour, easily available raw materials and other natural resources. Many business entities of other states try to exploit these conditions which are vital for flourishing their business. The companies often faces a dilemma regarding whether to maximize profits or take up social responsibility while making corporate decisions regarding production, distribution of services.

The increase in the number of TNC's and their power posed a great challenge for the states and its peoples. It is also seen as a major threat to human rights causes. TNCs are sometimes more financially influential than national economies. Some notable examples are Royal Dutch/Shell Group

Oil Company whose annual sale is close to twice more than New Zealand's gross domestic product ('GDP'). Similarly,annual sales of the British tobacco company, BAT Industries, are almost equivalent to the GDP of Hungary. The German electronics goods maker, Siemens AG, has annual sales that exceed the combined GDP of Chile, Costa Rica and Ecuador. Another example can be General Motors and Mitsubishi whose annual sales is more than double the GDP of Hong Kong or Israel (Dias 2011, pp. 496-497).

N. Eberstadt in his article, What history tells about Corporate Social Responsibility (1978) published in Business and Society Review, states that CSR had undergone various stages and he classifies its historical evolution into the classical (In this period businessman's positions in Greece was slightly above slaves), medieval (1000-1500 AD- churches branded profit motive as 'anti-Christian' and businessmen were expected to care for their guild members and for the well-being of the community. They also spcnsored municipal improvements such as educate the poor etc), mercantile (1500-1800 AD - Calvinist doctrine advocated profit maximization as the key to business success but still Business which provided outstanding social services to the community were given special privileges in the form of bestowing upon them the status of corporations) , industrial (1800-1920 AD- Laissez Faire economists rejected the proposition that businesses are responsible for the social welfare. This period felt the domination of the economy by business due to significant power and vested in the industrialists due to their wealth. Capturing new colonies by the industrialists was nothing new in this period) and corporate (This period includes the present day companies which are perceived as institutions discharging social obligations in society) periods (Sheikh 1996).

During the period of 1920-1970 as observed by Hay and Gray, there were three historical phases between 1920-1970 in which, CSR saw its gradual development. The highlight of the phase one was sole aim of the business to maximize profits. This behavior ends up in 1920s. Phase two was the development of the concept of 'trusteeship management' which emerged in 1920s and 1930s. According to this, business corporation acknowledged by their actions that money is important for the business organization but so are people, satisfying needs of the society is better goal than just minting money (Sheikh 1996, p. 8). The main attribute of Phase three was 'quality of life management'. According to this, economic objectives are not the sole objective of business organizations (Sheikh 1996, pp. 11-12). The world started talking about the one per cent clubs in UK (1986) and US (1970) with a main aim to make a significant contribution to the local communities in which they operate (Sheikh 1996, p.43). The next decades (1980s) forced the business organization to be more socially responsible due to the economic recession., There was a thought shift in this period which states that the primary responsibility of any business organization is too ensure that they behave as a good corporate citizen and should not only care about the shareholders but also about the other stakeholders like employees, customers, suppliers, general public, environment etc. (Sheikh 1996, p. 14).

In 20th century CSR has been seen as philanthropy, charity, and social-giving. But in late 20th century, the CSR concept was shaped in the form of a model to do sustainable business. Most companies had taken up topics of their respective interests and started investing in them. We also find a notable emphasis on elementary education in this period.

Conclusion

The concepts of CSR have shown its significant presence in the old religious text of almost of all the religions. There are many occasions when the concept of CSR has been mentioned in those texts though in subtle or indirect manner. However, there is no where we can find that the words corporation, company, corporate social responsibility is explicitly mentioned. We find that the main development of the concept of CSR took place in 19th century and the concept gradually started to become consolidated and clearer. The philosophy driving CSR discourses from the 1950s onwards was an attempt to cultivate civic virtue in corporations. In the 1980s, the focus was more on CSR as obligation ('doing good to be good'). Later on, the concept started flourishing as a corporate strategy with the idea, 'doing good to do well' (Banerjee 2007, p. 14). After 1990 we find that the concept of CSR took full shape as abusiness strategy and a mode of doing sustainable business.

Religious texts don't perceive CSR as an obligation or as a tool for business gain. CSR in India has gone beyond merely charity and donations. Today, it has become an integral part of the corporate strategy. Companies have specialized CSR teams that devise specific policies, strategies and goals for their CSR programmes and set aside budgets to support those programmes. CSR has become increasingly prominent in the Indian corporate scenario because organizations have realized that besides growing their businesses, it is also very crucial to create goodwill, build trust, and further sustainable relationships with the community at large, without which sustainable development of the corporation is not possible.

REFERENCES

Banerjee, Subhabrata B. (2007), *Corporate Social Responsibility: The Good, The Bad and The Ugly*, Edward Elgar Publishing Limited, New Delhi.

Blanchard, C. M., Islamic Religious Schools, Madrasas: Background, Available from: http://theroadtoemmaus.org/RdLb/33Rlg/Islm/Madrasas.htm [Accessed 1 October 2012].

Dias, C.J. 2011. Corporate Human Rights Accountability and the Human Right to Development: the Relevance and Role of Corporate Social Responsibility, *NUJS Law Review*, 4, pp. 495-521.

Christian Beliefs on Religion, Wealth and Poverty, (No date), *123 help me* [Online], Available from: http://www.123helpme.com/view.asp?id=122236 [Accessed 9 August 2012].

Dutta, M.S. & Bothra, R. 2009. Striving Towards a Green India INC.: A Critical Essay on the Environmental Policies of the Indian Corporations, NUJS Law Review, 2, pp. 243-265.

Jois, M. R. (2002), *Ancient Indian Law: Eternal Values in Manu Smriti,* Universal Law Publishing Co. Pvt. Ltd., New Delhi.

Muniapan, B. 2008. Kautilya's Arthashastra and Perspectives on Organizational Management, Available from: http://www.ccsenet.org/journal/index.php/ass/article/viewFile/2089/1968 [Accessed 2 October, 2012].

Muniapan, B. 2011. The Duty and Action for Corporate Social Responsibility from the Perspectives of Vedanta, Available from: http://www.aibuma.org/proceedings2011/aibuma2011_submission_45.pdf [Accessed 1 October 2012).

Niti-Sastra, C. (No date). The Political Ethics of Chanakya Pandit, *Available from:* http://philosophy.ru/library/asiatica/indica/authors/kautilya/canakya_niti_sastra.html [Accessed 3 October 2012].

Sheikh, S. (1996), *Corporate Social Responsibilities Law & Practice,* Cavendish Publishing, New Delhi.

Taman, S. 2011. The Concept of Corporate Social Responsibility in Islamic Law, *Indiana International & Comparative Law Review*, 21, pp. 481-508.

13

Rajbanshi People of North Bengal in India and their Livestock Management

Ashok Das Gupta

ABSTRACT

This chapter deals with indigenous livestock management of people from Rajbanshi Social Fold of North Bengal plains, watersheds, lowlands and sub-Himalayas (India). They use cattle in ploughing, carrying goods, and thrashing. Raising livestock is target of micro-finance. It has been seen that there is a scope of sustainable livelihood development through focusing on their interest. Various milk cooperatives could be there in small, medium or large scale.

Introduction

This article deals with indigenous livestock management of people from Rajbanshi Social Fold of North Bengal plains, watersheds, lowlands and sub-Himalayas (India).

This chapter deals with indigenous livestock management of people from Rajbanshi Social Fold of North Bengal plains, watersheds, lowlands and sub-Himalayas (India).

There are several steps in domestication - fodder gathering, carrying fodder to the home, grinding of feed, cutting and boiling of fodder, feeding the animals, watering to the animals, cleaning of mangers, grazing of animals, bathing of animals, cleaning of sheds, grooming, milking of animals, heating of milk, selling of milk, care of new born animals, care of sick animals and vaccination of animals. Cowpea yielding is a low-cost profitable production system. They know about local herbs that increase milk production. Cow is a part of their religious system.

They also use cattle in ploughing, carrying goods, and thrashing. Raising livestock is target of micro-finance.

Cow, *mithun*, buffalo, goat, lamb, duck, swan and chicken are livestock raised by Rajbanshis. They in general way avoid boar and pig. Evidences are there of Rajbanshis consuming pigeon, mollusk, frog, rabbit and tortilla.

They use their cattle as source for meat, milk and skin. Poultry yields meat and egg. Cow dung along with vermi-compost is good source of manure along with ash, semi-compost organic compounds and egg shells, snail shells and bone dust of cattle/poultry/fish. They know use of duck-snail-fish complex system that goes in fabour of their pond management.

Mithun is an indigenous hybrid of cattle.

North Bengal is a term used for the north-western parts of Bangladesh (Rajshahi and Rangpur Division) and northern districts of West Bengal and adjoining Bihar state of India. Cooch Behar, Darjeeling, Jalpaiguri, North Dinajpur, South Dinajpur and Malda districts of west Bengal state together constitute the North Bengal administrative zone and Bihar part includes Kishanganj district out of Purnea region. The entire trans-national region is within a particular natural boundary: west of Jamuna-Brahmaputra River of Assam-Bangladesh, north of Ganges-Padma River, east of Mahananda river and south of Sikkim-Bhutan Himalayas. It includes the Barind Tract and Teesta-Torsa river system. It also includes parts of Darjeeling Hills and Bengal Doors that are integral parts of Darjeeling and Jalpaiguri district. That hill and Doors buffer portions were once permanently included from influence of Sikkim-Bhutan-Tibet into Indian territory by the British during colonial rule: alternative economic opportunities and other transnational factors attract so many castes and communities to this region and provide it an essence of multiculturalism along with so many human shields along the borderland. My focus would be on the Rajbanshis of foothill region mainly covered up by Darjeeling district (Siliguri foothill) and Jalpaiguri-Cooch Behar continuity. These regions are made up of Barind ridge, uplands, lowland, rivulets, rivers, forest, bush, tea estates, agrarian sectors, rururban settlements, various townships and few municipalities besides Siliguri City Corporation. The region is an ample of so many indigenous peoples and Rajbanshi with regional variations is one of these.

A folk life consisting of production types and social system and belief system of a community living in an ecosystem can be discussed into several sectors are there like agriculture, animal husbandry, handicrafts, tools and techniques, nutrition, health care practices and bio-medicines, psycho-social care, natural and biological resource, management of environmental and bio-diversity resources, disaster mitigation, human resource management, saving and lending, poverty alleviation and community development as well as education and communication each with its respective area and manifestation of knowledge and the set of knowledge bearers in the community stratified on the basis of gender, age group, occupational groups and various personalities like local leaders, shamans, healers, medicine man, Wiseman, chiefdom, priest, magico-religious practitioners, craftsmen, art performers and so on. It also involves traditional ways of Environmental Management System, Disaster Management, Weather Forecast, Agriculture, Animal Husbandry and Poultry, Ethno-Fishery, Disease Treatment and Ethno-Medicine, traditional economic and political organizations and so on, at least to some extent (Banarjee et. al., 2006). The entire issue would be related to definite interrelationship among production and technical practices in a specific farming system, conservation of crop varieties, alternative agricultural production, production of various cash crop/vegetables/spice/ fruit and flower, maintenance of the nutrition level and traditional concepts of health, food preservation, labour-oriented handloom industry, traditional type of division of labour, ethno-fishery, animal husbandry and poultry, agro-forestry and use of forest products (timber and non-timber), sacred groove, agro-ecology and food web, bio-diversity with feed-back, water and soil management, house construction and kitchen garden, folk taxonomy, magico-religious performances, belief in super-nature, cultural lag, emerging socio-economic challenges, social transformation, sustainable rural and human resource development. Sengupta in 2003 wrote on perception of folk environment and folk taxonomy in land domain, plant domain, animal domain, color categories, hierarchical classification of folk food items and categories of food taste associated with natural environment. That perception was somewhat a direct interpretation of the folk cognition important for the study of ethno-science, but could not claim to be totally free from the external influences upon the language and some other contrasting urban phenomena as could be found there. Three villages in the industrial enclave of the west Singbhum district of Jharkhand comprising of two closely related folk communities, namely Santal and Kol were taken for the investigation.

Aspects of a Folk Life

1. material culture (including folk settlement patterns, house construction, folk architecture, folk craft, folk ornamentation and folk clothing, folk technological instruments, folk art and craft);
2. non-material culture (social values, ways of behavior, religious belief, folk dance, folk song, folk music, folk lore, folk tales, folk literature, folk play, folk notion of time and seasons, weather forecasting, folk cookery, folk painting, folk recreation, superstitions, myths, legends, riddles, folk religion;
3. and different kinds of organization (built upon taboo, prohibition, kinship bonds, sense of right and wrong (folk ways), morals, norms, leadership and priesthood);

4. norms (regarding kinship relations and rites-de-passage);
5. and folk linguistics folk customs (regarding household affairs, agricultural operations and other social behaviour);
6. folk language or dialect (including folk proverb, folk etymology and chants, dialectology of folk speech).

Together these indigenous knowledge traits of a tribal and a rural folk community (in close contact with a specific eco-system for long) behave like a useful system for utilizing the nature in the most nature friendly way with a feed back manner. This system is named as Indigenous Knowledge System. Though there is no universal scale for measuring indigenousness, the concern about Indigenous Knowledge System is day by day growing up in India since 1990s at various dimensions, for example, Peoples' Science, Traditional Knowledge System, Indigenous Technological Knowledge, Indigenous Agricultural Knowledge, Ethno-medicine, Folk life, Indigenous Environmental Knowledge and so forth.

There exist several knowledge gaps in agriculture related biodiversity. These traditional knowledge traits about agricultural system can be the way of fulfillment in following ways:

1. knowledge regarding agriculture: post and pre agricultural activities;
2. knowledge about wild and disease resistant varieties, weed management and pest control; bio-fertilizer and indigenous way of soil classification;
3. informal *ex situ* experiments of the farmers;
4. division of labor, barter system, reciprocity and community health;
5. water management, ethno-fishery, animal husbandry, poultry and animal product;
6. agro-forestry and forest produce including sacred groove;
7. house construction and cottage industry;
8. indigenous way of classification;
9. protection of agricultural biodiversity, issue of healthy food, and assurance to sustainable development through nature-friendly cultivation process and controlled and rechecked inputs.

Often the traditional knowledge traits under the domain of the Peoples' Science regarding the programmes like animal raring-cum-breeding as well as the production of good quality milk-meat-skin are too crucial in folk life more than we could ever expected. The forests in this region are the homes of various types of big and small animals, birds, snakes, insect, etc. The rivers are full of varieties of fishes, toads, frogs, crabs and so on. In North Bengal, different kinds of deer of which the principle variety is Sambar (*Carvus unicolor niger*), wild boar (*Sus scrofa*), hog deer, and barking deer are found in wood forests. Domestic animals like dog (*Canis familiaris*), cat (*Felis domesticus*), cow (*Bos indicus*), goat (*Capra hircus*), and pig (*Sus domesticus*) are very common.

Rajbanshi is an agrarian caste that like a huge social fold incorporates various tribal communities residing in transnational territory of northern West Bengal plains and watershed of India overlapped with sub-Himalayan foothills and hills of Sikkim and Bhutan Himalayas, Tibet plateau, Brahmaputra valley of North East India, Rajshahi Division of Bangladesh, Gangetic valley and Bengal delta. The place is full of biodiversity, of which the agrarian sector nourished by Rajbanshi Indigenous Knowledge System is distinct.

Animal Husbandry and Poultry

Rajbanshis rear cow, buffalo, bullock and ox as well as sheep and goat. As the fodder, Rajbanshis use rapeseed remains (*khoil*), paddy straw (*khor*), various types of grass (*ghash*), paddy seed coat (*tush*), paddy seed coat and cotyledon (*bhushi*), rice emulsion (*fen*), jungle leaves (*lotapata*), old corn grain (*makoi*), bad smelling millet (*marua,* wheat like substance), sugarcane (*ankh*) and if available solid crystallized sweet sugar cake of cane (*gur*). The rice seed coat is used as both manure and fodder. Often the rice cotyledon (detached from the rice grain) has been used as an important type of fodder. *Gangal* leaf is collected from the creeping vegetation inside the jungle and used as cattle feed so as to increase the amount, quality and taste of the cow milk. Water grass is considered to be good fodder for the cattle. Algae grown up in river can also be used as fodder. Hybrid grasses like *Guatemala grass* and *Napier grass*) and cowpea are necessary for increasing the quantity of milk. But these are not much utilized by the Rajbanshis folk.

The fear of blood sucking leach (*Dinobdella ferox*) and presence of excess jungle once resisted the Rajbanshis to bring in their cattle outside; however there are some preventive measures like moistening the body with oil, salt and soil, and pungent smelling creeping herbs collected from jungle.

The Rajbanshis often own large-scale poultries of duck; probably that is the effect of Vaishnavism which prevents them from eating hen. Whether hen or duck, they generally build up the poultry farm or the cage some heights above from the floor. They do this so as to reduce the chances of adverse effects from water, cold, snake bite and attacks of other bird-and-blood easting animals. Remaining byproducts and bone dust of the hen are used for manure. They use paddy straw, especially for the chicks to protect them from cold. Domesticated hens are often helpful in controlling the beetles, other insects and excess amount of earth warms in the soil. Ducks control the excess amount of snails in the pond eco-system. Rajbanshis consume bird meat in cooked manner with spices. They often consume the fresh egg yolk uncooked. Rajbanshis also rear goose. Rajbanshis are also fond of wild hens.

Ducks in pond help to control the number of snails that could be reason for scarcity in the amount of fish food and on the other hand, duck stool is a good source of food for the fishes.

A house may be looked as consisting of only outer courtyard with two sides open, children playing there under the banyan tree, women cooking meal at the southern corner with the help of fuel wood stored at a hut, cattle tasting the fodder under the temporary cow shade; but at the evening, the women would candle on the basil pedestal inside the inner court yard, cook food inside, males return back from the field, clean their feet and hands, cattle are brought inside, children prepare to go to sleep, grand mother tell them a folk lore, student studying under the lamp of cow dung/ bio-gas (sold from the market); in hot days, they often sleep in the *dhap* or inner courtyard or even under the shade of common gossip center outside the home.

The cowshed, kitchen and the store room are constructed very close to each other. It would be easier for the womenfolk to collect grains from the store and make food and fodder of it at the same time. Cattle are raised in a hot place near the hearth, which protects them from cold in the winter season and always keeps them and their cubs under close observation. A cowshed is generally kelp separate from cages for duck. Hen and pig are usually not reared by the Rajbanshis. Goat and sheep are sometimes domesticated and kept separately. Sheep or goat do not take much place and cover up of a region of maximum 16 feet. Sheep are fed with grass and so the goats along with jackfruit leaf. All these sheds are to clean up with lime or phenyl or bleaching power. Air and light should be permitted for easy entry. Feeding bowls should be kept clean. Cattle are to be bathed regularly. In drinking water, mulberry fruit extract (1%) or *tunt* is preferred to apply. For disease treatment, peasants have to communicate with veterinary hospitals. Gourd is a favourite for cattle. Gourd plant and clean paddy straw together increases immunity of the cattle. Leaf and twig of gadal creeper is milk increasing for cattle in a natural way vigorously used by the Rajbanshis and other caste people in their neighbourhood. Some Rajbanshis are associated with poultry of broiler chicken as their occupation. They usually buy feeder from market, build up a tier feeder system, and maintain their poultry on commercial basis. They construct the poultry outside the village or in wasteland or near the bamboo bush. They use high power electric bulb for the chicks. Sometimes, they use incubators. They use paddy straw and jute blankets within the bamboo made cage. Poultry waste is a good source of manure and fish feed. This is up to the poultry owner about food quality, hygiene, cage size and cleanliness that are to be maintained in ideal case. This is advised that they should provide liver tonic, vitamin and antibiotics (if needed) with clean water.

Rajbanshis in their kitchen/*rannagrar* (*annaghar*), use various types of cooking and cooking related utensils like jar/*ghot*, pitcher/*kalsi*/*kalas*, jug/*kunja*, pot/*hari*, small bowl/*bati*, big bowl/tub/*gamla*, basket/*tukri*, bucket/*balti*, glass/*gelas*, cup/*piala*/*pirich*, dish/*sarai*/*sara*, thatched plate with edge/*batai*, plate/*thala*/*thali*, cooking bowl/*karai*/*noya*, large spoon/*hata*, large flat spoon/*khunti*/*chilni*, spoon/*chamcha*/*chamche*/*chamuch*, rolling machine (to paste pulses)/*dalghata*/*phirki*, nutcracker/*janti*, match box/*shalai*, kettle/*ketli*, tong/*chimta*/*sharanshi*, box/*diba*, lid/*dhaka*/*dhakna*/*dhakni*, spice presser and grinder/*shil-pata*, husk/*chham*, sieve/*chalni*, winnowing fan/*dhama*, oven/*unan*, dry stick/*lakri*, cow dung/ *ghuta*/*ghute*, jute stick/*pat kathi*, paddy straw/*khor*, paddy seed coat/ *tush*, paddy cotyledon/ *bhushi*, lamp/*kupi*, wick/*sholta*/*polta*, bottle/*botol*, rope/*dori*/*roshi*, wooden seat/*piri*, thatched mat/*chatai*/*pati*, bag/*chot*/*bora*, and so on. Many of these utensils are used to serve fodder to the cattle. *Bhushi*, *khor*, *tush* and *pat kathi* are good fuel. *Bhushi* and *khor* are also used as fodder. Rajbanshis have used thatched semi-rounded baskets/*jhuri* both in kitchen and for their cattle. Rajbanshis call their cattle sheds are *goalghor*. Rajbanshis have stored various agricultural and soil cutting implements in their cattle sheds and these include spade/*kodal*, spade/*belcha*, sickle/*kaichi*/*kaicha*, dibble/*khurpi*/*poshani*, ladder/*moi*, rope/*dor*/*dori*, and plough/*langol* with *joal* (a wooden log that is fixed to the plough/ladder with the bullock pair) and *fauri* or *fal* (metal or wooden portion of *langol* that enters into the soil and cultivating the ground). Rajbanshis use hone and flat big stone piece with fine narrow cutting edges, so as to sharpen their metal/iron implements used either inside the house (knife/*chaku*/*boti*) or outside (axe/ *kurul*/*dao*) for construction of house and other occupational works. They use these implements to cut off the fodder like big grasses and straw into pieces and serve these as fodder to their cattle.

Fire wood is stored near the kitchen and the cow shade, often creating a barrier between these two. This is also stored separately in store or in the bamboo rack from the ceiling. Cow dung cakes (fuel) and dump of ash are again kept nearby. Worship of cow and earthen stove is also done at the same time by the Hindu Rajbanshis.

Milk collection from the cow shade, preparation of card (*goleya dahi*) from fresh milk (directly fermented non-boiled) and production of food items like *dahi-chura* (card with beaten rice), *ghee* (fat emulsion of milk), and *chhana* (clustered milk in lime) in the kitchen are related with each other. *Chhana* is however better prepared by sweet manufacturers basically belonging to Bengali community. In order to prepare card, the Rajbanshis keep milk directly from the cow in an earthen pot for several days in a clean, dust-free, cool dark room (with earthen wall and roof made by jute sticks and straw); hang it from the beams of the roof; and after some days, the card was formed due to the activity of the bacteria and then they pull in down and intake it with salt. They do not put any lime extract or swore fruit substances in it like the Bengalis do. Nor they even heat the milk on mild flame. When the cub is born, from the first milk this limed clustered milk or *chhana* is prepared, fed to the cub and taken also by the family members of the household. During crop failure or drought, *Yugis* are invited in the house and these magico-religious Wiseman conduct some performances in the cow shade, cook food there by their own hand and then after eating this go back on their ways.

Rajbanshis often burnt the leaves after piling them in a huge hip (bonfire). This started from evening and continued to late night. This increases the temperature of the neighborhood and provides warm both to the peoples and the animal husbandry and poultry to some extent. In the morning, the ashes are found wet due to the dew drops. Dogs made this ash as their sleeping bed. The wet ashes are good for organic manure. Ash is also layered on the cow or they are rugged by jute blanket. Ash, jute blanket, sand and paddy straw are important non-conducting agents. Ash is used in curing plant disease. The affected leaves are often collected along with pests and their larvae and eggs and burnt off in a dig before covering up with soil.

Mixture of cow dung and water is used each weak or once in every fortnight to plaster the yard, floor and lower portion of the wall for future protection of the earthen houses especially during the monsoon. The traditional husking machine is made up of bamboo- it has a whole on the dried muddy floor frequently plastered with cow dung and also a long wooden log used as a paddle or lever that press the paddy put inside the whole to make it free from the seed coat.

Cow dung is used as fuel. In order to so, the cow dung is mixed with water, softened; and as hand made cakes on wall or tree surface, sun-dried. It is also plastered on dried sticks and then sun dried. Both are efficient here. Rajbanshis are well concerned about need of cuttings and pruning- to check the risks of spreading infection; they use cow dung and lime at the cut tips of the branches of the shrub, mainly flowering plant.

They prepare the color brush from the tails of a cow or other animal fibers or hair. Rajbanshis used to prepare a kind of gum from pressing the fern between two stones. They prepare yellow color from turmeric, green from plant leaves, black from the lower portion under the *handi* pottery used in cooking food on earthen stove with the help of dry wood or dung cake. They use *haritaki* fruit rubbed on a stone to produce some kind of brown color.

Ash is used for preparation of ash color. Red is also prepared by mixing lime with powder of young turmeric rhizome. Wax is also produced from *bel* fruit. Once the Rajbanshis collected sponge (*shola*) from the water bodies of North Bengal and these light weight substances in dry condition were cut out to make various figurines. Carpenters collect burnish from teak extract. Brown colour is also collected from catechu bark. Lime is the natural source of white colour.

Application or re-application of bio-fertilizers like earth warms and degradable manures like cow dung in cultivation and production of organic foods in order to capture the foreign market have also been proved to be very much effective in protecting the environment and the bio-geo cycles and important aspects of research in the Agricultural Institutions and the Governmental Agencies.

Cow dung, half rotten and full rotten leaf manure, ash, nitrogenous soil, soil collected from the ground where the jungle was destroyed on fire, boiled tea leaves, rice emulsion, superfluity, rice dust, seed coat, cow urine, bone dust, egg shells, snail shells, remains of small fish-crab-prawn and even paste of rotten remains of mastered or other rapeseeds (after extracting the oil) are basically used as the organic manure. The collected cow dung from field is kept inside bamboo funnels and heated before applying as manure. In case of vegetable propagation in highland areas (*danga*), more or less 100 Kg of cow dung is used along with *Tricodarma viridi*, pseudomonas microorganisms, and fluorescence microorganisms per *bigha*[1] land. This could vary from five to ten vans of cow dung. This equals to 250-500 gm see weeds that could be used as powder in water emulsion and liquid form. But this is not a usual practice of the common Rajbanshis. Often cow dung manure is applied in part by part to the cropland. This process is known as *Chapan*. Quality of manure depends on the fodder. However, in these days various other manures are being added to the cultivation ground. In green house for vegetables and flower plants, again cow dung and microorganisms with different cakes, NPK, controlled vermicompost and even lime are added to produce the crops and flowers on regular basis. In mango tree, cow dung manure is highly needed. Cow dung is also to be added in ponds. After addition of lime in pond water that helps in controlling acidity, increasing supply of oxygen, pond bed management, organic manure (mostly cow dung) is the best option to improve the pond condition. *Mahua* cake 300-350 Kg and bleaching powder 70-90 Kg are actually to be added 7-day before addition of lime (300 Kg for pH 4-5, 250 Kg for pH 5-6, 70 Kg for pH 6-7, 35 Kg for pH 7-8). After application of lime in controlled manner, 500 Kg organic manure (50 vans) could be added. If only manure is to be added, then about 100-150 vans of cow dung to be added. These could be virtually applied to a pond of 1 *bigha*[1] size of minimum 1 meter depth. After a gap of 7 days, 30,000 to 40,000 small fishes of one inch size each in average can be added to this

---

1 In West Bengal, the *Bigha* was standardized under British colonial rule at 1600 sq.yd (0.1338 hectare or 0.3306 acre); this is often interpreted as being 1/3 acre (it is precisely 40D 121 acre). In Metric units, a *Bigha* is hence 1333.33 m^2.

pond. Paddy cotyledons, mustard cakes, cow dung manure, other superfluities, duck and fish feeds from market are to be added in the pond for their steady growth. Increment in nitrogen and phosphorus amount will also facilitate growth in number of plankton more than the waterweeds.

Rajbanshis preferred the earth warm, white ant and even ants as agriculture friendly organisms (obviously when under control). Earth warms do the same thing a plough does in order to prepare the land. White ants decompose the dead and other unnecessary organic compounds that help in sustenance of the bio-geo cycles. Ants also help in decomposition as well as allow air to enter within the soil through the channels they produce for their easy passage. They eat up the dead organisms, cut off the leaves into pieces, pollinate the flower, consume a decaying fruit, and construct underground chambers to live where air can pass into. Ants through their activities could make a weather forecasting; such as, their accumulation beneath the tree leaves or within the tree trunks indicates that the rain is coming. But now the ants are often found to fail from making a correct forecast. They have failed to adjust themselves with the rapid changes in weather and often denote wrong weather forecasting. Again, excess presence of ants, white ants and earth warm again reduces the fertility of the soil. But cow dung is the best organic manure to the Rajbanshi cultivators. Rajbanshis do not apply cow dung in the field directly, but actually in dried powdery condition. They also know how to make a compost of it. They take the cow dung along with paddy straw in pile and cover it with plastic sheet. Dung and urine of goat are also good fertilizers in small amount that the Rajbanshis and other local people apply in horticulture. In a dig, they store vegetable superfluity, some cow dung, paddy straw and ash layer by layer for one to two months and over the chamber under paddy straw sheet. This also gives them manure. They sometimes apply this manure with water of margosa and/or mustard cake. They use the manure in nursery or different times in the main cropland (before sowing, during sowing, after sowing). Various weeds from courtyard, kitchen garden, jungle and water bodies are collected and dried and applied with this manure. During preparation of the manure, they sprinkle water and cattle urine on the system. They generally produce this manure in their kitchen garden. They soil is very fertile there and often lattice is build up there where they plant creeping vegetables that again provide shade to this manure production unit. For each crop, stone free and germ free manure, pouring amount of the water, bone dust, boiled tea leaves, egg shells, cow dung or rotten leaves have been added. Two to three months before planting coconut sapling, in the dig cow dung has to be added and stirred from time to time to make it fine and fully prepared.

Thin ropes are produced from rolling the jute fibers constantly in the palms of two hands; by repeating the same process again and again from thin threads are produced thick and big ropes are manufactured. So, ropes thus produced are of various types and categories- thin to thick. Ropes they also used on domestic cattle, collecting water from the well through bucket, manufacturing of bullock cart and in bullock-plough cultivation.

Rajbanshis used to fence the kitchen garden not only with bamboo sticks or dried leaves, jute and slender branches as done today, but also with certain bushy shrubs with wooden stem, spine and bitter taste leaves. They in this way prevent the cattle to enter their kitchen garden of vegetable cultivation.

Exchange of goods is a kind of barter or reciprocity that involves the concept of property. Trade items and types of property could differ and that could include kind, gold, land, food items, animal husbandry, and cash). Rajbanshis consider cow as a valuable capital; they collect milk from this and cow dung is used in various ways, but they never east its meat. However, they are fond of other cattle like goat and sheep. They at a time sacrifice buffalo and pigeon to their cult. They also like duck more than goose and hen. They generally avoid piggery but can eat pig meat. They can consume egg and fish also for animal protein requirement.

Cattle horns were used as the simplest form of musical instrument where air from mouth had to be blown into it through the small pore made at the head of the polished and hollowed horn. Cattle horns were also used in preparation of comb. From bamboo, such type of musical instruments are now produced where again air from mouth has to be blown inside the polished hollow pipe and by regulating the coming out of air from various pores on the flint, music is created. Rajbanshis manufacture various types of musical instruments. One such example is the gourd shell with a string fixed with bamboo stick. The string is often prepared from dried, processed and tanned digestive organ from the abdomen of a cattle or goat or a ship. Tannin is usually extracted from the fruits like.

Haritaki, Amla, and tamarind are used in tanning the animal skin. Tanned animal skins are used in various kinds of wooden and bamboo drums like *khol, madal, dhol* and *dhak* of various types. Rajbanshis and other people connected with the agrarian production system supply these raw materials like bamboo and dead cattle to the shoe-makers who tan these skins and make so many items out of these. Cords were produced from animal organs or Muga silk moth cocoon. Such cord was used in musical instruments. Animal skins, bamboo and hard shell of cucurbit fruits are again used in manufacturing of drums. Some traditional musical instruments were *mokha-bansi, sarinja, ghuntung, ektara, dotara, dhol, dhak, dugdugi, singa,* metal instruments like bells and clappers.

Rajbanshis domesticate dog and cat. Dogs control attack of the rat in their granary. They also feed the mongoose that escapes them from snake attack. Snakes often shelter in cowshed and granary during monsoon season. Dogs act as guard to their house. Cats like fish and milk. Dogs are not generally fed with fish. They also serve water and food to the birds that are part of their village ecosystem and help in controlling pests in crop field. They however use net to protect their fruits from bats and other birds. They often domesticate parrot and other jungle birds. Parrots are fond of chili. They often catch various types of owl and sell them illegally to outside market. At a time, various fauna like monkey, python, porcupine, and turtle are found in their neighbourhood. They also get protein from mushroom, frog leg, and jungle fowl. Rich people often had horses and elephants. *Tangan* was a local horse breed. They had to protect their cattle from tiger, leopard, wild dog, fox and jackal. There were wild cats, civet and wild animals staying much close to the village. In search of food they came inside the village at darkness of night. Rajbanshis and other people buy cattle from local weekly markets. They choose cattle on the basis of teeth, mammary gland, body shape, belly and leg. They generally buy cow for milk and bullock for cultivation purpose and transportation. Bullocks are also used for thrashing of harvested crops. They carry piles of harvested crops from field, keep them in thrashing floor, and thrash the bundles by their hands. They set their bullock free on the thrashing floor and control its quick movement over the pile so that grains could be set free from the bundles and collected. A pair of bullock is needed for leveling and ploughing the cultivable ground, carrying the cart, and also extracting oil from rapeseeds in indigenous ways. These traditional practices have nearly completely gone away. Oxen are not domesticated and live free in nature. Hybrid cattle and cow with orange skin are the coastliest. Milk of the orange skin cattle is believed to be the best for health having various immunity powers. Banana tree is a secret for improving cattle health. Rajbanshis believe that local banana varieties containing seeds have medicinal powder to cure worm and stomach problem of both human and cattle. Local flora *bichilara* is believed to be efficient of curing skin disease of all the livestock. A Rajbanshi family may possess one cow (*goru* or *gavi*), two bullocks (*bolod*), one to two goats and a duckery (*hans*). *Mithun* is an indigenous variety of domesticated cattle found in hill and foothill region that are reared by local tribal groups and ethnic communities there. They are different from the plain cow usually domesticated by Rajbanshi and other caste people as well as from yak by high altitude Tibetans. Male goats are generally treated as *khasi* and sterile one as *patha;* whereas females as *chhagol*. But, in this fast life they are loosing their epicenes in animal husbandry and other livestock. Rather poultry of hen (*nurgi* for female and *morog* for male) is a profitable sector. Microfinance and Self-Help Groups could be the best option for boosting rural domestication. Goat and sheep are ready for breeding within two to three years. Sheep are mostly *garol* in type, but also other verities are domesticated. Sheep domestication is mostly confined in Jalpaiguri district. Rajbanshis do not domesticate pig or boar unlike many other communities in North Bengal.

They consider piggery unclean and also aware of high death rate of the babies. However, Rajbanshis also know about domestication of rabbit but there also high mortality rate affects the livestock. Swans are seldom domesticated along with ducks. Viral death of birds is a crisis and fatal to their poultry. They are preferred as source of red meat. Cow milk is favoured the most, but milk of goat and buffalo are more nutritious and costly. Rajbanshis rear their cattle for their own need and therefore this is nearly totally subsistent. Rajbanshis also serve salt to their cattle which is very necessary.

They also use cattle in ploughing, carrying goods, and thrashing. Raising livestock is target of micro-finance.

Livestock is not the primary economy in folk life of traditional Rajbanshi society. But it is actually an important part of their agrarian social system and folk culture. However, previously, Rajbanshis staying in the sub-Himalayan region used to produce paddy and jute in summer-monsoon-spring season time of the year and fallow their land during after-spring, winter and autumn. At that time, they fallowed their land and let their cattle graze the grassland. They also cultivate different vegetables in their kitchen garden, fences and bamboo lattice. They made plough by woods collected from nearby jungles from where they also got minor forest produces and also went for annual hunting of small games. So, cattle's rearing was an integral part of their bush-fallow type of cultivation. They are fond of milk items more than direct consumption of milk. They treat cow as *gai-goru* and being Vaishnavid do not eat the meat. But, they could eat duck, lamb, goat and pigeon that they sacrifice. In certain occasions, they sacrificed buffalo and even human blood. In some pockets, boar is consumed and for consumption purpose, they rear it. Those who worship, *Mashan* could consume pork but selectively. There are poultry farms of hen but outside the habitation area. They usually avoid eating chicken and jungle fowl. Fish-and-paddy and fish-paddy-duck are important part of their production system. Domestic cow or *gai-goru* is the most important livestock for a Rajbanshi traditional production system. In direct foothill region, the production system was mostly jungle oriented and livestock was very important part and parcel for folk life there. Mithun or *goru* was reared there by tribal groups like Toto and Dhimal. In Totopara village where the Toto Primitive Tribal Group is still living in within Madarihat block of Jalpaiguri district (Bhutan foothill pocket of Lucky Doors), Totos consume boar and mithun. So, they eat that goru (*Bos frontalis*) though it is not actually the domestic cow (*Bovid indica*).

Conclusion

Domestication of cow, goat and buffalo, domestication for milk, by-products of milk (curd, sweet card, red card, rice-card), cow dung as fuel, manure and construction material, grazing, all kind of fodder, disease cure for the animals, techniques for milk production increase, types of cow shed, special cure of calf (if any), meat, skin, bone and horn, social significance like reciprocity, acceptance of interbreeds, use in purpose of transportation and agriculture (with allied activities), domestication of dog and cat, domestication of pig (rare), domestication of mongoose, domestication of birds, poultry of hen, duck and goose, duck-cum-fish cultivation, feed for poultry, manufacture of hatchery and poultry farm, protection from disease and other animals, disease cure process, food and manure from farm, winter treatment and several other points are there exclusive for traditional Rajbanshi social life.

From this discussion on impact of livestock upon Rajbanshi way of living, I mean to say there is a scope of sustainable livelihood development through focusing on their interest. Various milk cooperatives could be there in small, medium or large scale. And I think that this is a common feature of entire sub-Himalayan belt with a transnational existence.

REFERENCES

Banarjee, S. Basu, D. Biswas, D. and Goswami, R. 2006. *Indigenous Knowledge Dissemination Through Farmers' Network: Exploring Farmer-to-Farmer Communication* in Choudhuri, B. and Choudhuri, S. (ed.) 2007. Iuaes Intercongress on Mega Urbanization Multi-ethnic Society Human Rights and Development (Vol. 4) *Indigenous People: Traditional Wisdom and Sustainable Development,* New Delhi: Inter-India Publications.

Sengupta,S. 2003. *Perseption of Folk Environment,* Kolkata: Classique Books.

Warren 1991.Definition of Indigenous Knowledge. www.worldbank.org/afr/ik/basic.htm_68k

Nurturing Youth Entrepreneurship to Tackle Youth Unemployment *A Case Study of Kerala*

Francis Kuriakose and Deepa Kylasam Iyer

ABSTRACT

Reducing Youth Unemployment is going to be one of the most important goals of nations in the coming decade. ILO estimates that out of the 1 billion youth, 180 million are unemployed. The UN has adopted reducing unemployment as Goal number 8 in the Millennium Development Programme.Though the benefits of entrepreneurship in creating wealth and job opportunities are well known, the study on youth entrepreneurship is relatively recent. Youth are bracketed under the adult population, but Youth unemployment is generally 2-3 times higher than the general unemployment rate. The purpose of the study is to examine the case of youth employment and its impact on a country's economy and evolve youth entrepreneurship as a viable solution to tackle the problem. In order to accomplish the objective of the study, review of relevant international and national literature has been involved to draw major conclusions and form a concrete proposal. Youth face specific constraints in business start ups due to their limited experience. The study takes a closer look at the financial, procedural and cultural factors that affect youth entrepreneurship. The entrepreneurial framework of a country also offers incentive to young entrepreneurs. By proposing a viable model for the unique case of Kerala, the study brings out that youth entrepreneurship as a viable option to reduce youth unemployment.

Keywords: Youth unemployment, Entrepreneurship, Vocational training, Business start-up.

Introduction

Unemployment has been an inconvenient truth from time immemorial. Ever since mankind began to make wealth, there were men standing in the streets idly as no one found them fit enough to be hired for work. Sometimes, supply of workers exceeded the demand, sometimes the workers were unwilling or incapable to take up the jobs offered. If we are to believe the numbers, at any given time, a reservoir of 2.5-3 per cent people remains unemployed. Thomas Carlyle once observed "Bubble periods with their panics and commercial crisis will again become infrequent and steady modest industry will take the place of gambling speculation." This prophecy has not come true. Riding on good fortune the public has come out with new aspirations, new needs and new preferences. Unfortunately, demand for a commodity has not translated into demand for labour. The prosperous years after war usually made people complacent and it was followed by severe depression. But statistics has never made it so urgent and ominous as it is today. 1 in 5 persons in the world is between the age group 15-25 years; that amounts to 1 billion people[1]. 85 per cent of them are in developing countries. According to the ILO, 74 million of the youth are unemployed, 310 million underemployed. In the coming decade, 500 million youth will be added to the global work force. The global financial crisis of 2009 eroded the real wages of 1.5 billion people[2]. Fixity of habits and reluctance to leave employment and enter the vagaries of labour market has led to seasonal unemployment. Fight against youth unemployment is a Millennium Development Goal of the UN covered under goal 8, target number 16. It is interesting to note that the unemployment rate of the youth is usually 2-3 times that of the adult population. Most of the young people are employed in the informal sector and take home 44 per cent less pay than their counterparts in the organised sector.

Unemployment goes with loss of production output, misallocation of resources and loss of labour market skills. Unemployment and poverty come from the same womb. The restlessness of the youth in such trying times may lead them to take up crime and anti-social activities. The story has been no different with India. As an economy in transition to free market ethos, unemployment rose in India from 6 per cent to 7.3 per cent in the nineties[3]. In a country where the poor[4] constituted a staggering 400 million, the recent financial crisis had its implications on the domestic economy even though it was sufficiently robust. When GDP[5] fell by 7.8 per cent from 8.6 per cent for the period 2008-2009, rate of unemployment shot up to 8.3 per cent[6].

Table 14.1: Unemployment Rate among Youth in India (15-29 Years)

(%CDS Basis)

Year	Male (Rural)	Female (Rural)	Male (Urban)	Female (Urban)
1993-1994	9.0	7.6	13.7	21.2
1999-2000	11.1	10.6	14.7	19.1
2004-2005	12.0	12.7	13.7	21.5

Source: National Sample Survey report number 515(61/10/1), Government of India.

Table 14.1 shows that unemployment among urban and rural youth is significantly higher than that of the general unemployment level. Current Daily Status (CDS)[7] is a measure used to analyse trends in workforce in India.

The youth of the country lack their desired skills to compete in the industrial domain. Traditional skills that are passed down generations are not recognised in the country. To add to their woes, outdated curriculum in Vocational training, lack of marketing strategies, remoteness of their villages, poor infrastructure deprive them of opportunities. A country like India that dreams to move towards a path of inclusive growth has to increase quality employment to absorb new entrants and facilitate absorption of surplus labour.

Role of the Government

The government being the caretaker of the needs of its people desires to address the distress call of the labourers through intervention and pro-labour schemes. In today's globalised world of 'survive or pack up', universal and permanently increasing wants of people have to be met. Government is a critical stakeholder in bringing in overall prosperity of its citizens and has monopoly in certain areas. Employment generation schemes taken up by the Indian Government like Mahatma Gandhi National Rural Employment Guarantee Scheme (MGNREGS) and Training Rural Youth for Self Employment (TRYSEM) are world's largest employment generation programmes that generate 5 million jobs annually. Social security measures like old age pensions, life or disability cover and health insurance are in place. In addition to Micro Financing Institutions (MFIs) and Self Help Groups (SHGs), a 5000 crore rupees (USD 1097.454 million) corpus fund is disseminated for those who could not access credit. In addition to this, the government offers to pay Rs5000 (USD 109.74) per person to any employer willing to provide one year training on job skill enhancement. There are 17 Ministries and various governmental departments providing vocational training to 3.1 million people per year. India's favourable demographic dividend of declining birth rate, increasing life expectancy and demographic bulge in the 15-29 age group makes it a young country and offers unprecedented opportunities for skill development.

Table 14.2: Average Annual Increment in Youth Population of India (in 1000s)

Year	Total	Male	Female
2001-2006	4028.8	2022.6	2006.2
2006-2011	2680.8	1330.0	1350.4
2011-2016	1312.6	621.2	691.8
2016-2021	226.4	76.0	150.4

Source: UN Population Database.

As the Table 14.2 clearly shows, India will reap the benefits of its favourable demographic dividend and increasing Youth population at least for the first two decades of the 21st Century.

But with a burgeoning population of 1.2 billion, only 2 per cent of the youth undergo formal vocational training compared to the corresponding figures of 60-90 per cent in developed countries. To foster competencies and encourage growth climate, creation of opportunities for self employment, augmentation of productivity and income of the poor and creation of durable assets is the way. In an era when public sector employment has taken a southward dip in the country, the role of government is limited. To attain these lofty goals, alternative employment generation has to be looked into in addition to the traditional ways. It is in this context that non-governmental players assume importance. They need to forge an aggressive and formidable alliance to create employment opportunities for young men and women.

Alternative Perspectives

With an ever expanding population and the downturns of economic cycles, it is natural that people are laid off from their work. Seasonal and cyclical unemployment is a truism that we have to live with. But long term unemployment can wipe off prosperity all together. A country cannot gallop its way to abundance when vast multitude of people cannot make both ends meet. The problem is made more acute if a large chunk of the young population is at the receiving end of such misfortune. Youth is an asset to a country if used intelligently; otherwise it becomes a liability. In developing countries and transitional economies like that of India, the demographic dividend[8] is advantageous. With consistent and moderately high growth rate of 9 per cent per annum over the past few years, India will be affluent and young in the years to come. About 20 per cent of the population of the country is in the 15-24 age group and that translates to 500 million in absolute numbers. By 2020, the average Indian will be 29 compared to the average American at 37 and the average European at 45. The potential of the favourable demographic dividend can be transformed into real time growth only if the economy is able to absorb the work force and ensure that the quality of the workforce is of the desired level.

There has been acceleration in unemployment rate among the youth in the country. This shows that the excess labour potential has not been exploited. A substantial population in the 15-24 age group declared their principal activity as education. This suggests that educated young men and women may be available for work but find none and hence revert back to education. This is a huge challenge that a country like India faces today- meeting the aspirations of millions of educated young Indians looking for a job. According to the 11th plan approach paper released by the Government of India, the service sector will offer 40 million jobs by 2020 and retail sector will absorb 115000 more people[9]. But even this optimistic projection fall short of our expectations. Demand - supply mismatch in providing jobs and the limitation of the government compel our attention toward alternative sustainable models of job creation.

Developing Youth Entrepreneurship

'I believe in the free market, competition and entrepreneurship.'

–Barack Obama, The Audacity of Hope

The onus today is not on merely earning wages but creating wealth. Only through the creation of wealth can you distribute it. Entrepreneurship is the process of identifying opportunities, gathering resources and exploiting these opportunities through action.[10] Entrepreneurship begins with the germ of an idea, takes form with the start up of business and flourishes with the expansion of the business venture. But it is easier said than done. We face endless difficulties to start a business- in the policies of the government, in the cultural climate of the country and also in accessing finance. About India, it is notoriously remarked that it takes eighty-nine days to open a business venture, 425 days to enforce a business contract and ten years to close down a business![11] India stands at the 122nd position in the ranking of countries based on their business environment[12] . Excessive complicated and stringent laws are the first stumbling block to venturing out for a novel enterprise in my country even today. In Kerala[13], in order to start a small venture, it takes 13 procedures, 41 days and the cost of completing the procedure was Rs. 20000 (USD 500) to simply get registered! Apart from obtaining the Permanent Account Number and Tax Account Number from an authorised franchise, Director Identification Number and a number of such cumbersome procedural formats delays the venture. Red tapism and the hierarchal structure of the bureaucracy impede the path of new dreams and new ideas. Often, we have to grease the palms of the officers along the way for speedy movement of our file through the ladder of hierarchy.

An unsupportive tax regime and bankruptcy laws add to the woes. Indian entrepreneurs have to pay approximately 60 different types of tax and the recovery rate on filing bankruptcy is poor. Non Resident cannot invest in India in a number of sectors and the 5 year business visa which helped the entrepreneurs as they had to frequently travel is no longer given. In fact, visas exceeding one year are not given for small and medium enterprises. Thus for starting a business, one has to deal with the construction permits, inspections, employing workers, registering property, file tax returns and enforce contracts with a mind boggling procedural format that was almost a disincentive for a young man or woman. Poor patent regulation and laws also deter young people from venturing out on their own. An academic approach to education effectively kills the spirit of entrepreneurship in the young minds. Even in vocational education, there is no focus on risk assessment, decision making, networking or innovation which is useful in the practical field. As a result, young men and women are educated but not employable. They are university friendly but not market friendly. Lack of access to finance acts as another choking point in business start ups and adequate flow of cash to sustain it long enough for it to succeed is hard to come by. The cultural factor that eulogises wage earning but condemns wealth creation discourages risk taking attitude in youngsters. Striving to meet the societal demands of success and status, enterprising youngsters qualifying out of the universities often bow down to pressure than venture out on their own.

The Indian labour market is another spectre that looms before a prospective entrepreneur. The job security legislations in the Indian labour market are tenuous. In India, there is a curious case of federalism giving a twist to regulations and amendments. The regulations are passed by the Central Government but the individual states can amend it. Therefore, the business climate of different states varies. There is a chasm that separates legislation from actual enforcements in a developing country. In Kerala, for instance, there are twice as many inspections a year for small and medium enterprises as compared to an investor friendly state called Gujarat[14]. In Indian states public expenditure can turn into private capital formation. In my state, frequent strikes and lock outs deter prospective investors. Thus poor labour relations and labour management trust deficit do not augur well for a new business enterprise.

Entrepreneurship Development Programmes (EDPs)

It is understood that the young entrepreneur who ventures out with a new business idea faces considerable difficulties in starting a business and sustaining it long enough to taste success. Dual training that involves vocational training and apprenticeship is the bed rock on which entrepreneurship building programmes are built. The onus is on enterprise, apprenticeship and vocational training. Programmes focussed on nurturing young entrepreneurs have to keep in mind that their training must be demand driven and suitable to the needs of the market. Emphasis should be on core skills and competencies like risk assessment, decision making and networking that are useful in the practical fields. Teacher in-service training can be helpful in this aspect. The curricula should be framed in such a way so as to be appealing to learn and relevant to employment. In a market ruled by permanent innovation and lifelong learning, mere cramming up of theory will not do. The ability to work in functional context is more important than the knowledge of useless isolated facts. Stress should be on comprehensive understanding of how the market works. The concept of Reflective Learning[15] will go a long way to address the problem. The Model of ATB[16] in Netherlands that makes good use of Information Technology, The European Model that provides insertion contracts that help the prospective entrepreneurs to get a strong foot hold in the market and enterprise based training that uses productive assets simultaneously in training and production are excellent examples of training with functional utility. 'The Start and Improve Your Business' promoted by the ILO believes in the dictum that small business provides better employment in developing countries. In any entrepreneurship development programme, the thrust should be on demand of the markets, reflective learning, the mode of teaching and the curricula and the financing. We need industry consensus, well defined courses, employment opportunities and strong trade unions to protect the labour before we begin a programme to train the youth on entrepreneurship.

Kerala Model EDP – A Proposal

We have seen how unemployment affects youth and prospects of youth entrepreneurship as a solution to the problem. Despite all the travails that a young man or woman has to face, there is a suitable sustainable model that can be applied with a great degree of success in a particular area. I have chosen my home state Kerala as my laboratory for my experiments. Kerala is a small state in the southern tip of India. The indices of the social sector here are comparable to those of the Scandinavian countries. Kerala excels in healthcare and education and its per capita consumption is one of the highest in the country. It is also a hundred per cent literate state. The unique problem that plagues Kerala is that of educated youth unemployment. Of the 40 lakh (4 million) people unemployed, over 20 lakhs are graduates and are technically qualified. Lack of a business culture and diversion to risk taking has been the major deterrents preventing the youth from making it as entrepreneurs. We need to cultivate a business culture, training ground for prospective candidates and a support system for business start ups. We have chosen two most important potential areas where immense opportunity beckons for Keralites. With its lush greenery and backwaters, Kerala is described as 'God's Own Country'. There is an unrealised potential in the Tourism Sector that encompasses Ayurveda[17], Health and Eco-tourism[18]. Another exciting field for the computer literate graduates of Kerala is the Information Technology Enabled Services (ITES) that focuses on software development, molecular biology data and computer aided drug designing.

The working class group can be broadly divided into unskilled, semi skilled and skilled group that has a potential for training. Therefore the types of intervention will be structural for the unskilled, interventional for the semi skilled and log end training for the skilled but unemployed. Unskilled refers to an education level below that of high school with no vocational training, semi skilled refers to those with the necessary qualification and a short and sketchy on the job training but no formal vocational training. A skilled person has the necessary educational qualification and a new idea but is unable to convert it into productive business value. Structural training refers to a comprehensive programme for skill development, interventional training is aimed at apprenticeship programme and log end help refers to help in accessing finance, start up a business with less hassles. The aim of this project is to reduce the inactivity in the working age group and promote entrepreneurship in youth as an answer to unemployment.

The major participants involved are the Non Governmental Institutions that can help to reach out and provide post placement support, private players who can impart skills, governmental agencies that can subsidise training and provide social protection and financial institutions for credit assistance. The programme comprises training, financial assistance and policy advocacy to create a sustainable model for entrepreneurship. For this, the cost of the training has to be borne by the Government, the industry with the help of NASSCOM[19] and partly by the individual. Tie up with market players are essential to ensure a foothold in the market. Post placement support services are also necessary to survive and expand after establishment of the venture. Labour protection is another component necessary for a sustainable model of job growth. The five components of the Entrepreneurship Development Programme (EDP) are described below:

1. Training

The training has to be a targeted initiative for the semi skilled and unskilled group. Capacity building through local regeneration has to be the key factor. For the semi skilled group, English language skills and computer training has to be a part of the curriculum. Excellent communication skills is mandatory to succeed in both the sectors chosen. The agencies involved in imparting targeted initiative can be Job Assistance Centres and personal advisers trained in Employability, Client Progress Model and Re-Integration and Assessment Model[20]. For the unskilled group, a basic programme that includes the alternative therapies of Ayurveda or eco- tourism specific to their locality will be suitable.

2. Intermediary Assistance

Intermediary assistance broadly comprises certain pilot projects of six months to one year that can provide temporary jobs and intermediate relief to the youth after the training and before embarking on a successful venture. If these projects are found sustainable, these projects can be expanded to cover a longer period.

3. Employment Support Programmes

Tie up with market players are very important to provide employment support facilities. Universities can collaborate with industries to evolve apprenticeship projects and on the job training. An analysis of the local labour market will be useful in modifying the programme according to market needs.

4. Partnership with Stakeholders

It is a good idea to include the local community as a stakeholder in such ventures. Local, voluntary and community organisations can organise seminars and disseminate information and awareness of such projects.

To ensure gender parity, a suitable percentage of the vacancies in the training programme should be reserved for women. In a state where girls exceed boys in number with a favourable sex ratio, it is imperative that women are encouraged to be in the forefront.

5. Financing

As mentioned earlier, the training cost will be shared by the Government, Industry and the individual. seed capital for business start ups can be provided through Micro Financing Institutions (MFIs). For other innovative ideas with a higher potential for growth, Venture Capitalists may be approached. Kerala has a formidable record with phenomenal success in Self Help Group involving women. In eco-tourism and rural tourism projects, group undertakings are likely to be more successful. The successful record of Kudumbashree[21] stands testimony to such observation.

Apart from financing and training, studying from the best models throughout the world is of utmost importance. It is by learning from others that we rectify our mistakes and improve for the better.

Conclusion

Unemployment will persist as long as the giant wheels of the economy move our world towards prosperity and wealth creation. Poverty is there not because we do not have sufficient means, but we do not distribute the fruits of the labour sufficiently. Unemployment is nothing but an offshoot of such unequal distribution of wealth and hence that of poverty. There is no magic cure to such material problems. Even the mammoth hands of government cannot wipe off the tears of every eye. Therefore alternative methods of wealth creation and employment have to be a part of the solution in addition to the government interventions and market mechanisms.

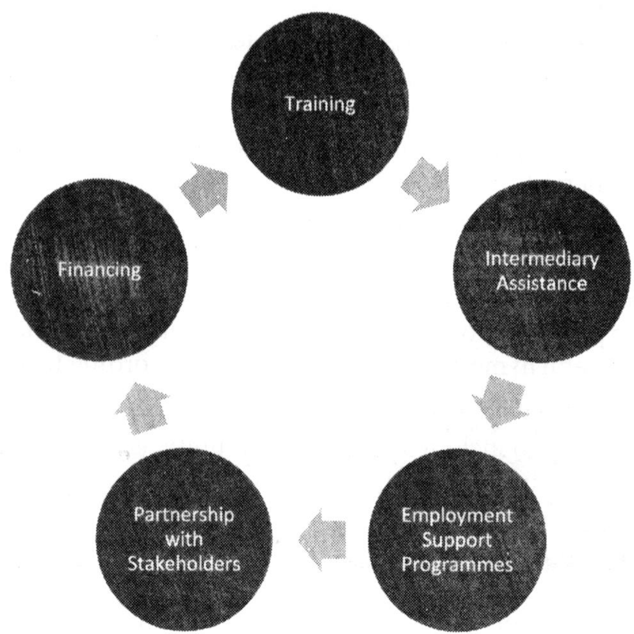

Fig. 14.1: Pictorial Representation of Entrepreneurship Development Programme (EDP)

Youth entrepreneurship holds a promising avenue for growth and development especially in the developing countries with a favourable demographic dividend like India. Innovative ideas need to be nurtured, risk taking to be encouraged and a favourable environment for sustainable development has to be ushered in. The new capital is the human capital and investment is on 'Ideas'. As they say, ideas will indeed rule the world.

NOTES

1. 'Facilitating Labour Market Entry for Youth through Enterprise based schemes in Vocational Education, Training and Skill Development, Seed Working Paper No. 48, ILO, Michael Axmann, 2004.
2. Global Wage Report 2008/09, ILO.
3. 'The Impact of Economic Liberalisation on Employment and Wages in India', Paper Submitted to International Policy Group, ILO, Sonia Bhalotra, 2002.
4. Poverty Line Estimated by the 10th Five Year Plan, Government of India, Measures the Degree of Deprivation based on 13 parameters.
5. Gross Domestic Product (GDP) – Sum Total of all Final Goods and Services Produced in a Country in a given Year.
6. 'The Impact of Economic Liberalisation on Employment and Wages in India', Paper Submitted to International Policy Group, ILO, Sonia Bhalotra, 2002.

7 Current Daily Status (CDS) is a Tool used to measure Employment Trend by National Sample Survey Organisation (NSSO), India. A Person is Considered Working for an Entire Day if he has Worked for Four Hours or more on any Day of Reference Preceding the Date of Survey.

8 Demographic Dividend Refers to the Rise in the Rate of Economic Growth due to Rising Share of Working Age Population.

9 Study Conducted by Retailers Association of India.

10 Definition by Sexton and Bowman- Upton, 1991.

11 Murthy, N.R Narayana (2009). A Better India, A Better World, , Penguin Allen Lane, New Delhi, pp. 40.

12 Ease of Doing Business Index/Economy Rankings, World Bank 2009.

13 Kerala is a State in the Southern most Part of India Widely Acclaimed for its Phenomenal Social Indicators Comparable with the U.S and Scandinavian Countries.

14 Gujarat is a State on the Western Coast of India. It is Famed for its Industry Friendliness.

15 Reflective Learning Refers to Greater or Deeper Degree of Processing of Material to be Learned.

16 Amsterdam Trade Bank N.V. (ATB) is a Fully-owned Subsidiary of Alfa Bank, one of the Largest Russian Private Financial-industrial Conglomerates.

17 Ayurveda is the Traditional Indian System of Medicine.

18 Ecotourism Refers to Travelling to Fragile, Pristine and Protected Ecological Areas to Increase Awareness about Conservation.

19 The National Association of Software and Services Companies (NASSCOM), the Indian Chamber of Commerce is a Consortium that Serves as an Interface to the Indian Software Industry and the BPO Industry Maintaining a State of the Art Information Database of IT Software and Services Related Activities, for use of Both the Software Developers as well as Interested Companies Overseas.

20 Reintegration and Assessment Model was introduced by the Task Force on Employability and Long Term Unemployment Implementation Group, North Ireland , to Study the Extent of Reintegration of Socially Isolated Groups into Mainstream Society.

21 Kudumbashree is a Mission Formed in the Indian State of Kerala to Eradicate Absolute Poverty within a Decade.

15

Ethics and Values in Business and Management

Dr. (Mrs.) Asha Sharma

ABSTRACT

Values are the rules by which decisions is made about right and wrong, should and shouldn't, good and bad. They also tell us which are more or less important, which is useful when we have to trade off meeting one value over another. Here is clearly a balancing act to develop policies that define the ethics of the corporation, while understanding that codes of conduct vary greatly around the world assignments. It is essential for business to follow practices, code of conduct and social responsibility.

Keywords: Ethics, Work Culture, human values, management, corporate social responsibility

Introduction

Ethics tend to be codified into a formal system or set of rules which are explicitly adopted by a group of people. Thus you have medical ethics. Ethics are thus internally defined and adopted, whilst morals tend to be externally imposed on other people. Ethics refers to standards of conduct, standards that indicate how one should behave based on moral duties and virtues, which themselves are derived from principles of right and wrong. In order to apply this definition to practical decision making it is necessary to specify the nature of the moral obligations considered intrinsic to ethical behaviour.

Ethics is concerned with how a moral person should behave, whereas values simply concern the various beliefs and attitudes that determine how a person actually behaves. Some values concern ethics when they pertain to beliefs as to what is right and wrong. Most values do not.

Ethical commitment refers to a strong desire to do the right thing, especially when behaving ethically imposes financial, social or emotional costs.

Values are described as a professional's obligation to comply with rules of one's conduct, ethics, etiquette, and professional values and attitudes. Ethics is the study of the concepts involved in practical reasoning: good, right, duty, obligation, virtue, freedom, rationality, choice.

The different values are as: ambition, competency, individuality, equality, integrity, service, responsibility, accuracy, respect, dedication, diversity, improvement, enjoyment/fun, loyalty, credibility, honesty, innovativeness, teamwork, excellence, accountability, empowerment, quality, efficiency, dignity, collaboration, stewardship, empathy, accomplishment, courage, wisdom, independence, security, challenge, influence, learning, compassion, friendliness, discipline/order, generosity, persistency, optimism, dependability, flexibility.

Human values are necessary in today's management. Business is no longer confined to a national state but is really borderless. Hence business from the international viewpoint cannot be regulated by Governments unless international agreements can be reached. In this "lawless land" the responsibility of the executive is greater than ever. On a national level we find similar concerns with ethics and values in management. It is believed that the manager of today has a wider responsibility than that. We believe that it is in the interest of the managers themselves to have a heightened awareness of the values of humankind and also to promote them.

Role of Values and Ethics to Society

For an Individual

At the base of this character are personal values and ethics. These are different in every individual even in as small a unit as a family. Initially, these personal values may be adopted from family or cultural mores. They develop based on personal strengths and preferences and may be driven by self interest.

For Society

As a person grows and develops into an individual, social values and ethics come into play. This occurs as the person begins to leave the confines of an immediate family group and is influenced by the society in which a person is surrounded by. Although the values development is internal and personal, external societal forces contribute to the change as an individual begins to care more about what others think about them.

For Nation and its Economy

Modern organizations promote shared values and ethics of their members by creating mission statements, corporate slogans, written rules of conduct, policies, and procedures for encouraging productivity leading to economic gain. Organizational values serve many purposes. They set the tone in the environment by bonding people together, facilitating work behaviour, and producing achievements of shared goals

For Career Success

Professional values and ethics are valuable assets that can take a person a long way in developing success. Skills that aid in a career, whether learned on the job or not, can be what keeps a person separated from anyone else. The way a person conducts the workload or rapport built with clients, results in greater marketing for the company. This is a two sided win because a person not only represents the company, but also has now turned from an employee into an asset, a benefit factor for the employee and the business. Ethics alone, in business, has to come from a place of selflessness and integrity.

For Professionals

Professional values do not determine who a person is, but will add to one's worthiness as a person. Ethics can be an asset in the success of a person's careers because a person is choosing what is in the best interest of the company or business. A person with strong values and ethics will always have a path of accomplishment, because one can see the big picture. A person has achieved career success by allowing the mind to venture outside of its betterment and to the betterment of others that affect a team or group as a whole.

Human Values in Work Culture and Business

Many business practices are neither black nor white but exist in a gray zone, a moral free space through which businesses and their managers must find away to deal with. It seemed to have helped managers by treating company values as absolute and insisting that their suppliers and customers do the same. How this was addressed by these companies, was the development of detailed codes of conduct that provides clear direction on ethical behavior, but leaves room for managers of these companies to use moral imagination that allows them to resolve ethical problems appropriately.

Firmslike Levi Strauss and Motorola, not only define their policies, they understand that their managers must be able to adapt to a great deal of moral uncertainty in international.

Donaldson argues that companies must be guided by three principles in the shaping of ethical behavior: respect for core human value, respect for local traditions, and the belief that context matters when deciding what is right and wrong. These principles help in establishing a moral guide for business practice.

James Rachel's The Challenge of Cultural Relativism, argues that different cultures have different moral codes. He is obviously taking the opposite approach to Donaldson's absolute approach, that of a relativist approach.

The relativist concludes that there is no objective "truth" in morality, therefore right and wrong are merely matters of opinion that can vary from culture to culture. The problem with this argument is that the stated conclusion does not necessarily need to be the case if the premise is given. The premise states what different people believe to be true, and the conclusion assumes that this belief must be the case.

One consequence of practicing relativism, is that culture determines what is functionally right and wrong. Meaning that an individual has no say in the matter, and if there is a conflict between the two, the individual's ethical belief is not given any consideration. Just because a culture deems an action right, it does not mean that the action is correct for that culture. The second consequence is that it is impossible to judge the actions of any culture as to their morality. Because a relativist believes that what is right is what is functional for a specific culture, there is no room for comparing one culture's actions to another. For example, a culture that practices infanticide, and another culture believed that babies are to be protected from all harms. In the relativist view neither culture is more correct in its views; both societies are performing the functionally right action for their culture. Based on this observation, it seems that infanticide is wrong, and therefore, the culture that practices it, is also morally wrong.

Just as one culture cannot criticize another, there cannot be criticism from within it. Rachel's argues that a relativist would not allow for an individual in the aggressive culture to speak out against their inhumane actions. Because, as mentioned previously, the relativist, states that one culture's actions cannot be judged to their morality.

Human Values in Business

Values and ethics are very much related in the work place for human beings because it creates capacity and it helps in improvement of leadership skills and abilities. It also helps in improvement of the performance and brings the decision making theory and the decision making goals in the organization. Values and ethics helps in developing the human behavior, the origin and scope of the human values which adds values and ideas in the human behavior and also in the human application of power. It illustrates the framework of the systematic approach of managers and leaders who can perform well keeping in mind with all the positive effects.

Values and ethics in human resource management are very much related to each other because the company's main motive, the company's goals are all remain same with each other. It remains constant when it gets continued by the management hierarchy because it provides the continuation of management and it goes on and moves on as per the level of management.

Values and ethics are very much related to each other and it is very much related concepts which let us know about its importance, about its techniques, about its uses and benefits that matters a lot for the people who are working in the organization, that matters a lot who are associated with the organization and that is what matters most is for the benefits and uses of organization and also the capabilities of the management and its people. Values is most important in the organization because it talks about the stability of the organization, it does not say about the complexity, misconceptions, misunderstandings and misbehavior but here value talks about the morals, the culture, the importance, the growth and development of the people who are working in the organization and so on.

Values related with behavior which describes about the behaviour of an individual which talks about the values, about the behavior of an individual who respect each other, it is related with the concept of respect and individualism which says about the people who respect each of an individual in the organization and they maintain dignity and respect which express the best and wonderful culture in an organization, which talks about the organization goods and about the goodwill and reputation of the organization so values and ethics matters a lot. In terms of culture, when there is full respect for an individual, they get high source of effort for business, and then clients feel good about the strategy.

Values talks about the core values of an organization when someone shows professionalism attitude and when company grows with high integrity. It is related with the vision of the company and also honesty and values matters lot. For example: when we look at Wipro, Mr. Premji have done a great job to maintain the integrity of this high known reputed and esteemed organization where culture values comes first and really matters. Values also can be related to the importance when someone gives importance to other's true feelings and other's true honesty as well as innocence.

In case of work place when if employees are feeling problem in their work, from the work place they decides to go to the senior management or authority like HR people to discuss their issues and concerns and if that person will not be given an opportunity and freedom to speak, if that employee will not get the right to tell their views and ideas, opinions they will not feel bad but if the same person if gets the full freedom, full opportunity then surely they will feel valued, surely they will feel good and motivated. The environment will be high on energy and also there will be lot of motivation in the mind of the employee for that work place which will help both the perspectives and also it will help the employee to sustain and become stable in that organization because the values, the morals, the ethics all are been given to that employee. So for sure this organization focus on both the two terms which are important and understand the feelings, the issues and concerns of each employee

Human Values and Corporate Social Responsibility

Corporate social responsibility (CSR, also called corporate conscience, corporate citizenship, social performance, or sustainable responsible business/ Responsible Business) is a form of corporate self-regulation integrated into a business model. It is basically developed and inspired by concept of human values.CSR policy functions as a built-in, self-regulating mechanism whereby a business monitors and ensures its active compliance with the spirit of the law, ethical standards, and international norms. CSR is a process with the aim to embrace responsibility for the company's actions and encourage a positive impact through its activities on the environment, consumers, employees, communities, stakeholders and all other members of the public sphere who may also be considered as stakeholders.

Steps to Encourage Ethical Behaviour

The first step toward encouraging our workers to be more ethical is to establish a code of ethics. Th writing of this should be an organization-wide project to ensure that the code is comprehensive in addressing issues applicable in all areas of the organization. We can, however, develop a code of ethics for our own department employees.

The writing of the code of ethics is only the beginning. It must be communicated to all the workers in order to be effective. The best written code that is not well-known to all the workers is no better than the total absence of a guideline for ethical behavior.

Communicating the code to employees gives more weight to it. Managers are viewed as more serious about their expectations for ethical behavior if the guidelines have been extensively communicated. This can be accomplished through department announcements, bulletin board postings or individual memoranda. The method of communication is not as important as the fact that the code definitely be well-known to all the employees of the firm. Workers cannot be expected to behave in a prescribed manner if they have not been appropriately apprised of the guidelines.

When employees are familiar with their code of ethics they have a very clear idea of management's expectation of them. The guidelines for ethical behavior minimize the area of uncertainty for employees. The "right" course of action is more clearly obvious to workers when there is a code of ethics in place. It provides direction for our workers' behaviour.

The first step in any recovery process is admitting you have a problem, and businesses have a problem with ethics. It is not just a matter of some arrogant, immoral executives at a few companies getting greedy and cooking the books. The problem is more basic than that. The hard truth is that natural, unavoidable tension is inherent in the term "business ethics"—a tension that stems from conflicts between the interests of companies and their employees, customers, and the greater society (Columbia, 2001).

Although society wants companies to create many well-paying jobs, those same organizations want to limit compensation costs and raise productivity levels. Customers want to purchase goods and services at low prices, but businesses want to maximize profits. Society wants to reduce pollution levels, but businesses want to minimize the cost that environmental regulations add to their operations.

Because these conflicts are fundamental to the nature of business, managers must continuously and consciously balance the needs of the organization and its stockholders with the needs of other stakeholders, including workers, customers, and the larger community. Managers must also balance their personal needs and desires against those of their organizations.

Balancing such factors in a stable economic environment is tough enough. What makes it even trickier these days is factors such as globalization, technological innovation, and the quickening pace of business change. There are just too many new developments for traditional ethical standards to keep up. At what point, for example, does using cloning technology in medical research become unethical? Are executive stock options a principled way of linking performance to pay, or do options actually encourage unethical decision making? When does offshore outsourcing become a form of labor exploitation and a repudiation of community responsibility?

There are no easy answers, but this does not mean managers should throw up their hands and turn over the problem of ethics to corporate lawyers, saying, "Just keep us out of court." Business and HR leaders can model behaviors and create corporate practices that reduce unethical business practices even while making their firms more competitive in the marketplace. Despite the impression that U.S. companies are less ethical than ever, they have actually enjoyed progress in this area over the last couple of years, a trend that will continue if employers remember the lessons of the recent past.

Business Ethics and Future Management

The first step in any recovery process is admitting you have a problem, and businesses have a problem with ethics. It is not just a matter of some arrogant, immoral executives at a few companies getting greedy and cooking the books. The problem is more basic than that. The hard truth is that natural, unavoidable tension is inherent in the term "business ethics"—a tension that stems from conflicts between the interests of companies and their employees, customers, and the greater society (Columbia, 2001).

Although society wants companies to create many well-paying jobs, those same organizations want to limit compensation costs and raise productivity levels. Customers want to purchase goods and services at low prices, but businesses want to maximize profits. Society wants to reduce pollution levels, but businesses want to minimize the cost that environmental regulations add to their operations.

Because these conflicts are fundamental to the nature of business, managers must continuously and consciously balance the needs of the organization and its stockholders with the needs of other stakeholders, including workers, customers, and the larger community. Managers must also balance their personal needs and desires against those of their organizations.

Balancing such factors in a stable economic environment is tough enough. What makes it even trickier these days is factors such as globalization, technological innovation, and the quickening pace of business change. There are just too many new developments for traditional ethical standards to keep up. At what point, for example, does using cloning technology in medical research become unethical? Are executive stock options a principled way of linking performance to pay, or do options actually encourage unethical decision making? When does offshore outsourcing become a form of labor exploitation and a repudiation of community responsibility?

There are no easy answers, but this does not mean managers should throw up their hands and turn over the problem of ethics to corporate lawyers, saying, "Just keep us out of court." Business and HR leaders can model behaviors and create corporate practices that reduce unethical business practices even while making their firms more competitive in the marketplace. Despite the impression that U.S. companies are less ethical than ever, they have actually enjoyed progress in this area over the last couple of years, a trend that will continue if employers remember the lessons of the recent past.

The problems of actually practicing cultural relativism are numerous. They include the fact that the culture determines what is right and wrong, that it is impossible to judge a culture morally, and there can't be any moral progress in a culture The minor benefits of cultural relativism such as tolerance, lacking of an absolute standard, and an open mind can only be applied to a limited number of instances. There are some things that can be learned from this form of ethical theory. One is the idea of not being overly critical of other cultures. If more cultures tempered their tolerances with wisdom, then many of the problems we encounter when dealing with cultures other than our own could ultimately be eliminated.

Conclusion

In conclusion, overall values and ethics come in a variety of ways throughout one's life. Through personal, social, and economical experiences, a person can learn values and ethics which transfer into the person's success in careers, ventures, and life. By understanding and learning the meaning behind values and ethics, a person can become a more active and complete individual in life. This essay has made a better understanding of the definition of values and ethics, the sources where they are derived from, and how professionally applied, can lead to a person's successful career.

The manager significantly affects, and is affected by, the value culture of the society, through the mediating agency of organizations and other social institutions. Proper appreciation of this value dynamics requires understanding, and interiorisation, of the operation of human values at the societal and ecological levels of our categorization.

REFERENCES

Bharati, D. (1990). Mnav Mulya Aur Shitya (in Hindi; transl.: "Human Values and Literature") Delhi, Bhartiya Jnanpith.

Chakraborty, S.K. (1991). Management by Values. Delhi: Oxford University Books.

Chakraborty, S.K. (1995a). Human Values for Managers. Delhi: Wheeler Publishing Co.

Chakraborty, S.K. (1995b). Ethics in Management. Delhi: Oxford University Press.

Devaraj, N.K. (1988). Humanism in Indian Thought. Delhi: Indus Publishing Co.

Fromm, E. (1981). To Have or To Be. New York: Bantam Books.

Mesaroric, M.D. and Pestel, E. (1974). Mankind at the Turning Point. New York: E.P. Dutton, quoted from Fromm, 1988, p. 148.

Mukherjee, R. (1965). The Social Structure of Values. Delhi: S.Chand.

Rokeach, M. (1973). The Nature of Human Values. New York: Free Press.

Schwartz, S.H. (1994). "Are there Universal Aspects in the Structure and Conduct of Human Values?"

Journal of Social Issues, 50, No. 4, 19-45.

Swami Ranganathanand (1991). Human Values in Management. Delhi: Bharati Vidya Bhavan.

16 Feminization of Poverty and Inequality

Mary Princess Lavanya

Introduction

The feminization of poverty is a phenomenon that has been observed in the United States since 1970 as female headed households accounted for a growing proportion of those below the poverty line. A large majority of these women are divorced or never-married mothers. In 2000, 11 per cent of all families in the United States lived in poverty, but 28 per cent of families headed by single mothers did so. The burden of supporting a family is difficult for single mothers because of low salaries relating to the lack of previous work experience and low educational attainment and is often exacerbated by meager or unavailable child supports. In the United States, divorce is a primary factor leading to the filing for economic bankruptcy. In the India, poverty is defined as not having enough income to pay for basic needs, such as food, clothing and shelter. Poverty is a family attribute. In other words, if a family is classified as poor, all the members of that family are also poor. To determine whether or not a family is poor, the Census Bureau sums the income of all the members of the family and divides by the "need standard" or "poverty thresh hold" for a family of that size. The "needs standard" or "poverty threshold" was developed in 1964 by Mollie Orshansky, an economist at the Social Security Administration (Ruggles, 1994).

The poverty measure implicitly assumes that money is equally shared among members of a family. This assumption is not necessarily correct. It is certainly plausible that the person who earns the money may have more control over its use, or a man might control the money as part of his breadwinner identity, or there might be some other unequal arrangement.

A criticism of the poverty line measure is that it is based on an absolute rather than a relative standard. A poor family today is much worse off, relative to the average family, than a poor family was in the 1960s (McLanahan 1995). This is because the living standards of the median family have increased dramatically during the past 35 years, while the poverty thresholds still assume that families need only three times their basic food needs. Some scholars have suggested setting the poverty line at a given proportion of the median income, rather than having it reflect a fixed amount of money. For example, families with incomes below 50 per cent of the median family income (adjusted for family size) would be classified as poor. With a relative measure, poverty measures economic standing in the society, rather than marking economic destitution or the inability to feed, clothe, or house one's family. Many other countries use a relative standard for poverty (Smeeding, Higgins, Rainwater, 1990). As we will see in the cross-national comparisons below, if the U.S. adopted a relative standard, poverty rates would be significantly higher than they are under the official poverty measure. The difference reflects different ideas of what poverty is — relative economic disadvantage or the inability to cover basic needs.

Female-Headed Households and Women's Poverty

The term "feminization of poverty" originated in the United States in the late 1970s, when it was discovered that the fastest growing type of family structure was that of female-headed households (Pearce, 1978). Moreover, because of the high rate of poverty among these households, their increase was mirrored in the growing numbers of women and children who were poor. By the mid-1980s, it was believed that almost half of all the poor in the U.S. lived in families headed by women in various stages of the life-cycle. According to one study on the subject, in 1984, 16 per cent of all white families, 25 per cent of all families of Hispanic origin, and 53 per cent of all black families were headed by women (Gimenez, 1987).

The term feminization of poverty focuses our attention on sex differences in poverty rates and the fact that they have grown in the last half-century. Feminization describes both the unequal state of men's and women's poverty rates and the processes by which women's risk of poverty has increasingly exceeded that of men's. In Pearce's articles (1978, 1984), she focused on the proportion of the poor who were female. Other scholars, including England and McLanahan and her colleagues, have focused on the ratio of women's poverty rates to men's rates (Casper, McLanahan, Garfinkel, 1994; McLanahan, Casper, Sorensen, 1995; McLanahan et al, 1989). A sex-poverty ratio greater than one means that women have a higher poverty rate than men. For example, a poverty rate of 1.50, which is close to the number today for all adults, means that women's poverty rate is about 50 per cent higher than men's.

Sex differences in poverty rates are a function of the differences in poverty rates among single men and single women weighted by the proportion of adults who are single (i.e. not married). Since poverty is measured at the family level, sex differences in poverty can only exist among unmarried men and women. If all adults were married, and if boys and girls were evenly distributed across households, the sex-poverty ratio would be 1:0. Of course, some families would still be poor, but there would be no sex differences in poverty because each poor man would be linked to a poor woman. The sex-poverty ratio, our measure of the feminization of poverty, can change when either the percentage of single adults changes or when the poverty rates of single men and women change.

Feminization of Poverty

While discussing there many questions that arise in our mind, few such important questions are: Why has the sex poverty ratio grown so rapidly over the last fifty years? Why were women only slightly more likely than men to be poor in 1950, whereas today they are about 50 per cent more likely? What accounts for the leveling off, and the possible reversal, of the feminization of poverty among some age groups after 1980? There are three changes that have profoundly altered the social and economic conditions of men and women during the past forty years: changes in the family, changes in the economy, and changes in the welfare state. As described below, some of these changes have clearly benefited men more than women. Others have benefited women more than men, and still others have had different effects at different times.

Changes in the Family

Starting with changes in the family, several demographic trends are important. The first of these is the delay in the age of first marriage. Throughout the 1950s, the typical young woman married when she was about 20 years old and the typical young man married when he was about 23. This situation prevailed throughout the 1950s. By 1990, however, the median age at first marriage-the age at which half of the population has married for the first time - was 24 for women and 26 for men. (McLanahan, Casper, 1994).

A second major change is the rise in divorce. Whereas, in 1950, most people married and remained married until they (or their spouses) died, today over half of all couples end their marriages voluntarily. The divorce rate — the number of divorces each year per 1,000 married women — rose steadily during the first half of the twentieth century and increased dramatically after 1960. Over half of all marriages contracted in the mid-1980s were projected to end in divorce (Castro Martin, Bumpass, 1989). The divorce rate leveled off during the 1980s, but this was not necessarily a sign of greater stability. We would have expected such a leveling off, given the increase in the average age at first marriage, and given the fact that the large baby boom cohorts have reached middle age and passed through the period of their lives when they were most likely to divorce (Bumpass, Sweet, 1989).

The increase in divorce, coupled with the decline in marriage, meant that an increasing proportion of adult women were living separately from men and relying on themselves for economic support. Since women generally earn less than men for various reasons, single women have a higher risk of being poor than single men. In short, if nothing else changes, declines in marriage will lead to increases in the sex poverty ratio.

A third trend affecting family arrangements is the increase in children born outside marriage. In 1960 about 6 per cent of all births were to unmarried couples whereas by 1996 over a third fell into this category. The increase is even more dramatic among black families-from 22 per cent in 1960 to nearly 70 per cent in 1996. These changes in fertility are due to several factors, including the decline in marriage which increases the pool of women at risk for having an out-of-wedlock birth, the decline in the birth rate of married couples which was especially steep during the 1960s and early 1970s, and the increase in the birth rate of single women which has risen since 1980.

The net result of the changes in fertility and the increases in divorce among couples with children has been the growth of single mother families (Garfinkel, McLanahan, 1986). In 1960, only 8 per cent of families were headed by a single mother; today the number is about 27 per cent. Blacks are much more likely than whites to fall into this category, with over half of all black families now consisting of a single mother and her dependent children. However, the trends are similar for all race and ethnic groups.

Single parenthood has affected women's poverty rates much more than it has men's. Whereas in principle, responsibility for children could be evenly distributed between mothers and fathers after a divorce or a non-marital birth, in practice, women almost always have custody of the child (about 90% of single parents are women). Thus, not only do single women earn less money than single men, their needs, as defined by the poverty threshold, are greater than men's because they have more dependents. Again, we should point out that most mothers, when faced with a divorce or a non-marital birth, prefer to have custody of their child, despite the economic hardships associated with single motherhood. However, as noted above, these women pay a high financial price for their independence.

A fourth demographic trend affecting the family life of men and women is the increase in "non-family" households, particularly, the increase in one-person households. In 1940, only 10 per cent of all households were classified as "nonfamily" households, whereas in the early 1990s, over 30 per cent were of this type (Sweet, Bumpass, 1987). Until recently, nonfamily households were more common among blacks than among whites. Today, however, the proportions are nearly the same for both races. Hispanics, in contrast, have always had lower rates of nonfamily households.

Young adults and the elderly are especially prone to living in nonfamily households. For young people, this change is associated with the decline in marriage and the increase in cohabitation. Interestingly, couples who are cohabiting are not counted as families by the Census Bureau, even though they may be pooling their incomes and sharing expenses. Thus the poverty rates of many of these couples are likely to be overstated. Since young women are somewhat more likely to cohabit than young men, treating co-habitators as nonfamily households leads to an overestimate of women's poverty rates relative to men's (McLanahan, Casper, 1994).

The elderly are also much more likely to live independently today than they were fifty years ago (Treas, 1995). This change is generally viewed as a sign of progress, and most elderly people report that they prefer their independence. Whereas in the past, a majority of elderly people lived with their adult children once they were widowed, today, more and more widows and widowers live alone. The increase in the proportion of elderly living alone is due in part to increases in Social Security income.

A final trend affecting the sex differential in poverty rates is the increase in life expectancy. More specifically, women are likely to live longer than men and so their retirement income has to stretch over more years. The differences in men's and women's life expectancies have grown over these years. In 1940, men at age 65 had a life expectancy only 17 months shorter than that of women aged 65. In 1993, men at age 65 had a life expectancy 47 months — almost four years — shorter than that of women aged 65 (Advisory Council on Social Security, 1996).

Changes in the Economy

Changes in family composition reflect changes in the needs of the family — the denominator of the poverty function. Women's labor force participation has increased over most of the twentieth century (Bianchi, 1999). The changes have been larger in recent decades than in the early 1900s, with many American women seeking and finding employment since 1960. The increase in women's employment means that women are gaining more experience in the labor market, which, all else being equal, should increase their ability to support themselves and their families. Equally important, women are also gaining on men with respect to their hourly wages (Bianchi, 1999). From 1960 to 1980, full-time women workers averaged about 60 per cent of full-time male workers' earnings. Since 1981, however, the ratio of women's earnings to men's earnings has increased to about 70 per cent. If changes in women's earnings (relative to men's) are largely responsible for the reversal in the sex poverty ratio, we would not expect to observe a reversal among the age groups who are less likely to be working, namely among retired persons. From 1970 to 1996, the sex-poverty ratio did not decline for women over 65 years.

Suggestions to Improve the Status of Women

- Women should undergo compulsory vocational, life skills and self-protection (karate) Training.
- Schools should conduct activities and programmes based on gender equality and women empowerment and the curriculum should ensure that women empowerment is possible when men are part it.
- Government should initiate better welfare programmes for female headed families.
- Women empowerment should be the focus of any Governmental programmes, schemes and welfare measures.

Conclusion

The changes in poverty rates and sex differences in poverty have occurred in two major periods, from 1950 to 1970 and from 1970 to 1996. In the decades after World War II, poverty rates declined dramatically. This was a period of strong economic growth, including rising wages, and expansion of government benefits, such as Social Security and welfare programmes. Both of these forces pushed poverty rates down. As poverty rates declined, the sex-poverty ratio increased for all groups. The growing inequality in men's and women's poverty rates was caused by several factors. First, the wage growth that pushed poverty rates down benefited men more than women because they were more closely attached to the labor market. Second, changes in family structure hurt women more than men, mainly because women bore more responsibility for children in the growing number of unmarried households.

After 1970, poverty rates stopped declining. During the 1970s, the economy stagnated and when it recovered in the 1980s, the main beneficiaries were college graduates rather than less-educated workers living near the poverty line. The sex-poverty ratio continued to increase among the elderly, but stopped increasing among working age adults. An examination of the "feminization of poverty" around the world is approached in terms of the three contributing factors that have been underscored in the women-in-development and gender-and-development (WID/GAD) literature:

1. the growth of female-headed households;
2. intra-household inequalities and bias against women and girls; and
3. neoliberal economic policies, including structural adjustments and the post-socialist market transitions.

The growing visibility of women's poverty, it is argued, is rooted in demographic trends, "cultural" patterns, and political economy. It is high time that our country focuses on women empowerment through education, definitely this will bring about a great deal of change.

REFERENCES

Advisory Council on Social Security, Volume 2, 1996, p. 261.

Bumpass, L. L. and J. A. Sweet (*1989*). Children's Experience in Single-Parent Families: Implications of Cohabitation and Marital Transitions. Family Planning Perspectives 21, 256-260. American Journal of Sociology 85, 49-65.

Constance F. Citro and Robert T. Michael, (1995). *Editors,* Panel on Poverty and Family Assistance: Concepts, Information Needs, and Measurement Methods, National Academy Press, Washington, D.C.

McLanahan, Sara and Lynne Casper. (*1995*). "Growing Diversity and Inequality in the American. Family." In R. Farley (ed.)

Ruggles, Steven, (*1994*). The Transformation of American Family Structure. American Historical Review, vol. 99 pp. 103-128.

Smeeding, Timothy, Michael O' Higgins, and Lee Rainwater, eds, (1990). Poverty, Inequality and Income Distribution in Comparative Perspective. London: Harvest Wheatsheaf.

Suzanne M. Bianchi, (1999). Feminization and Juvenilization of Poverty: Trends, Relative Risks, Causes, and Consequences, Annual Review of Sociology, Vol. 25: 307-333.

Castro Martin, & L. *Bumpass,* (*1989*). "Recent Trends in Marital Disruption" Contraceptive. Colorado: West View Press. Demography. 26(1):37-51.

Treas, J., & Torrecilha, R. (1995). The Older Population. In R. Farley (Ed.), State of the Union: America in the 1990s (pp. 47-92). New York: Russell Sage.

17

Special Economic Zone (Sez) the Catalyst of Agro and Food Processing Industries in Nagaland

Dr. Mithilesh Kumar Jha

ABSTRACT

A single SEZ can contain multiple specific zones within the boundaries. Indian policy maker realised it and initiated to do the experience with this concept of development. India becomes the pioneer country in Asia when she set up the Asia's first SEZ in Kandla(Gujarat). The policy intended to create SEZs as an engine for economic growth supported by quality infrastructure complemented by an appealing fiscal package, both the Centre and the State level, with the minimum possible regulations. An SEZ may be set-up in the public, private, or joint sector and/or by a state government, subject to compliance with the Policy and guidelines issued by the Ministry of Commerce ("MoC").

Concept of SEZ

Special Economic Zone (SEZ) has the magical power to transform the any developing areas into developed areas through the multiplier effect on developmental process in the region. A single SEZ can contain multiple specific zones within the boundaries. Indian policy maker realised it and initiated to do the experience with this concept of development. India becomes the pioneer country in Asia when she set up the Asia's first SEZ in Kandla (Gujarat) in 1965. It did not fulfill the expectedtion of the nation. China's experiment with SEZ has brought the worldwide revolution in this concept. In the people's Republic of China,SEZ were founded by the central Government under the Leadership of Den Xiaoping in the early 1980s.The most successful SEZ in China, Shenzhen, has developed form a small hamlet into a city with a population over 10 million within a limited period of time i.e. 20 years.

Manycountries have followed this successful experiment of china and SEZ have been established by them namely Brazil, Iran, Jordan etc. In the same process of development Peru has been the ZONA ECONOMICA by its dynamic president Alan Garcia. Taking the lesson from China, with a view to overcome the shortcomings experienced on account of the multiplicity of controls and obviousness; paucity of world -class infrastructure, and volatile fiscal regime and with a view to attract enormous foreign investments in India, the Special Economic Zones (SEZs) policy was announced in April 2000.

The policy intended to create SEZs as an engine for economic growth supported by quality infrastructure complemented by an appealing fiscal package, both the Centre and the State level, with the minimum possible regulations. SEZs in India functioned from 01.11.2000 to 09.02.2006 under the provisions of the Foreign Trade Policy and fiscal incentives were made effective through provisions of relevant statutes.

To impulse confidence in investors and signal the Government's dedication to a stable SEZ policy regime and with a view to impart stability to the SEZ regime thereby generating greater economic activity and employment through the founding of SEZs, a comprehensive draft SEZ bill formulated after extensive discussions with the stakeholders. A number of meetings were held in sundry parts of the country both by the Minister of Commerce and Industry as well as senior officials for this purpose. The Special Economic Zones Act, 2005 was passed by parliament in May 2005 which received Presidential approval on the June 23, 2005. After extensive consultations, the SEZ ACT, 2005 supported by SEZ Rules, came into effect on February 10, 2006, providing for drastic simplification of producers and for single window clearance on matters relating to Central as well as State Governments.

Definition of SEZ

Special Economic Zone (SEZ) is a specifically delineated duty free enclave and shall be deemed to be foreign territory for the purposes of trade operations and duties and tariffs. Thus the zone in India is treated as a foreign territory and is designated duty free enclave In the premises of SEZ treatment occurred as:

1. Supplies from Domestic Tariff Area (DTA) are treated as exports and entitled for all benefits of exports.
2. SEZ products sold in DTA are treated as import and applicable duties of customs are payable.

An SEZ may be set-up in the public, private, or joint sector and/or by a state government, subject to compliance with the Policy and guidelines issued by the Ministry of Commerce ("MoC"). The policy requires the minimum size of an SEZ to be 400 hectares. A SEZ is considered to be a territory outside the customs territory of India for the purpose of undertaking the authorized operations. There are several special fiscal provisions such as duty free goods for development of SEZs as well as for SEZ units, exemption from Income Tax to SEZ units for 15 years.

Main objectives of the SEZ Act are:

1. Generationof additional economic activity;
2. Promotion of exports of goodsand services;
3. Promotion of investment from domestic and foreign sources;
4. Creationof employment opportunities;
5. Developmentof infrastructurefacilities;

It is anticipated that this will activate a larger, uninterrupted flow of foreign and domestic investment in SEZs infrastructure and productive capacity, towards to generation of additional economic activity and creation of employment avenues in the entire region.

The SEZ Rules provided for:

1. Simplified procedure for development, operation, maintenance for the SEZs and for instituting units and conducting business in SEZs;
2. Single window clearance establishing of SEZs;
3. Single window clearance on matters relating to Central as well as State Governments;
4. Simplified compliance procedures anddocumentation with prominence on self certification.

Incentives and Facilities Offered to the Units in SEZs

After creation of the SEZs incentives and facilities offered to the units in SEZs for attracting investments into the SEZs, including foreign investment and as intended:

1. 100 per cent Income Tax exemption on export income for SEZ units under Section 10 AA of the Income Tax Act for first 5 years, 50 per cent for next 5 years thereafter and 50 per cent of the ploughed back export profit for the next 5 years.
2. Exemption from minimum alternate tax under section 115JB of the Income Tax Act.
3. External commercial borrowing by SEZ units upto US $ 500 million in a year without any maturity restriction through recognised banking channels.
4. Exemption from Central Sales Tax.
5. Exemption from Service Tax.
6. Exemption from State Sales Tax and other levies as extended by the respective State Governments.

Project Background

In pursuance of the pronouncement made in Shillong on January 21-22,2000 by the Prime Minister of India in respect of scales for the development of exports from the affluent North Eastern Region, especially to give the boost to its natural resources and its product. The Government of Nagaland has notified the Nagaland Industrial Development Corporation Limited (NIDC), Dimapur as the authourised Export House in order to deal with all correlated matters. The State Government has approached the Ministry of Commerce to approve and sanction Special Economic Zone (SEZ) for the State and correspondingly, a multi- products SEZ was approved and to be implemented under private sector by M/s H.N. Company, Dimapur which is the first one in the NER. A notification is awaited from the respective Ministry for implementation.

In the midst of, M/s Nagaland Industrial Development Corporation Limited (NIDC) has recognised Dimapur as another location for a product specific Agro and Food Processing SEZ by transforming already created an Export Promotion Industrial Park (EPIP) in the proposed location. The EPIP has been developed with all necessary modern facilities like road, power, administrative building, guesthouse, residential complex, few standard Design Factories and warehouses.

NIDC is a Government of Nagaland undertaking mandated with a mandate to assist, develop and promote industrial growth in the State. NIDC through the state Govt. has sought clearance from the Ministry of Commerce for conversion of the EPIP into a product specific Agro & Food processing Special Economic Zone (SEZ). The GoI has approved the proposal and sanctioned the second one for which a Notification has already been issued by the Ministry of Commerce. Implementation of the project by NIDC is in steps forward

The Proposed Project

The proposed project for SEZ is planned across an area of 125 acres at Ganeshnagar adjacent to the Industrial Growth Centre (IGC) under Dhansiri Sub-division in Dimapur District. At present it spreads over 52 hectares. The MoC & I, and Government of India has notified on July 9, 2009 that 50. 70 hectares of land of the Ganeshnagar,SEZ. It is the first of its kind in the entire North Eastern Region.

Infrastructure

NIDC would develop an integrated industrial, commercial, residential, and social infrastructure of internationalstandards and world class facilities aimed at boosting exports and propelling the economy of the entire region. The NIDC had mooted the plan to give the boost Agro and Food Processing Industries in Nagaland through the SEZ with Export Promotion Industrial Park (EPIP). NIDC had proposed under section 3 of SEZ Act, 2005 to set up a sector specific SEZ for Agro and Food processing Sector. Now the dream to establish the SEZ has come true. The SEZ is proposed to develop State-of art infrastructure.

Status of Agro and Food Processing Industries in SEZ

Nagaland is having the varying altitude from 194 to 3048 metres and its favourable agro-climatic and geophysical conditions which promote a wide variety of organic sub-tropical & temperature fruits and vegetables grow abundantly. In Nagaland, almost all agricultural and agro-horticultural products are produce naturally, chemical free, i.e., Organic. Till date, 63,000 hectares of land have already developed and over 40,000 hectares being developed further, namely, Oranges, Passion fruits, Pineapples, Bananas, Plums, Pears, Ginger, Chilies, Topioca and other many other exotic fruits and vegetables are grown on extensively.

Being a hilly State Nagaland is known as treasure trove of a number of rare plants, plethora of medicinal plants, medicinal and aromatic herbs and other valuable plants, namely, Geranium, Patchouli, Citronella, including aloe-Vera and worlds best quality of Ginseng, a valuable medicinal plant, etc. These plants and herbs grow well and produce the considerable quantities. The climate is suitable for Jatropha known as Bio-diesel.

Meaning of Agro

The word agro has been from the Greek word Agros meaning field or soil or pertaining to agriculture, and used for Latin Agri (from ager) which is combination form (Forming ns and adjs) of farming; agriculture. Thus the meaning of agro is obvious that the work of agriculture and farming and the produce of these activities comes under this to feed the human and other creatures.

Agro and Food Processing

The meaning of the word Food has been used here as source of nutrients: All material that provides living things with the nutrients they need for energy and growth or as solid nourishment: substances, or a particular substance, providing nourishment for people or animals, especially in solid as opposed to liquid form. The word processing meant to prepare something using a process: to treat or prepare something in a series of steps or actions, e.g. using chemicals or industrial machinery.The meaning of the word Agro is already defined before. Ergo, Agro & food processing could be defined as set of techno economic activities carried out for conservation and handling of agricultural produce and to make it usable as food, feed, fibre, fuel or industrial raw material. Food processing is generally understood to encompass all methods by which raw foodstuffs are rendered suitable for cooking, consumption, or storage. Food Processing generally includes the basic preparation of foods, the alteration of a food product into another form (as in making preserves from fruit) and preservation and packaging techniques. There are a number of food - processing innovations have even developed in new products, such as concentrated fruit juices, freeze- dried coffee, and instantaneous foods. Foods and food supplements have also been processed from such hitherto unexploited sources namely oilseeds (chiefly protein-rich soybeans and cotton seeds); mutant varieties of crops; leaves, grasses, and aquatic plants; and highly nutritious fish meal and concentrates. Henceforth, the scope of the agro- processing industry encompasses all operations from the stage of harvest till the material reaches the end users in the desired form, packaging, quantity, quality, and price meant that it cross the several processes which provides employment opportunities to all types of the persons. Ancient Indian Scriptures contain distinct account of the post harvest and processing practices for preservation and processing of agricultural produces for food and medicinal uses.

Agro-processing is now known as the sunrise sector of the Indian economy in view of its large potential for growth and likely socio-economic influence specifically on employment and income generation. Some estimates puts forward that in developed countries, up to 14 per cent of the total work force is betrothed in agro-processing sector directly or indirectly. However, in India, only about 3 per cent of the work force finds employment in this sector indicating its developing state and vast untapped potential for employment. Properly advanced, agro-processing sector can make India foremost player at the global level for marketing and supply of processed food, feed, and a wide range of other plant and animal products.

On account of poor post-harvest management, the losses in farm produce in India have been assessed to be of a very high order. Sundry studies have estimated post production losses in food commodities to the tweak of Rs. 75,000-100,000 Crore per annum.

Commodity wise agro processing consists of the following:

- Processing of grains namely, rice, wheat, maize and other course cereals.
- Processing of pulses
- Processing of Oilseed
- Processing of fruits & vegetables
- Processing of Sugarcane
- Processing of Jute
- Processing of animal produce
- Processing of Fish & the product of Fish
- Processing of Plantation crops
- Processing of Commercial crops including spices and condiments
- Processing of medicinal and aromatic crops
- Processing of Floriculture
- Processing of Apiculture produce
- Processing of traditional foods

Agro and Food Processing Industries: An Overview

The food industry is the multifaceted, worldwide collective of varied businesses that together supply much of the food energy devoured by the world population. The food processing industry is one of the biggest industries in India. It has occupied the fifth ranked in terms of production, consumption, export and expected growth. After seeing the growing importance of this industry it is widely accepted as a 'sunrise industry' in India. It has got the tremendous potentiality to boost the agriculture to uplift the economy of our country, creation of large scale processed food manufacturing and food chain facilities, and the subsequent generation of employment and export earnings. At the present time India is the second largest food producer and it is projected that very soon it would be the world'snumber one producer.

Food processing industry is of colossal significance for the development of India because of the fundamental linkages and collaborations that it promotes between the two pillars of the economy, viz., industry and agriculture. It covers a spectrum of products from sub-sector comprising agriculture, horticulture, plantation, animal husbandry and fisheries. Essentially, the food industry involves the commercial movement of food from field to work.

The country's food processing maker is commencing upto a wide range of investors from corner to corner of the globe. Analysis antedated that the total market for food processing goods in India will yield approximately US $ 69.4 billion in 2004-2005, of which value-added products comprises US $ 22.2 billion. Processed food exports and value-added agricultural products are expected to witness rapid growth in their respective industry segments in the coming years.

Prominent Features of the Food Processing Industries

1. At the present timeagro and food processing industry is generally unorganised and operating on a small scale level.
2. Presently, the Indian food processing industry is mainly export oriented although domestic consumption of processed food is low but it is fast picking up with growing income levels and fast changing consumer comportment due to economic growth.
3. Indian food processing industry endows comparative & competitive advantages over the other countries because of:
    - cheap workforce;
    - fiscal initiatives (tax holidays); and
    - availability of raw materials.
4. Existence of untouched large consumer base with growing income levels.

Technological Innovations

Techniques for food processing from natural deterioration, following harvest or slaughter, date to prehistoric times. Among the oldest methods of preservation are drying, refrigeration, and fermentation. Modern methods consist of canning, pasteurization, freezing, irradiation, and the addition of chemicals. The modern technological innovations have brought the revolution in the field of food processing technique. The foremost technological innovations contain as:

- Agriculture product modification paraphernalia such as cleaners, graders, and driers for on-farm operations as well as industrial operations.
- Processes and tool for parboiling of rice, preparation of puffed rice and flaked rice.
- Development of techniques and tool for processing of pulses to produce dal for higher recovery and superior quality.
- Adoption and development of processes, tool for output of high protein concentrated produces, namely full fat soy flour, soy drink/soy milk soy paneer (TOFFU) and soy fortified baked products.
- Development of driers using agricultural remains, by -products and solar energy.
- Development of equipment, viz., leaf cup and Dona making machine, multipurpose mills, mini flour mill, grain pearlers, maize dehuskers, shellers, groundnut decorticators, fruit graders, juice extractors, high recovery mechanical oil expellers and improved storage structures for cereals, pulses, oilseeds, onion and potato.

Processes and tool for output of high quality ground spices and spice mix, development of raw materials and processes for output of instant sweets, curries snack foods, instant soft drinks, idly, dosa, sambhar mixes/powders, egg powder, production and packaging of milk products namely, butter, skimmed milk, full cream milk, ghee, paneer, curd, lassi and different types of sweets.

- Equipment to squeeze and high recovery of sugarcane juice, processes for production of high quality jaggery and liquid jaggery.
- Processes, tools & equipment and pilot plants for production of sundry industrial raw materials from lac and dyes and pharmaceutical products.

Improved technology for processing of jute sticks to produce jute fibre and impregnation, preparation of jute based textile materials and bags.

- Control of stored grain insects by using chemical and physical methods, storage structures for on farm, trade and process plant level operations.
- Processing and canning of meat, meat products and fish.

Brief History of Food Processing

The practice of food processing can be traced to prehistory,when fruits and vegetables were dried, cereal grains were parched, and fish and game were salted and dried. These age old methods developed very slowly and were purely empirical-fermentation, drying, smoking, and curing with salt being the prime techniques. AS the biological causes of food spoilage became better taken into account, rapid advances followed, and suitable methods were soon developed for dealing with the causative agents.

In late 20th century an electric appliance developed and practiced for a variety of food - preparation functions including kneading, chopping, blending, and pulverizing. Food processing got momentum when the food processor was invented by Pierre Verdon, whose Lee Magi-Mix, a compact household version of his own restaurant-scaled Robot-Coupe, was first displayed in Paris in 1971. Since then many inventions have added the flavour with refined version and modification in this industry.

Present State of the Industry

India is blessed by the nature specially favourable climate to grow the all seasons agriculture, horticulture and floriculture in adequate amount. Unfortunately the food processing industry is still in infancy: only 2 per cent of fruit and vegetables: and 15 per cent of milk produced are processed. Despite, of this the processed food industry ranks fifth in size in the country, constituting 6.3 per cent of GDP. It accounts for 13 per cent of the country's exports and 6 per cent of total industrial investment. At present the size of the industry is estimated at US $ 70 billon, including US $ 22 billion of value added outputs This industry has been attracting FDI across different categories:

- India is one of the biggest food producer producing 600 million tonnes of food grains yearly. Its warehouses had a buffer stock of nearly 50 million tonnes of food grains (wheat and rice) in 2003-2004.
- The second largest exporter of rice and 5th largest exporter of wheat in the world. Its agricultural exports account for nearly 14.2 per cent of its total export figures.
- India ranked first in the world in production of cereals and milk. It is the second biggest fruits and vegetables producer and is among the top five producers of rice, wheat, groundnuts, tea, coffee, tobacco, spices, sugar and oilseeds.
- India is the 7th biggest producer of fish in the world and ranked 2nd in inland fish production.

It is estimated that the Indian food market is approximately US $ 69.4 billion out of that value added food products constitutes US $ 22.2 billion. In spite of food production in the country is projected to double by the year

2020.It shows that the sector has become the alluring sector for huge investment and to upgrade the technologies, skills and equipments.

Future Prospective

Albeit the food processing industry of India is in infancy but it offers great opportunities to attract FDI. It accounts for US $ 29.4 billion, in a total estimated market of US $91.66 billion. There is a rapidly growing demand for processed food due to the high urbanization and enhancing income levels. To meet this growing demand, the investment required is about US $ 28 billion. Keeping this thing for future perspective GoI has declared it as a priority sector and formulated the integrated food policy to explore the potentiality of the sector in the competitive world. To harness the value-generating agro and food processing, superior market mechanism and infrastructure are required to be prepared immediately.

State governments have already commenced to actively encourage the preparation of aggregators by encouraging companies to engage in agriculture marketing.

The outlay in this sector has been swelled from US $19.5 million in 2004-05 to US $41.35 million the next year, more than twice the earlier amount. The government is also considering to invest US $ 22.97 million in minimum 10 mega food parks in the country as well as working towards offering 100 per cent FDI and income tax benefits in the sector.

As the Confederation of Indian Industry (CII) has estimated that food processing sector has the high potential to attract Rs. 1,50, 000 crore (US $ 33) of investment in 10 years and create employment of 9 million persons. A Goldman Sachs report (Dreaming with BRICs: The path to 2050) said that among Brazil, Russia, India, and China (BRICs) will grow the fastest over the next 30 to 50 years by leveraging its demographic advantages and through continued development. At its present rates of growth, the burgeoning market in the country "would be adding nearly one France every 3.5 years and one Australia every year."

Thus, when deemed from the national perspective as well, the industry has a huge potential to develop.Value addition of food products is anticipated to grow from the current 8 per cent to 35 per cent by the end of 2025.Fruit and vegetable processing, which is presently around 2 per cent of total production will grow to 10 per cent by 2010 and to 25 per cent by 2025. This shows the large scope for both investors and exporters.

Prospect of North Eastern Region in the Food Processing Industry

As it is well known that the NER's agro climatic condition is favourable for the cultivation of wide variety of fruits and vegetables though this potential is to be optimally utilize. In addition to this the region is a stockroom of varied aromatic and medicinal plants, which are yet to be commercially utilized in the real sense of the term. The area under cultivation and production of horticultural yields would better highlight the potential of the area as it is shown in table 17.1.

Table 17.1: Horticultural Production in North East

	2003-04		2004-05	
	Area ('000ha)	Production ('000MT)	Area ('000ha)	Production ('000MT)
Assam	415.4	3158.2	410.1	3189.6
Arunachal Pradesh	78.3	218.9	80.8	218.8
Manipur	79.1	417.0	79.1	417.0
Meghalaya	85.2	555.8	8.25	555.8
Mizoram	35.8	107.1	35.8	107.1
Nagaland	29.8	163.7	29.8	163.7
Sikkim	58.2	112.7	57.4	118.3
Tripura	74.0	871.1	76.2	908.3
NER Total	855.8	5,604.5	854.4	5,678.6
All India	19,449.0	1,57,834.9	20,198.9	1,69,828.8

Source: Project Report for setting up of agro & food processing SEZ at Dimapur in Nagaland.

The region has 4.2 per cent of the total area under cultivation of horticulture crops in India, while the output consists 3.34 per cent out of all India production. There is thus a need to boost productivity, which can be successfully done through proper marketing of its valuable produce as at present distress sale and low price of horticultural outputs is working as a deterrent to this. The whole region is rich in the production of citrusfruits, pineapple, passion fruits etc., medicinal and aromatic plants are abundantly available here and people used it since the olden age which is unknown to outside the region till today.

Prospect of Food Processing Industry in Nagaland

As the aforesaid description of the NERs candidly explained that the agro climatic condition support the cultivation of wide variety of fruits and vegetable though this potential is to be optimally exploited, same condition applied for Nagaland too.

The economy of the State is primarily agrarian with more than 70 per cent of its population dependent on agriculture and related activities. Paddy is the major food crop and other food crops viz., maize, wheat millet pulses, grams, potatoes, chilly, ginger, garlic, large cardamom, Soya-bean, sugarcane, cabbage tomato oil seeds, etc. are also produced in modest quantities Since the creation of the state, the state has made an impressive food-grain production from an annual food-grain production of 62,000 MT only to the present annual production capacity of 4,22,870 MT with a productivity grow from 700 kg per hectare to 200 kg per hectare showing an overall growth of productivity by 186 per cent. Ergo, the state agriculture policy is aiming to achieve the vision of food-grain for all by 2020.

The Horticulture TechnologyMission has tried to exploit the potentiality of the fertile land of the State for that Mission formulated the policy to provide the required things. The mission has facilitated for up gradation of orchards better yields which has resulted in a surplus production in fruits. The current production of fruits is estimated at above 2 lakh MT and the projection for 2010-11 is about 3lakh MT. The production of some products in recent years are as follows:

The economy of the State is primarily agrarian with more than 70 per cent of its population dependent on agriculture and related activities. Paddy is the major food crop and other food crops viz., maize, wheat millet pulses, grams, potatoes, chilly, ginger, garlic, large cardamom, Soya-bean, sugarcane, cabbage tomato oil seeds, etc. are also produced in modest quantities Since the creation of the state, the state has made an impressive food-grain production from an annual food-grain production of 62,000 MT only to the present annual production capacity of 4,22,870 MT with a productivity grow from 700 kg per hectare to 200 kg per hectare showing an overall growth of productivity by 186 per cent. Ergo, the state agriculture policy is aiming to achieve the vision of food-grain for all by 2020.

The Horticulture Technology Mission has tried to exploit the potentiality of the fertile land of the State for that Mission formulated the policy to provide the required things. The mission has facilitated for up gradation of orchards better yields which has resulted in a surplus production in fruits. The current production of fruits is estimated at above 2 lakh MT and the projection for 2010-11 is about 3 lakh MT. The production of some products in recent years are as follows.

The aforesaid table candidly depicts the production of the sundry fruits, medicinal, aromatic and spices in the state. At the present time the food processing industries has been gaining the popularity worldwide. Ergo, the ongoing SEZ can enhance the scope of development in the said organic agricultural products. To support the peasants Government of Nagaland can easily set up the following food processing industries:

- Banana based processing industries
- Ginger and Cardamom processing industries
- Passion fruit processing industries
- Citrus and Pineapple processing
- Medicinal and Aromatic distillation and fractionalization industries

Table 17.2

Name of the Crops	Year (HA)	Area (MT)	Production (MT/HA)	Productivity
Citrus	2001-02	1169	5525	4.73
	2005-06	3683	20,500	5.57
Orange	2008-09	5,650	32,000	5-66
	2009-10	8,500	48,110	5.66
Pineapple	2001-02	1535	16,885	11.00
	2005-06	3695	40,720	11.02
	2008-09	6,545	70,550	1078
	2009-10	7,695	82,952	1078
Passion Fruit	2001-02	620	1,135	1.83
	2005-06	3040	9500	3.13
	2008-09	5,190	10,800	2.08
	2009-10	6,000	13,000	2.20
Banana	2001-02	1,768	13,980	7.91
	2005-06	3,042	36,538	12.01
	2008-09	4,650	38,900	8.37
	2009-10	5,200	N.A	N.A
Vegetables	2008-09	7,200	63,000	8.75
	2009-10	8,000	1.20 lakh	–
	2010-11	–	1.50 lakh	–
Ginger	2001-02	720	5,226	7.26
	2005-06	1,865	21,500	11.53
	2008-09	383	3,447	9.00
	2009-10	300	2,760	9.20
Turmeric	2001-02	300	650	2.17
	2005-06	850	9,000	10.59
	2008-09	358	3,222	9.00
	2009-10	200	1,900	9.40
Large Cardamom	2001-02	203	148	0.73
	2005-06	1300	850	0.65
	2008-09	2,791	1,395	0.5
	2009-10	3,191	2,967	0.52
Black pepper	2001-05	100	39	0.39
	2005-06	585	700	1.20
	2008-09	1200	1,116	0.93
	2009-10	1400	1,302	0.93
Garlic	2001-02	100	550	5.50
	2005-06	1,000	7,550	7.55

(Contd...)

Name of the Crops	Year (HA)	Area (MT)	Production (MT/HA)	Productivity
Chillies	2001-02	450	3,500	7.78
	2005-06	600	4,000	6.67
Naga Chilly	2008-09	248	992	4.00
	2009-10	400	1600	4.00
Medicinal	2001-02	427	371	0.87
Aloe Vera & Taxus Baccata	2005-06	1350	2000	1.48
Aromatic	2001-02	147	126	0.86
Patchouli & Geranium	2005-06	1200	1500	1.25

Source: Compiled the data from.

1. Govt. of Nagaland, (2010), 2years of Dan's 2nd ministry A RECORD OF Achievements.
2. Govt, of Nagaland, Year of the entrepreneur 2010-11, Guide to enterprise promotion, Deptt. of Industries and Commerce.

For this there is an essential to create the support structure in terms of infrastructure development and making provisions for the promotion of such industries. Poor infrastructure is the main obstacle in the development of these industries. So it isurgently required to bridge the gap to make the optimum utilisation of the abundant available resources. It is possible when the following requirements will be fulfilled.

- Developed infrastructure with sound transportation system,continious power supply with adequate voltage and water facilities.
- Common infrastructure for research laboratory,laboratory testing, and quality standardization, which can make the products a better market on reasonable price.
- Robust storage facilities of both raw produce as well as processed foods
- Well developed communication network.
- Support facilities that can grow well a industrial cluster.

Infrastructure Evaluation

NIDC would make an integrated industrial, commercial, residential and social infrastructure of international standards envisioned at boosting exports and propelling the economy of the whole region. The SEZ is spread across 125 acres. It is suggested to develop state -of- the art infrastructure facilities. The industrial park is being recommended as a agro and food processing Special Economic Zone. An assessment of necessary infrastructure within the SEZ is candidly explained as follows,

Development Vision and Positioning

The suggested SEZ is aimed to position Nagaland on the map of global Agro and Food Zone through the provision of an internationally competitive, hassle-free environment and world class infrastructure facilities. The prime rudiments of the SEZ vision are mentioned below as:

- Creation of a podium for domestic export oriented agro forestry companies to expand into global players at each level of the value chain.
- Awake the latent talent of locally available manpower and up grade their skills through the development of training, latest know-how, proper education and research facilities for processing activities of the agriculture produce.
- Creation of world class trade promotion amenities for B2B (Business to Business) and B2C (Business to Consumer) like Exhibition Mart, Convention centres, EXIMT trade acceleration, etc.
- Build high- end retail and hospitality infrastructure to entice good players and develop a sustainable and monetarily viable business model for the SEZ.

Processing and Non-processing Analysis

The prime attention of the SEZ should be on development of medium scale industries, as trading & services, training & research, and research & development too. All facilities needed for industries together with housing for the entrepreneurs and employees working in the domain will be planned for the SEZ. Thus, the suggested SEZ will operate as an integrated package with all the necessitated facilities, which will make sure sustainable development of medium and large-scale industries and service activities with adequate provision for future growth and development.

The SEZ shall be developed as a service oriented, self contained estate concept which can satisfy the need of the SEZ. It will be a premier SEZ offering full sub structure and dependable utilities complete with supporting facilities and amenities. Supporting and robust infrastructure shall compliment the industrial and business activities and this will broadly range from logistics and warehousing hub to social, commercial, residential and recreational facilities. Prominence will be placed on creation a functional and highly aesthetically fabricated urban environment within the SEZ premises with proper landscaping and signature plazas at the entrance. The purpose is to create value with product and service differentiators.

At least 50 per cent of the total project area in SEZ must be utilised for processing activities, namely, production or manufacturing, while the balance can be utilised for other non-processing activities.The processing area shall be a custom-bonded zone and must be adequately confined with stern access control. The comprehensive components under processing and non-processing domain are being mentioned subsequently.

Land Use and Zoning in SEZ of Nagaland

The proposed land usage for the projected site of SEZ is as presented in table 17.3.

Table 17.3

Sr. No.	Description	Land Use in (Acres) Processing	Land Use in (Acres) Non processing	Total Area in (Acres)	Percentage (%)
1.	Industrial	60.00	–	60.00	48.00
2.	Social infrastructure	3.00	15.75	18.75	15.00
3.	Specialised Infrastructure	6.25	6.25	12. 50	10.00
4.	Utilities		1.25	1.25	1.00
5.	Roads and Foot Path	7.75	5.25	12.50	10.00
6.	Greenery		12.50	12.50	10.00
7.	Residential		6.875	6.875	5.50
	Total	77.00	47.875	125	100

Source: NIDC, (2007), Project Report for setting up of Agro & food Processing Special Economic Zone at Dimapur in Nagaland.

Project Cost Estimates

A quick approximate of the project cost for the purposes of this report has been formulated based on some assumptions. As per typical site planning principles, about 60-70 per cent of the total area in an integrated industrial estate may be considered as vendible domain. The remaining land is 125 acres, the total vendible area would be about 80 acres.

NIDC points towards to bestow more of built up facilities than providing land for individual development. On the other hand, strategic associations would be work out to create world class processing and non processing infrastructure. The following table shows the estimated cost of the proposed SEZ:

Table 17.4: Estimated Project Cost

Sr. No.	Component	Amount ('in Million)
1.	Cost of Land	1.25
2.	Site and Infrastructure Development	180.00
3.	Built-up area	172.80
	Total	354.05

Source: NIDC, (2007), Project Report for setting up of Agro & food Processing Special Economic Zone at Dimapur in Nagaland.

The aforesaid projected cost mentioned in Table 17.4 is just a initial approximation and more accurate cost of development shall be worked out later on.

Funding Plan

The SEZ is conceived to be developed under the aegis of NIDC and NIDC would be accountable for its proper design, funding, planning, construction, marketing, maintenance, administration and management. Government of Nagaland has provided land on long term lease foundation to NIDC and NIDC would be developing the SEZ including the provision of the infrastructure and the creation of the uprights for the development of the SEZ.

To boost the developmental process if NIDC needs to have a private developer at any stage of the projects, the private sector developer and designer would be selected through a transparent & translucent, competitive and reasonable bidding process. At present the proposed funding plan is mooted as:

Table 17.5

Sr. No.	Particulars	Amount ('Million)
1.	Equity	100
2.	Debt	150
3.	Accruals/Lease Deposit	104.05
	Total	354.05

Source: NIDC, (2007), Project Report for setting up of Agro & food Processing Special Economic Zone at Dimapur in Nagaland.

Revenue Generation

The proposed SEZ project would be obtain a posy of upfront and annual revenue streams from sundry revenue sources such as:

(a) Lease Premimum and Rental as plotted land, flatted factories, residential properties, commercial properties.

(b) Income from Commercial ventures

(c) Revenue from specialised industrial facilities

(d) Operations revenue from Infrastructure facilities; and more suitable revenue generation model would be framed as per the requirement of time.

Appraisal of the SEZ of Ganeshnagar

Economic Appraisal:

The prime aim of India's SEZ policy is to obtain the forexthrough foreign trade. It is possible when the export will be enhanced. The SEZ of Ganeshnagar can boost it through its organic produce.

The SEZ would create huge employment avenue and opportunities as direct employment and adjuvant employment from units supplying to SEZ and booking orders from the SEZ. It is assumed that its cascading effect would generate direct employment and a significant number through back and forth linkages essential for industries installing units within the SEZ.

The SEZ Act has dispensed with the minimum 10 per cent forex value addition clause that was earlier germane to the conformist EPZ and 100 per cent EOU schemes. Though, presuming that the units across industries which were earlier installing within the EPZ/EOU units would now be setting up units in the SEZs on a green field basis. It is possible that 10 per cent netforex would be now accumulating from the units within the SEZ.

Its actual benefits would be visible in the long run when it will commence functioning in full swim. A few significant dimensions of the assistance of the SEZ as an economic growth model are talked about as follows:

Wealth Maximisation: SEZ policy hovers around two main principles namely, Trade Libralisation and Minimisation of transaction costs/ tariffs that otherwise apply in the domestic tariff zone.

Tariffs increase exorbitantly domestic prices and reduce consumption of goods from the natural equilibrium point to demand and supply. Tariffs also cause economic inefficiencies, especially by distorting the balance of market shares between international players and domestic suppliers. It decrease the overall value of goods in the hands of the consumer. Consequently, the economic loss to consumers is greater than the revenue earned by government plus the additional benefits gained by the producers.

Trade Liberalisation focuses towards local comparative advantages, with each player and country pondering on what is completed and what is the finest way to adopt? In the wake of it, everyone is better off and obtaining profit as per their capacity.

Total Factor Productivity: Generally developing countries thrive for suitable technology and know-how to give the boost in production sector and support innovation in industrial and service activities. The SEZ structure opens huge possibilities in this regard by minimising the risks of ownership of intellectual property and complete control on business assets. It paves the way to flow the adequate capital over and above technology while applying nativelabour skills and step by step modernising the technological productivity. Ultimately, SEZ area becomes the outgrowth of skilled and unskilled labour, network of complementary suppliers and service providers and a critical mass of customers for a wide range of products. The SEZ of Ganeshnagar will provide the ample of opportunities for Dimapur and its vicinity to expand its economic choices while connecting with the world economy.

Environmental Appraisal

There is no environmental threats from this SEZ as it is obvious from the notification of the MoEF vide 14th September 2006 that clearance from

MoEF is not required for setting up of the Agro and Food Processing SEZ. Environmental Clearance required for installing specific units within the premises of the SEZ would be obtain by the respective promoters of those units from the state pollution control board or MoEF.

Social Appraisal

The establishment of Agro and Food processing SEZ in Ganeshnagar will have a catalysing impact on the socio- economic, political and Cultural Revolution of the locality. The land use pattern will endure a prominent modification and there along, the economic sources, means of livelihood,community life and traditional way of living will also undergo a transformation. It is assumed that the following positive impacts are likely to happen.

During the construction phase, there will belabour intensive work opportunities. Once the zone will be completed white collar jobs will surpass the blue collar jobs and the scope of self employment, trade and commerce will be more. As it is said that self employment is the best employment, SEZ provides this opportunities to the native.

SEZ will develop the rurban and outgrowth in that region which will create the adequate demand of agricultural products. It might provide opportunity to native artisans to diversify and commercialise their agricultural production to cater to the production of the region. There is a scope for animal husbandry, to fulfill the growing demands of dairy products and other products namely, poultry, fisheries, etc., from the population of the region and new schools, hospitals, colleges and other institutions to foster the need of the people of that locality (rurban and outgrowth).

The rapid development of various infrastructure facilities including smooth communication and transportation facilities is expected to boost the local economy. The local population is expected to have its own share in such developmental activities. Besides, the service organisations, commercial institutions (bank, market, hospital etc.)will have their own impact on local population.

To sum up: SEZ of Dimapur alone cannot transform the entire region and become the engine of growth. Therefore, there is a need to bring about a balance between SEZ and non-SEZ units and thus, rationalization of incentives and tax concessions has to be undertaken, rather than tilting the balance only in favour of SEZ units of Dimapur. If it happens, definitely this SEZ can bring the tremendous change in food processing industries and becomes the catalyst for the region and nation too.

REFERENCES

Datt, Rudra and K.P.M. Sundhram, (2007), Indian Economy, S.Chand & Company Ltd., New Delhi, 56th Revisied Two Colour Edition., pp. 788-794.

Dhingra, Ishwar C., (2006), The Indian Economy Environment & Policy, Sultan Chand & Sons, New Delhi, pp. 525-526.

Economic Times, (2009), Nagaland to get First SEZ in North East, 24.07.09.

Encarta ® World English Dictionary © & (P) 1998-2005 Microsoft Corporation.

Encyclopaedia Britannica, (2003), The New Encyclopaedia Britannica, Micropaedia, Vol. 11, Edition 15, Encyclopaedia Britannica, Inc. London, p. 75.

—The New Encyclopaedia Britannica, Micropaedia,Vol. 4, Edition 15, Encyclopaedia Britannica, Inc. London, pp. 869-70.

—The New Encyclopaedia Britannica, Macropaedia, Vol. 19, Edition 15, Encyclopaedia Britannica, Inc. London, pp. 339 & 371.

Government of India, (2011), Economic Survey 2010-11, New Delhi, pp. 176-78, 216.

Govt. of Nagaland, (2010), 2 Years of Dan's 2nd Ministry A Record of Achievements.

Govt. of Nagaland, Year of the Entrepreneur 2010-11, Guide to Enterprise Promotion, Deptt. of Industries and Commerce.

NIDC, (2010), Naturally Nagaland, Agro & Food Processing Special Economic Zone.

—(2007), Project Report for Setting up of Agro & Food Processing Special Economic Zone at Dimapur in Nagaland.

Webster's Comprehensive Dictionary, (2003), The New International Webster's Comprehensive Dictionary of the English Language, Encyclopedic Edition, Trident Press International, Naples Florida.

Shrinking Livelihoods
A Case of a Tribal Group in Kerala

Mr. Vineeth Sahadevan

ABSTRACT

Bamboo as an eco-friendly raw material capable of meeting multifarious needs of the people at large is gaining global acceptance now a days. The raw material which known as the *"poor man's timber"*, bamboo is currently elevated to the status of *"the timber of the 21st century"*. India has the largest area under bamboo which is estimated around 9.6 million hectares. It is estimated that 8 million bamboo artisans are depended on this craft for their livelihood. This craft has been practiced by the North Eastern States for centuries as their prime source of income and, in the process; the weaving skills of the artisans had evolved to levels comparable with the craftsperson from more affluent societies like Japan, China etc.

Bamboos were found abundant in the forest and home gardens in Kerala. Bamboo is a source of income of the Paraya community in Kerala, who belongs to the Scheduled caste, is considered to be the subsistence crop. The present paper focuses on traditional occupation of Parayans and the role played by the state for a sustainable livelihood of the community.

Introduction

In every community there is a set of institutionalized activities which combine natural resources, human labour and technology to acquire, produce and distribute material goods. There are wide varieties of cultural arrangements with an economic system. They live according to the values and norms that have grown among members through time. These norms, values and procedures became embedded in the social structure of the community and helped its members to manage the natural resources on a sustainable basis. Environment plays an important role in the formation and development of society and culture. In order to fulfill the needs people exert power on the nature. Every community has their own developing mechanism of managing natural resources to meet their needs and greed and they inhabit definite geographical area. To maintain the livelihood, the community has directly utilized the natural environment. The Parayans of Kerala are such community still depending on natural resources particularly the bamboo for their livelihood.

The Scheduled Castes and Scheduled Tribes of India have remained socially, economically, educationally and politically backward. There is a close relationship between caste and occupation. The caste system has not allowed weaker sections to shift more productive occupations. There has been a growing tempo of developmental activities for them to facilitate their mobility. The Parayan (the Scheduled Caste) are also known as Sambavar. Parayans are mainly found in Tamil Nadu and Kerala. They are divided into different categories such as Payyorma Paryan, Parambu Parayam, Thekkan Parayan, Pula Parayan. The place of origin of Parayans was Balussery and Ulleri regions of Calicut district. The word 'Parayan' is derived from *'para'*, which means 'drum'. The delight in drum beating, and are thus generally called Paraya. About the origin of Parayans, is that they belong to a particular vamsam (lineage) and are descendents of the Nambuthiri Brahmins. This get further support from the account given by Thurston (1975): 'A legend runs to the effect that Vararuchi, the famous astrologer, and son of a Brahmin named Chandragupta by his Brahmin wife, became the king of Avanthi, and ruled till Vikramaditya, the son of Chandragupta by his wife, came of age, when he abdicated in his favors. Once, he was resting under an *ashwastha tree* (Ficus religiosa), invoking the support deity living therein, he overheard the conversation of two *Gandarvas* on the tree, to the effect that he would marry a Paraya girl. He tried to prevent this by requesting the king to enclose the girl in a box, and float it down a river with a nail stuck into her head. Though this was done, Vararuchi finally did marry the Paraya girl without knowing their identity. When he realised the truth, he resolved to go on pilgrimage with his wife, bathing in rivers, worshipping at temples. At last, they came to Kerala, where the women bore his twelve sons, all of whom, except one, were taken care of by members of different castes. One of them was Pakkanar, who is believed to be the ancestor of the Parayan. (Singh, 2002)

Occupation of Parayans

Basketry was the traditional occupation of the Parayans. Reeds and bamboos are the main raw materials used for the manufacture of the basketry items. The local communities especially the Parayans have been making bamboo/reed products for themselves and for the sale in the local market. Earlier the Parayans collected these materials from the forest where it was in plenty. There is no restriction on its collection; later the state Government has imposed restrictions in the cut and removal of the bamboos. They make different type of baskets which includes winnower (*muram*), different types of mats and other household items. In addition to the Parayans and the members of the Pulaya is the another community (Scheduled castes) who are engaged in making the bamboo products.

The manufacture of different product from the bamboos and reeds is an excellent manufacture. The product will look as if it may make of machine even though they are handicrafts. Reeds are soaked in water and then dried so as to make clean and soft, with the help of sharp knife, the reed smoothened and split into long pieces. The long pieces are then cut uniformly for certain length. Reed splits are then arranged or knitted on the ground cross- wise in such a way that the centre of all the splits passes across one another.

Bamboo Production

Bamboo is an important commodity at many different levels of global economy, right from the bottom of sheer subsistence use by forest-dwellers in several countries to being chosen by the global Common Fund for Commodities (CFC) for a grant of USD2 million aimed at improvement of resource base, quality, durability and market opportunities in two least developed countries (LDCs) (CFC 2004) (CFC, Common Fund for Commodities, *http://www.common-fund.org as viewed on 18 February 2004*). Bamboo has been widely used for traditional purposes. It is a source of income to resource extractors and farming community people who often have very limited opportunities to earn other cash incomes. The causative factors behind the decimation of the bamboo resource base and the consequent destruction of the livelihood of millions of people associated with bamboo have been many and interrelated. Subsistence activities by local people aimed at meeting their basic survival needs for biomass, water, food and raw materials for value addition also have been regarded as inflicting harmful impacts on the forests, though the extent of damage caused by them remains debatable. Bamboos being primarily a forest resource are mostly owned by central and state Government.

For many centuries, bamboo had been a readily available resource that met various requirements of the economically weaker sections of the society especially, the Parayans. The local communities have been making the same type of bamboo/reed products for a long time. The winnower (*muram*), and basket were the major products made of bamboos. There are two different types of winnowers — one-cornered and two-cornered winnowers. It is mainly used for separating husk and dust from the grains. These products were in demand in the village and the nearby towns, but the demand was highly seasonal. *Korambakkuda* and *Marakkuda,* two types of umbrellas made out of bamboo leaves and reeds were also used traditionally by the communities while working on the fields to protect the body from sunlight and rains. However, of late, plastic sheets have largely replaced the use of the *Korambakkuda.* The Paraya community members in the village who were earlier weaving mats have almost stopped doing this due to difficulties in getting adequate quantity and quality of reeds and the penetration of cheaper mats from local markets. Even though the plastic winnowers are available in market, the demand for the winnowers made of bamboos does not have any set back in the local market.

Distribution of Bamboo and Reeds through Kerala State Bamboo Corporation (KSBC)

Kerala State Bamboo Corporation (KSBC) was set up on 13 March 1971 with the objective of supporting the traditional bamboo and reed weavers in Kerala and gets rid of the middlemen in the sector who exploited the weavers. Ensuring cheap and adequate supply of raw material to the weavers was one of the prime objectives of setting up KSBC. To this end, an agreement was signed between the corporation and the Government in 1977. The organized traditional reed weaving activities carried out under the Kerala State Bamboo Corporation is concentrated in the Angamaly-Kalady region of Ernakulam district and the Nedumangad-Aryanad region of Thiruvananthapuram district.

A large number of cooperative societies were formed in the bamboo sector during 1960s.Around 40 cooperative societies with total membership strength of around 5,000 bamboo/reed artisans existed in the 1980s [(Nair and Muraleedharan 1983) Muraleedharan, P.K and Rugmini, P, 1988]. A majority of members of these societies belonged to Scheduled Caste communities traditionally dependent on mat and basket production. These cooperative societies organized on the principles of self-help and mutual help, thus cooperative societies have not been successful in ensuring adequate distribution of raw materials to bamboo artisans. Within the hierarchy of bamboo user-groups in Kerala, the position of the unorganized bamboo/ reed artisans is at the lowest rung socially, economically and politically with regard to rights over resources. The majority of such artisans belong to the Sambhava (Paraya) community, downtrodden castes in the Hindu caste system that has prevailed in Kerala to this day. By the term 'unorganised' what is meant here are the groups of bamboo/reed artisans who fall outside the KSBC supply chain. Even those artisans who obtain reed supplies through KSBC's reed distribution centres are also unorganized in all other aspects of production including technical, financial and marketing support.

Table 18.1: Distribution of Bamboo/Reed Craft Workers in Kerala

Sl. No.	Districts	No. of Panchayats in which Bamboo Craft Continued	No. of Panchayats in which Bamboo Craft Faced Crisis	No. of Panchayats where Bamboo Craft did not Exist/not Mentioned
1.	Thiruvananthapuram	12	13	53
2.	Kollam	15	11	44
3.	Pathanamthitta	33	2	19
4.	Alappuuzha	22	1	51
5.	Idukki	23	1	27
6.	Kottayam	33	1	24
7.	Ernakulam	35	14	25
8.	Thrissur	57	17	20
9.	Palakkad	53	15	2
10.	Malappuram	62	22	10
11.	Kozhikode	40	11	22
12.	Wayanad	8	11	5
13.	Kannur	23	21	38
14.	Kasaragod	9	15	13
	Total	425	155	353

Source: From 'Plan Reports' (*Vikasana Rekha*) of various LSGIs in Kerala.

The Bamboo Corporation's 13 Reed Distribution Centers (RDCs) are concentrated mostly in central and south Kerala and thus do not cater to a large proportion of traditional bamboo/reed artisans in the state. There are only three RDCs in north Kerala namely the ones at Perinthalmanna and Nilambur both in Malappuram district and Vadakara in Kozhikode district.

The study focus on the Paraya community of cherumala colony in Perambra Grama Panchayat, Kozhikode district. The colony consists of 35 houses which were constructed by the government. They mainly depend on bamboo for making baskets and winnower and it is considered as source of livelihood. The community's subsistence and way it organizes its consumption needs play an important role in social relationship. Occupation and caste are interlinked in the traditional social structure. As bamboo is a subsistence resource they prepare baskets, winnower, mat and umbrella. They were selling the products in nearby local market. It is a Sunday market, every Sunday they will sell their products in the market which is locally known as *chandha*. The Paraya women are engaged in selling the products in the market. The market plays a significant role in their socio- economic life of the Paraya community.

Since there was unscrupulous cut and removal of the bamboos from the forest and since the same will affect the ecological balance, the state Government has restricted the cut and removal of the bamboos by certain enactments. In order to help the community who are engaged in the manufacture of bamboo products for their livelihood, the state Government took initiative for the distribution of these resources through Kerala State Bamboo Corporation (KSBC).

The bamboos and reeds are distributing by the Kerala State Bamboo Corporation (KSBC) through it's the co-operative societies. These reeds are collecting from the Nilambur forest. In Kozhikode district there is one distribution centre which is situates in Vatakara. The said co-operative society was started in the year 1994. For getting the bamboo and reeds one should be a member of the society. Now there are 75 members. The materials will be distributed on every Thursday. A bundle of reed which will consist of 20 in numbers will cost rupees166 at present. Both the paraya and the Pulaya communities were collecting reeds in the distribution centre. The distribution is highly erratic in time and quantity allotted would be in proportion to the stock available with the corporation.

Conclusion

Now a days the members of the Paraya Community face various problems in the field of collection and marketing of the raw materials and the products respectively. Prior to the Governmental restrictions in the collection of bamboos and reeds from the forests, the members could have got their materials free of costs. After the restriction made through the enactments the members have to pay the price and the cost of transporting the same. Now they are compelled to sell their products at the production cost. They are also facing competition with product made of plastics in the market. Even though the raw materials are distributing through co-operative society of Kerala State Bamboo Corporation (KSBC), there is no statutory agency to help the marketing of bamboo products.

Therefore, the concerned authority has to take appropriate statutory measures for the marketing of the bamboo products and there by the upliftment of the community who are engaged in the production and marketing of bamboo products. The standard of living of the members of the Paraya community can be improved by way of giving subsidies to the raw materials (bamboos and reeds) and rebate to the products. Governmental action in this aspect is invited for the promotion of the standard of living of the paraya community and there by the advancement of an eco-friendly market. An action in this regard will be a step forward in the elimination of polluted plastic market.

REFERENCES

Barua, Indira and Anita Devi.2004. Women Market of Manipur: An Anthropo-historical Perspective. In Journal Human Ecology, Vol. 1512, New Delhi: Kamala Raj Enterprises.

C, Surendranath. 2004. Constraints in Sustainable Development: A Case Study of Intersectional Allocation of Bamboo and Reed Resource in Kerala. Trivandrum: Centre for Development Studies.

Gudeman, Stephen, 2001. *The Anthropology of Economy: Community, Market and Culture* USA: Blackwell Publishers Inc.

Muraleedharan, P.K and Rugmini, P. 1988. Problems and Prospects of Traditional Bamboo based Industry in Kerala, Proceeding of the International Bamboo Workshop, November.1988.

Nair, C.T.S.1986. Bamboo based Industry in Kerala State. Rom: FAO Forestry Paper.

Singh, K.S., 2002. People of India. New Delhi: East West Private Ltd.

Thurston, E., (1909) 1975. Castes and Tribes of Southern India. New Delhi: Cosmo Publications.

19

Pattern of Use of Training Programme for Human Resource Development by Non-Government Organizations in Nagaland, India

M.N. Odyuo, N.K. Patra, S. Das and L.Y. Longchar

ABSTRACT

Importance, potentiality and efficacy of training were established gigantic way during Second World War due to its success in military training. Later on the re-construction and rehabilitation work also achieved with the help of trained civil workers. The aim of the process is to develop in the organization's employees the knowledge, skills and attitudes that have been defined as necessary for the effective performance of their work and hence organizational aim and objectives by the most cost-effective means available. All over the country as well as in Nagaland Non Government Organization (NGOs) are running with insufficiency of fund except few reputed and high profile NGOs.

Introduction

Importance, potentiality and efficacy of training were established gigantic way during Second World War due to its success in military training. Later on the re-construction and rehabilitation work also achieved with the help of trained civil workers. However, remarkable inclusion of training as a prominent tool in development sector was came into reality slowly. According to Mishra (1990) the vital role of the training for human resource development was regarded worldwide and as the single most important resource for speedier socio-economic development being attempted in the developing countries.

Patra et. al. (2011), viewed that for any developmental work the first and foremost requirement is financial arrangement, and second important requirement is sufficient manpower for developmental work. In reality, all over the country as well as in Nagaland Non Government Organization (NGOs) are running with insufficiency of fund except few reputed and high profile NGOs. Financial status is directly related to staff strength and again staff strength is directly related to selection of extension activity. In other side, efficacy of the extension activity towards the implementation of the work is another technical consideration for selection of extension activity. When any organization is continuing in such a way i.e. lack of man power and insufficient financial arrangement, then that organization tries to adopt such type of extension activity where requirement of man power and involvement of fund is limited. In this juncture training is a unique extension activity where financial and manpower involvement is limited and effectiveness is up to the mark, because within low budget and less manpower it covers wide numbers of beneficiaries.

According to Khemmani (1983), training is a planned communication process which results in changes of attitudes, skills and/or knowledge in accordance with specified objectives relating to desired patterns of behaviour.

Tyson and York (1989), describe training in a work organization is essentially a learning process, in which learning opportunities are purposefully structured by the managerial, personnel and training staffs, working in collaboration, or by external agents, acting on their behalf. The aim of the process is to develop in the organization's employees the knowledge, skills and attitudes that have been defined as necessary for the effective performance of their work and hence organizational aim and objectives by the most cost-effective means available.

The training for development worker or extension worker can be described as organized, systematic and planned way of initiative to improve the knowledge level about the activity or technology, up-scaling of the existing skill to desirable skill and favourable attitude formation in the development personnel.

According to NSSO (2005), despite a large, well educated, well trained and well organized agricultural manpower, around 60 per cent of farmers in the country remain untouched. So, Government sector is unable to reach quantitatively to all the resource poor and backward people for upliftment of their existing condition.

As per Central Statistical Organisation survey (2009) in India, as on March, 2008 there were about 3,174,420 registered NPIs i.e., Non- profit organizations (broadly synonymous with Voluntary Organizations or NGOs) and in Nagaland, around 7330 NPIs were present and engaged for all round development of the society. To overcome the hindrances of development mainstreaming of all the NPIs / NGOs and Government - NGOs collaboration,

In development sector, Non-Government Organizations (the organizations which are outside the direct control of government agencies or autonomous bodies and are engaged in providing financial and non-financial services to the community are called Non-Government Organization or NGO) are playing major role since time immemorial. NGOs adopted various extension activities including training for staff and beneficiaries for the purpose of up-scaling of staff and all round development of beneficiaries. The present investigation aimed at identifying and measuring the extent of adoption of training by NGOs for staff and beneficiaries.

Materials and Methods

Nagaland State was inaugurated as the sixteenth State of India on 1st December, 1963. It is bounded by Assam in the West, Myanmar on the East, Arunachal Pradesh and part of Assam on the North and Manipur in the South. The State is lies between 25°60° and 27°40° latitude North of Equator and between the Longitudinal lines 93°20′E and 95°15′E and having an Geographical area of 16527 sq km (Govt. of Nagaland, 2006) and total population is 1,980,602 (as per 2011 census). Density of population is around 120 per sq km. Average annual rainfall ranges from 2000-3000 mm and temperature ranges from 4°C to 31°C. The topography of the state is undulating, full of hill range which breaks into wide chaos of spurs and ridges. The altitudes vary between 194 to 3840 meters above the mean sea level. The state has a beautiful landscape and it consists of 11 administrative districts viz., Kohima, Dimapur, Kipheri, Longleng, Mokokchung, Mon, Peren, Phek, Tuensang, Wokha and Zunheboto. Out of the total 11 districts, 6 districts have been selected purposively for the present study, namely, Dimapur, Kohima, Mokokchung, Peren, Tuensang and Wokha.

In this study 85 NGOs were identified by obtaining list from reliable sources. Out of the total identified NGOs, 45 NGOs were finally selected. From every selected NGO, one respondent from the higher level of employees and minimum one respondent from the lower level of employees were considered for this study. Higher level of employees of NGOs includes the top level of functionaries, like Director, Secretary, Topmost functionaries of sub-office of the large NGOs. A lower level employee of NGOs includes those which are not designed in higher level of position and directly involved in grass root level implementation work. Accordingly, 45 higher level of employees and 75 lower levels of employees were interviewed as the final respondents. The respondents were asked and facilitated by the researcher to inform the status and pattern of participation in training programmes during last one year (from the date of data collection) by them for up-scaling the skill and capacity to disseminate and implement the different development programmes more proper way. Simultaneously, they were also asked and facilitated to inform the numbers of training programme organized by them for beneficiaries. The collected information was analyzed and interpreted as per suitability.

Result and Discussion

The participation in training programme as a participant for skill up gradation and capacity building by respondents during last one year and training programme for the beneficiaries organized by the respondents were taken into consideration and analyzed.

Participation in Training Programme by NGOs Employees

Training has achieved wide acceptability to increase knowledge, upgrade skills and for persuasion of favourable attitude towards any work or development/extension work and it is widely accepted one of the important tool for speedier and sustainable all round development. In other words training is a bridging device in between present and desirable performance of the employees or workers. Chaturvedi (1979) broadly states that, training aims to maintain and increase the employee's effectiveness in his present job, prepare him for promotion by stimulating his potentials, and develop his skills and knowledge for greater organizational effectiveness.

Table 19.1: Participation in Training Programme by Higher Levels of Employees of NGOs

Participation in Training Programme	Total	%	Local	%	State	%	National	%	Inter-national	%
Not participated	8	17.77	6	22.22	1	8.33	1	33.33	0	0
Upto 3	7	15.55	6	22.22	1	8.33	0	0	0	0
Upto 6	13	28.88	4	14.81	6	50.00	1	33.33	2	66.66
Upto 10	8	17.77	6	22.22	1	8.33	0	0	1	33.33
Upto 15	3	6.66	2	7.40	0	0	1	33.33	0	0
Upto 20	1	2.22	1	3.70	0	0	0	0	0	0
Above 20	5	11.11	2	7.40	3	25.00	0	0	0	0
Total	45	100.00	27	100.00	12	100.00	3	100.00	3	100.00

Table 19.1 contains the information about the participation in training programme by higher level of employees of NGOs and shows that 18 per cent of higher levels of employees had not undergone any training programme during last one year where 16 per cent of employees attended upto 3 training programme. About 29 per cent of employees had participated training programme upto 6 times whereas another 18 per cent of higher levels of employees attended training programme upto 10 times. Table also shows that about 7 per cent, 2 per cent and 11 per cent of higher levels of employees of NGOs attended training programme upto 15 times, 20 times and more than 20 times respectively.

Further table shows that 22 per cent of employees of Local level of NGOs, 8 per cent of employees of State level of NGOs and 33 per cent of employees of National level of NGOs having no participation in any type of training programme whereas another 22 per cent of employees of Local level of NGOs and 8 per cent of employees of State level of NGOs participated training programme upto 3 times. According to the table, 15 per cent of Local level of NGOs' employees, 50 per cent of employees of State level of NGOs, 33 per cent of National level of NGOs' employees and 67 per cent of International level of NGOs' employees attended training upto 6 times. Table also shows that 22 per cent of employees of Local level, 8 per cent of State level and 33 per cent of employees of International level of NGOs attended upto 10 numbers of training during the last one year followed by 7 per cent of employees of Local level and 33 per cent of employees of National level of NGOs attended training upto 15 times during last one year. Table also shows that, about 4 per cent and 7 per cent of employees of Local level of NGOs attended training upto 20 times and more than 20 times respectively.

Table 19.2: Participation in Training Programme by Lower Levels of Employees of NGOs

Participation in Training Programme	Total	%	Local	%	State	%	National	%	Inter-national	%
Not participated	12	16	10	22.72	1	5.26	0	0	1	20
Upto 3	29	38.66	15	34.09	9	47.36	2	28.57	3	60
Upto 6	20	26.66	10	22.72	6	31.57	3	42.85	1	20
Upto 9	5	6.66	3	6.81	2	10.52	0	0	0	0
Upto 14	0	00	0	0	0	0	0	0	0	0
Upto 15	6	8.00	5	11.36	0		1	14.28	0	0
Above 15	3	4.00	1	2.27	1	5.26	1	14.28	0	0
Total	75	100.00	44	100.00	19	100.00	7	100.00	5	100

Table 19.2 contains the information about the participation in training programme by Lower level of employees of NGOs during the last one year and shows that 16 per cent of Lower levels of employees had not undergone any training programme during last one year where 39 per cent of employees attended upto 3 training programme. About 27 per cent of employees had participated training programme upto 6 times where another 7 per cent of Lower levels of employees attended training programme upto 9 times. Table also shows that about 8 per cent and 4 per cent of Lower levels of employees of NGOs attended training programme upto 15 times and above15 times of training respectively during the last one year period.

Further table shows that 23 per cent of Local level of NGOs' employees, 5 per cent of State level of NGOs' employees and 20 per cent of International level of NGOs' employees not participated any training programme where 34 per cent of Local level of NGOs' employees, 47 per cent of State level of

NGOs' employees, 29 per cent of National level of NGOs' employees and 60 per cent of International level of NGOs' employees participated training programme upto 3 times. According to the table, 23 per cent of Local level of NGOs' employees, 32 per cent of employees of State level of NGOs, 43 per cent of National level of NGOs' employees and 20 per cent of International level of NGOs' employees attended training upto 6 times. Table also shows that 7 per cent of employees of Local level and 11 per cent of State level of NGOs' employees attended training programme upto 9 times. Table also shows that 11 per cent of local levels of NGOs' and 14 per cent of employees of National level of NGOs attended upto 15 training during the last one year. Followed by, 2 per cent of employees of Local level and 5 per cent of employees of State level and 14 per cent of National level of NGOs attended training above 15 times during the last one year of period.

Training Organized by the Employees of NGOs for the Beneficiaries

Training is one of the most important extension tool to skill up-gradation and capacity building of the target people which directly related to human resource development and capitalization of human resources for national growth. In Nagaland, maximum NGOs are working for weaker section and/or backward people of both rural and urban areas of Nagaland. These peoples having relatively low level of understanding, poor educational background, non accessibility of every day modernization of outer world and slower rate of adoption of innovation. According to Patra et al. (2011) out of 5 extension activities "training" has the highest scale value and considered as the first and most important extension activity which perceived by the employees of NGOs of Nagaland, India and which is most widely accepted tools or extension activity throughout the world for implementation of all types of developmental work.

In this respect researcher tried to explore the extend of organizing training programme by the employees of the NGOs for the beneficiaries with reference to higher and lower levels of employees separately.

Table 19.3 contains the information about training programme organized by the higher level of employees of NGOs for their beneficiaries. Table shows that around 84 per cent of higher level of employees of NGOs had organized training programme for beneficiaries during last one year whereas remaining 16 per cent of employees did not conduct any training programme during last one year. Table clearly shows that 16 per cent of employees had conducted training programme upto 3 only for the beneficiaries during the last one year whereas another 20 per cent and 22 per cent of employees conducted upto 6 and upto10 numbers of training programme respectively during the same period. Table also shows that a considerable percentage i.e. the 11 per cent of employees conducted training programme upto 15 numbers and another 4 per cent of employees conducted upto 20 numbers of training programme and the remaining 11 per cent conducted training programme more than 20 numbers during the last one year for their beneficiaries.

Table 19.3: Organized Training Programmes for Beneficiaries by Higher Levels of Employees of NGOs

Organized Training Programme for Beneficiaries	Total	%	Local	%	State	%	National	%	Inter-national	%
Not Organized	7	15.55	4	14.81	2	16.66	1	33.33	0	0
Upto 3	7	15.55	5	18.51	1	8.33	0	0	2	66.66
Upto 6	9	20.00	6	22.22	2	16.66	1	33.33	0	0
Upto 10	10	22.22	5	18.51	4	33.33	0	0	1	33.33
Upto 15	5	11.11	3	11.11	1	8.33	1	33.33	0	0
Upto 20	1	4.44	0	0	1	8.33	0	0	0	0
Above 20	5	11.11	4	14.81	1	8.33	0	0	0	0
Total	44	100.00	27	100.00	12	100.00	3	100.00	3	100

Taking into consideration the status of the NGOs, 15 per cent, 16 per cent and 33 per cent of higher level employees of NGOs from Local level, State level and National level of NGOs did not conduct any training programme during the period of last one year. In case of higher level of employees of International level of NGOs, cent per cent of employees organized training programme, where 67 per cent and 33 per cent of them organized training upto 6 and upto 10 numbers respectively for their beneficiaries. Apart from the employees of International level of NGOs, pattern of conducting training programme for the beneficiaries were relatively similar with total NGOs' employees performance.

Table 19.4 contains the information about training programme organized by the lower level of employees of NGOs for their beneficiaries. Table shows that 32 per cent of lower levels of employees of NGOs did not organize any training programmes for beneficiaries during last one year, whereas remaining 68 per cent of employees conducted training programmes during last one year. Table clearly shows that 31 per cent of employees conducted training programmes upto 3 only for the beneficiaries during the last one year whereas another 13 per cent and 16 per cent of employees conducted upto 6 and upto10 numbers of training programme respectively during the same period. Table also shows that a considerable percentage i.e. 5 per cent of employees conducted training programme upto 15 numbers, whereas 1 per cent each of employees conducted training programme upto 20 numbers and more than 20 numbers separately during the last one year of period for their beneficiaries.

Table 19.4: Organized Training Programmes for Beneficiaries by Lower Levels of Employees of NGOs

Organized Training Programme for Beneficiaries	Total	%	Local	%	State	%	National	%	Inter-national	%
Not Organized	24	32	16	36.36	5	26.31	1	14.28	2	40
Upto 3	23	30.66	10	22.72	9	47.36	2	28.57	2	40
Upto 6	10	13.33	6	13.63	2	10.52	2	28.57	0	0
Upto 10	12	16	8	18.18	3	15.78	1	14.28	0	0
Upto 15	4	5.33	4	9.09	0	0	0	0	0	0
Upto 20	1	1.33	0	0	0	0	0	0	1	20
Above 20	1	1.33	0	0	0	0	1	14.28	0	0
Total	75	100.00	44	100.00	19	100.00	7	100.00	5	100

Taking into consideration of the status of the NGOs, 36 per cent, 26 per cent and 14 per cent and 40 per cent of lower level of employees of NGOs from Local level, State level, National level and International Levels of NGOs did not conduct any training programmes during the period of last one year. In case of lower level of employees of International level of NGOs, 40 per cent of employees organized training programme upto 3 numbers whereas remaining 20 per cent of them organized training upto 20 numbers for their beneficiaries. Further table shows that 23 per cent of employees of local level of NGOs, 47 per cent of State level of NGOs and 29 per cent of National level of NGOs' lower level of employees conducted training programmes upto 3 times. It is clear from the table that 14 per cent, 18 per cent and 9 per cent of lower level of employees of local level of NGOs conducted training programmes upto 6, upto 10 and upto 15 numbers of trainings respectively during the last one year of period. Whereas 11 per cent and 16 per cent of employees of State levels of NGOs conducted training for the beneficiaries upto 6 and upto 10 times respectively during the said period of time. Table also shows that 29 per cent of employees of National level of NGOs conducted training upto 6 times and 14 per cent each of employees conducted training for beneficiaries upto 10 times and above 20 times respectively during the considerable period.

Conclusion

A considerable numbers of employees from higher and lower levels of NGOs had not undergone any training programme and at the same time they did not conduct any training programme for their beneficiaries also during study period. To convince and to lead the people, maintaining up to date knowledge base is very much essential, and similarly, performing as a trainer also gave an opportunity to learn the real problem of the target group.

So, conducting training for beneficiaries and participation in training programme by the employees irrespective of their status are most important alternatives for maintaining up to date knowledge base of the functionaries and quick implementation of development works. So, such type of organizations may take initiative accordingly for faster and quicker development.

REFERENCES

Census of India 2011a, "Rural Urban Distribution of Population (Provisional Population Totals)", *http://censusindia.gov.in/2011-prov-results/paper2/data_files/india/Rural_Urban_2011.pdf*

Central Statistical Organization (2009), "Compilation of Accounts for Non Profit Institutions in India in the Framework of System of National Account (Report of Phase-1 Survey)". National Accounts Division, Central Statistical Organization, Ministry of Statistics and Programme Implementation, Government of India.

Chaturvedi, T.N. (1979), Institution Building for Training, in Mathur et al. (Eds.) (1979) (q.v.), Chapter 12, pp. 141-150.

Govt. of Nagaland (2006) *'Nagaland'* Department of Tourism, Government of Nagaland, Kohima, Nagaland, India.

Khemmani, M. (1983), "Turning Thoughts Towards Training", Manila, Philippines, Asia and Pacific Programme for Development Training and Communication Planning (DTCP), United Nations Development Programme. Training Tips No. 1, Editor: Andrew P. Bartlett. TT 601.

Mishra, D.C (1990), "New Direction in Extension Training: A Conceptual Framework" Directorate of Extension, Ministry of Agriculture, West Block 8, R.K. Puram, New Delhi - 110 066.

National Sample Survey Organization (2005), "Situational Assessment Survey of Farmers: Access to Modern Technology of Farming", Report No. 499(59/33/2), NSSO, Ministry of Statistics and Programme Implementation, GOI, New Delhi.

Patra N.K., M.N. Odyuo, Sagar Mondal and A.K. Makar (2011) "Prioritization of Extension Activities for Development Work by the Non-Governmental Organization in Nagaland, India," SAJOSPS, Vol. 12, No. 1, July-Dec, pp. 44-47.

Tyson Shaun and Alferd York (1989), "Pernnel Management, made Simple, Oxford, England, Made Simple Books, An Imprint of Heinemann Professional Publishing Ltd., Second Edition. First Published, 1982.

Urbanization and its Impact on Youths
A Study of Shillong City

Dr. Surojit Sen Gupta

ABSTRACT

The term 'urban area' is used in two senses – demographically and sociologically. Sociologists do not attach much importance to the size of population while defining city because the minimum population standards vary greatly. As such, they give more importance to characteristics other than the population size. The urbanization process is often accompanied with the movement of people from rural areas in search of non-agricultural employment in urban centers. Such a movement of people from village to city affects both the migrants and their families in an urban environment as well as the villages that they had migrated.

Introduction

What is an 'urban area' or a city or a town? This term is used in two senses – demographically and sociologically. In the former sense, emphasis is given to the size of population, density of population and nature of work of the majority of the adult males; while in the latter sense, the focus is on heterogeneity, impersonality, interdependence, and the quality of life. The German sociologist, Tonnies (1957) differentiated between rural and urban communities in terms of social relationships and values. The rural *gemeinschaft* community is one in which social bonds are based on close personal ties of kinship and friendship, and the emphasis is on tradition, consensus and informality, while the urban *gesellschaft* society is one in which impersonal and secondary relationships predominate and the interaction of people is formal, contractual and dependent on the special function or service they perform. The emphasis on *gesellschaft* society is on utilitarian goals and competitive nature of social relationships. Other sociologists like Max Weber (1961) and Geroge Simmel (1950) have stressed on dense living conditions, rapidity of change and impersonal interaction in urban setting. Louis Wirth (1938) has said that for sociological purposes a city may be defined as 'a relatively large, dense and permanent settlement of socially heterogeneous individuals'. Scholars like Ruth Glass (1956) have defined city in terms of factors like: size of population, density of population, main economic system, type of administration, and some social characteristics.

Sociologists do not attach much importance to the size of population in the definition of city because the minimum population standards vary greatly. As such, they give more importance to characteristics other than the population size.

Theodorson (1969) has defined 'urban community' as "a community with a high population density, a predominance of non-agricultural occupations, a high degree of specialization resulting in a complex division of labour, and a formalized system of local government. It is also characterized by a prevalence of impersonal secondary relations and dependence on formal social controls". According to Robert Rdfield (American Journal of Sociology, January 1942), 'urban society' is characterized by a large heterogeneous population, close contact with other societies (through trade, communication, etc.), a complex division of labour, a prevalence of secular over sacred concerns, and the desire to organize behaviour rationally toward given goals.

"Urbanization may be defined as a process of concentration of nonagricultural occupations and land uses around a single nucleus or multiple nuclei" (Rao, Prakesha. V.L and Tiwari, V.K., 1986). The settlements thus emerging create a distinctive physical and social environment, different from the adjoining regions. It provides contrasts in terms of occupations, socio-economic value systems, way of life, degree of socio-economic awakening and level of social and economic interaction (Chandna and Sidhu., 1980). The urban centres are also characterized by the concentration of socio-economic and political power and tend to influence the 'whole socio-economic milieu of the area'. The urbanization process is often accompanied with the movement of people from rural areas in search of non-agricultural employment in urban centres. Such a movement of people from village to city affects both the migrants and their families in an urban environment as well as the villages that they had migrated.

The study of the processes of urbanization and urban growth thus, is primarily concerned with the recognition and analysis of the basic economic and sociological factors that are responsible for the physical growth of a settlement to an urban centre. Urbanisation as Berry (1962) suggests, therefore, is essential associated with the economic development and diversification of occupations caused by the 'movement of people out of agricultural communities into other and generally larger non-agricultural communities' (Carter: 1982).

The dynamics of urbanization is complex one. The natural increase in the existing urban population add to the total number of people on the one hand while, on the other the migrants from adjoining regions tend to enter the urban space already crowded. Migration of people from rural to urban areas is guided both by push factors in the adjoining regions and pull factors operating in the urban centres. Thus, one significant aspect of urbanization pertains to the migration of people from rural areas leading to the process of change in values, attitudes and styles of those people migrate to cities and towns from villages. Philip M. Hauser (1965) in his "Review of Urbanization" observes that the "Urbanization in the developing regions of the world provides an opportunity for significant research which not only may help to explain the process and consequences in specific under developed regions but also may shed light on the antecedents and consequences in the west". The process of urbanization in India has been studied by scholars of different disciplines like anthropology, geography, sociology, history, economics, demography, political science and town planning. While reviewing the available literature on urban India,Victor D' Souza (1974) arrives at the conclusion, "... that the treatment is mostly descriptive and studies by Indian sociologist are conspicuous by their virtual absence". This observation seems to be valid even today.

Although the studies pertaining to urbanization have increased tremendously in the recent past, yet not much attention has been paid to the analysis of the factors that promote the process of urbanization. Urbanization has been increasing ever since the emergence of the first urban agglomerated settlement. Castells (1977) rightly observes that the magnitude of urbanization is directly correlated with the rate of proliferation of urban functions, wherein, the role played by technology is undisputable. In the beginning, the urban places have limited functions and the urban culture remains confined to a few places. The advancement in science and technology results in the multiplications of functions of urban centres which leads to further diffusion of urban culture.

Urbanization as a Change Process

Urbanization is the function of socio-economic changes that take place through time. The determinants of urbanization can broadly be categorized into three categories of economic, social and demographic determinants. The economically rooted determinants are the type of economy, the degree of commercialization of agriculture, the extent of diversification of economy, the changing size of agricultural landholdings, the stage of economic advancement and the degree of development of means of transportation and communication. The social factors that determine the nature and magnitude of urbanization are the degree of socio-economic awakening, the social value system, the stage of technological advancement, the public policies and the governmental decisions. Among the demographic factors, the rate of population growth, magnitude of migration and pressure of population are significant.

Since the economic base of urban places is very much different from that of the countryside, the economic factors gain prominence among the determinants of nature and magnitude of urbanization. No wonder, the agrarian societies with a high incidence of subsistence economy, small and dwindling agricultural landholdings, primitive agricultural technology and very little diversification of economy display very low degree of urbanization where the urban places are small-sized, widely spaced administrative headquarters. On the contrary, the societies, which have an industrial base and where even the agricultural sector is highly mechanized, commercialized and scientifically rationalized, exhibit a high degree of urbanization with urban centres having a large size. Thus, the stage of economic advancement which is closely related with the stage of scientific and technological advancement is also a crucial determinant of degree of urbanization.

Development of means of transportation is also a vital factor in the urbanization. Much of the interaction envisaged in the processes of urbanization depends largely upon the degree of regional mobility. Even the processes of economic development are accelerated by the regional mobility. Generally, the incidence of regional mobility has a two way effect upon the process of urbanization. In the initial stages, the development of means of transportation and communication may break the rural isolation which may result into the increased urban concentration. At a later stage, the means of transportation and communication may help in accelerating commuting activity between cities and small towns as also between countryside and urban places. When the region gets highly urbanized, the means of transportation and communication may facilitate outward migration from large congested cities to the peripheral suburbs.

The degree of socio-economic awakening is the most important among these. This factor finds its expression through the desire for improving the living standards, the appreciation for the benefits of urban living, the changing value system and the breakup of the joint family system. The technological advancement works as a catalytic agent in this process of socio-economic awakening. The process of urbanization is also influenced greatly by the government policies and decisions.

The demographic factors like growth of population, the pressure of population upon agricultural resources and the migratory trends also play their role in determining the magnitude of urbanization. The five-staged model of urbanization process envisaged by Gibbs (1966) emphasizes the role of rate of natural increase and migration in determining the degree of urbanization. The regional differences in the rate of natural increase and the consequent migratory trends give a particular direction to the process of urbanization in any area. Above all, the role of increasing population upon the agricultural resource base in giving birth to urban settlement has been universally recognized. Thus, the nature and the magnitude of urbanization in any area is governed largely by the nature of its economy, social life and demographic character.

The changes occurring due to urbanization are not restricted to occupational and economic structures, but also have a considerable impact on the way of living, dress, manners, attitudes and values of the people. The Cultural dimension is covered under the concept of urbanism. There has been an increased tendency, among the Indian scholars to use this term as a synonym of 'urbanization', providing only a partial understanding of the phenomenon. Louis Wirth (1938) was probably the first to make a systematic and detailed analysis of 'urbanism' and 'urbanization' by considering the former as that complex of traits which makes up the characteristic mode of life in cities, and urbanization, as a process of development and extension of these factors. He explained the relationship between the two in the following way:

- "Urbanization no longer devotes merely the process by which persons are attracted to a place called the city and incorporate into its system of life. It refers also to that cumulative accentuation of the characteristics distinctive of the mode of life which is associated with the growth of cities and finally to the changes in the direction of modes of life recognized as urban which are apparent among people, whenever they may be, who have come under the spell of the influences which the city exerts by virtue of the power of its institutions and personalities, operating through the means of communication and transportation (Wirth, 1938).
- The degree of openness, which is direct outcome of the values of equality and rationality, can be measured through the changing basis of social networks in the city. The declining role of family, kinship and caste as the houses of social networks is also an indicator of the urban value system, based on a rational attitude, abandoning the superimposition of caste regulations. It also reflects an increased value for individuality, equality and secularism. The role of urbanization in transforming the basis of networks has been brilliantly brought out by K.N. Sharma (1975).

Defining Youth

Youth is a much debated term and there is no wide agreement on its meaning. It is no use going into the various meaning attached to the term by psychologists, educationists and physiologists. The major emphasis in psychology seems to be on regarding youth as a category of biological age with its characteristic drives and tendencies. The fact of biological age is, however, not ignored in the sociological definition of youth, but here age is viewed as sociological rather than biological category. Understood as a sociological category, age is a period of transition in the life of a man, transition from one stage of life to another. Specifically for sociologists youth stands for a collectivity belonging to a particular age group which marks the transition from childhood to adulthood. It is a period when one ceases to be a child but does not yet acquire the status of an adult. Hollingshead (1949) has remarked: "Sociologically adolescence is the period in the life of a person when the society in which he functions ceases to regard him (male of female) as a child and does not accord him full adult status, the role and functions. In terms of behaviour, it is defined by the roles the person is expected to play, is allowed to play, is forced to play or prohibited from playing by virtue of his status in society.The U.N. definition of youth covers the age group 15-24 both inclusive. In Indian census the age group 15-29 is taken to comprise youth population.

In order to safeguard the basic buoyancy of youth it is necessary to find out from time to time what they are thinking. It is only by learning more about the current youth psychology that the guardians of society can discharge their true obligations to the rising generation. Social surveys conducted into the affairs of youth have revealed their interesting notions and views about political, economic and social matters. Some of these show the contamination of their sources, the cynicism and skepticism which are rampant in the life outside. But the great majority of youth has been found to be of one mind in their total rejection of the many evils that surround us today.

The Youth Phase

From the sociological point of view, it is considered to be an unified and separately identifiable segment of life in so far as, in it the process of integrating into the essential membership roles of society starts and runs its course to the end. From this point of view, the youth phase has the function of further developing and expanding the elementary social skills and capabilities, acquired in childhood to the extent that the complex degrees of competence necessary to achieve adult status are adapted and acquired in the fields of school and vocation, interacting partnership, politics and ethics, culture and use of consumer goods.

In respect of access to position and privilege, the youth phase represents an age-group which, as compared with adulthood, is discriminated against and, as far as whole course of life is concerned, represents an underprivileged sector of it. The justification for this discrimination lies according to the predominant social definition, in the fact that young people have first to acquire skill and degrees to competence which are prerequisite if adult status is to be competently maintained. Youth is characterized by the step-by-step acquisition of rights in various areas of behaviour and the expectations, demands and duties connected with these rights.

The youth phase is a sector of life characterized by juxtaposition of two kinds of action demands: the dependent one related to childhood and the independent one related to adulthood. The transition from the youth phase is achieved only when, in all the relevant spheres of action, a complete or at least, an extensive degree of autonomy and personal responsibility in action is attained. As a rule, the decisive step towards adult status is taken only when, in the public sphere, the scholastic and the subsequent vocational training relationship are left behind and the young people proceed to the vocational and gainful sector; and again the 'private' sphere, only when the parent home is left and the foundation of firm partnership and a family has ensued. In the youth phase the decisive pre-programming of the reproduction of the social and economic structures of society is done immediately, after taking up a vocation, marriage or the establishment of a firm partnership can be seen as the second dominant event which noticeably marks the transition from youth to adulthood.

In the demarcation between children and adult, young people are those who with puberty have reached biological sexual maturity without having achieved by marriage and vocation the general rights and duties which enable and compel them to participate responsibly in the essential basic processes of the society. Youth must also be analyzed as a socially produced phenomenon, the outlines of which are determined by social pre-conceptions. Correspondingly, the end of the youth phase cannot be tied to a definite age/date and does not necessarily occur in a closed sequence.

Youth is a phase in life with its own quality of experience; at the same time it is a 'product' of society and its culture which can be determined by reason of its characteristic place value in human-life and its specific importance in the reproduction of society. Friebel (1983) aptly expresses this fact when he calls youth a phase of life necessary for personal development and social placement, made possible by social measures and necessitated by the structural problems of society.

The youth phase is to be regarded as neither a mere prolongation of the childhood phase, nor as a characteristic situation of transition to the adult phase. Undoubtedly, the basic patterns of personality are formed in childhood but, because of the radical changes, in the characteristics of the youth phase, there arises a different situation which considerably alters the previous patterns because they are fitted into a total structure which is qualitatively different. Undoubtedly, too, youth is characterized by having to acquire the capacities and skills which are typical and obviously necessary for the adult status which is to follow, but, because youth has to undergo its own processes of adapting and argument there can be no mechanical reproduction of social personalities from one generation to another.

City of Shillong

Shillong is the capital of Meghalaya at an altitude of 1561 meter above the mean sea level. On its west and south lies the Bangladesh plain, to the east the Barak valley and to the north the valley of the Brahmaputra (Assam plain). The region enjoys a sub-tropical monsoon climate. The amount of rainfall within the region varies, ranging from between an average 300 to 400 cm, annually. Despite its undulating topography, the rejuvenated parts of the plateau leads to quick soil formation combined with high average annual rainfall that permits thick and quick vegetal growth.

Shillong is situated in the East Khasi Hills District and is linked by National Highway No. 40 with the state capital of Assam at a distance of 103 km. In the past it was a few cluster of scattered hamlets under the jurisdiction of the Syiem of Mylliem. Since the year 1866, Shillong became the provisional headquarters of the Khasi and Jaintia Hill districts. Again in 1874, Shillong was made the capital of the Assam province. Between 1905 to 1912 Shillong was turned into summer capital of newly created province of Eastern Bengal and Assam. Since then Shillong had remained the capital of Assam. However, in 1972, Meghalaya attained its full statehood and Shillong became the capital of the state.

Shillong City is the regional headquarters of a number of Central government establishments, Army, Air Force, Assam Rifles, Border Security Force, various All India Surveys such as Anthropological, Botanical, Geological etc., North Eastern Hill University, North Eastern Council, various Scientific bodies like Atomic Energy Commission, Indian Council of Agricultural Research etc, all chose Shillong as their regional headquarters. These developments resulted in influx of a sizeable non-local migrants to the city.

During the last three decades or so the city has undergone a radical transformation from a hill resort to a multifunctional service centre, catering to a host of administrative and other service functions not only for the State but for the entire North East Region. From a small village in 1866 to a class-I city in 2001, the city has grown to cater to the needs of the state as an enclave of modernization in the midst of the rural-tribal hinterland that continued without any significant change. The modern transport network and expansion of the city infrastructure have influenced the tribal social order but only to a limited extent thereby giving rise to a dualistic economic organization.

With the increase in the population, urban expansion of Shillong has taken heavy toll on the forests. Many localities have come up in forest clearings and urban invasion has engulfed steep forested slopes.While city has outgrown to occupy isolated places, forest clearings and even steep slopes in all directions under increasing population pressure, open space, stream beds, and steep stream banks have been encroached upon within the central localities. Today Shillong is expanding at a very fast rate and taking within its ambits the peripheral areas.Thus, urbanization is spreading rapidly in Shillong and its population is becoming more cosmopolitan in nature which is not only affecting the social condition but the economic life style of the people. Due to its varied functions and high rate of urbanization the population of Shillong has increased at a rapid pace.

Objectives of the Study

The impact of urbanization on the youth today cannot be denied. Youth is the period of life which is considered as crucial and significant period of an individual's life. Youth is the period of rapid changes in the individual's physical, mental, moral, emotional, social and sexual aspects. In the present day scenario the process of globalization has been influencing in the urbanization process which has an impact on the youth of today.

Keeping the above conditions in mind, an attempt has been made to study the impact of urbanization on the youths of today in the city of Shillong, with the following objectives.

1. To examine the attitude of the youths in various societal issues.
2. To study the recreational facilities among the youths.
3. To investigate the impact of urbanization and the life style of the youths.

The data for the present study have been collected with the help of random sampling method from 87 youths from two urban localities i.e., Laban and Laithumkhrah of Municipal area of Shillong City. Questionnaires were circulated to more than 100 youths, but those that returned the duly filled in questionnaires were only 87.

Result and Discussion

The form of human life is determined by the environment where he lives. In relation to the environment, age has played a very vital role for the development of personality. An individual acquires experiences through the ages.

Out of the total 87 respondents, the majority of the respondents 49, that is 56.32 per cent falls in the age group between 21-23, 26 respondents, that is 29.88 per cent fall in the age group 18-20. Whereas 12 respondents, that is 13.79 per cent fall in the age group 24-26. Therefore, on the basis of the data it can be seen that majority of the youths come from the age group between 21-23.

Regarding the sex composition of the respondents, out of the total 87 respondents, 51 that is 58.62 per cent are males and 36 that is, 41.37 per cent are females. About the marital status of the respondents it is reported that all the respondents were unmarried.

The religious background of the respondents, shows that majority of the youths are Christians that is, 64.36 per cent. Hindus constituted 27.58 per cent, which is followed by Muslims 5.74 per cent. And a small section of 2.29 per cent constituted the Sikhs.

About the birth place of the respondents, it was found that, 87.35 per cent were born in the state of Meghalaya and 12.64 per cent have reported that they were born in states other than Meghalaya. In response to the information about whether their place of birth was rural or urban, it is seen that majority of them were born in urban areas which accounts for 89.65 per cent and the rest 10.34 per cent of them were born in rural areas.

The ethnic composition of the youths under study is that, a considerable number of them were Khasis 37.93 per cent. Next to them were the Bengalis 16.09 per cent, which is followed by 11.49 per cent of Nepalies and 10.34 per cent of Marwaries. Among the others which constituted less than 10 per cent includes, Mizo 9.19 per cent, Naga 6.89 per cent, Behari 5.74 per cent and Assamese 2.29 per cent.

As regard the family background of the respondents, it was found that 87.35 per cent comes from the nuclear family background and only 12.64 per cent come from the joint family system.

The educational status of the youths under study reveals that all of them are pursuing their studies in the colleges situated in the Shillong city. Regarding their stream of studies in the college, it is found that, majority of the respondents that is 59.77 per cent were from Arts stream. 31.03 per cent of the respondents were from science stream and 9.19 per cent were from commerce stream.

Further it was enquired from the respondents about their class of study in the college at the Three Year Degree Course, and to this, 42.52 per cent of the respondents were from Second year, which is followed by 36.78 per cent of the respondents from First year. And another 20.68 per cent of the respondents were from Third year.

With a view to understand the leisure time activities of the respondents, we enquired as to how they spent their leisure time. To this, it was found that, 44.82 per cent of the respondents spend their leisure time in internet surfing. 17.24 per cent preferred watching Television, which is followed by Games and Sports 12.64 per cent. Going to Cinema and Theater accounted for 14.94 per cent and another 10.34 per cent of the youths revealed that they spend their leisure hour by attending Clubs.

To understand the social circle of our respondents with people they most often met, it was found that 43.67 per cent of the respondents meet their friends, 31.03 per cent have reported that they meet their peer groups. Meeting the members of their own community and neighbours accounted for 13.79 per cent and 11.49 per cent. Thus, the youths under study meet limited groups of people in a closed circle.

It was interesting to know from the youths about their habit of prayers at home. To this, it was found that 67.81 per cent of the respondents do not have the regular habit of praying and only 32.18 per cent prays regularly. Similarly, it was interesting to know about their visit to the religious places. The answer to this by the respondents is that, 56.32 per cent visit occasionally. 29.88 per cent reported that they visit regularly and 13.79 per cent said that they do not visit at all in the religious places.

An enquiry was made to know from the respondents about their food habit, because food plays an important role in the individual's life. Thus, we enquired from our respondents about their choice of food habit. The responses received for this, is that, 55.17 per cent of the youths prefer modern food items such as, Pizza, Burger, Momo, Hot Dogs etc. 29.88 per cent of the respondents said that, they prefer both traditional and modern food items. And only 14.94 per cent have reported that they prefer only traditional food items.

Enquiring further from the respondents about their opinion on Dresses they prefer to wear, it was found that, 33.33 per cent of respondents prefer to wear the latest up to date fashionable dresses, which is followed by formal dresses 28.73 per cent. The respondents who prefer causal dresses accounted for 21.83 per cent. And only 14 respondents out of 87, that is, 16.09 per cent prefer the traditional costumes.

It was interesting to know from the respondents, whether they possess mobile phone or not. The answer in returns was that, 100 per cent of the respondents reported that they possess mobile phones. Further, it was asked whether they have 2G and 3G connection in their mobiles. To this, 49.42 per cent have said yes, that they have this facility in their mobile phone. Then again 79.31 per cent of the respondents have reported that they even have internet facility in their mobile phones.

Our curiosity was also to know from the respondents about their usages of modern gadget. Our query to this, shows that, 32.18 per cent of the respondents have got Bikes, followed by 25.28 per cent of the respondents with Laptops. 20.68 per cent and 16.09 per cent of the respondents reported that, they have in possession the Ipod and Tablet. And only 5 respondents out of 87, that is, 5.74 per cent constitutes for other things like Hair drier, Digital Camera, Video Games etc.

We were also interested to know from our respondents about their attitudes towards helping their parents in the family. The responses received was that, 44.82 per cent of the youths replied that they help sometime or occasionally. Respondents who always help accounted for 36.78 per cent. And another 18.39 per cent of the respondents have revealed that they do not help at all, as there is no need and they are engrossed with other things. We further enquired from the respondents, the extent of their service at the community level. Out of total 87 respondents, 3.78 per cent said that sometimes they extend their service. 24.13 per cent of respondents always extent their service for the community. Respondents who not at all come forward for the community service accounted for 20.68 per cent. Depending on the mood was another response by 18.39 per cent of the respondents.

Regarding the involvement of the youths is social function, the majority have reported for the Birthday Party which accounted for 48.27 per cent. This was followed by 22.98 per cent of the respondents for visiting any types of Fairs like Trade Fare, Industrial Fair, Book Fair etc. Attending any cultural events like Musical Show, Rock Concert etc was responded by 17.24 per cent. And 11.49 per cent of the respondents has accounted for Picnic, Outing etc.

It was interesting to know from our respondents about their educational aspirations after they complete their Graduation. For this, 36.78 per cent of the respondents have reported that, they would pursue professional education like M.B.A, Journalism, B. Ed, LL.B etc. 19.54 per cent of the youths would like to study upto the Post Graduation Level. This was followed by 16.09 per cent of the respondents who would like to continue their education beyond Post Graduation with Research Degree in the University. Respondents who do not want to continue their studies after Graduation accounted for 27.58 per cent.

Regarding the job aspiration or what they want to choose as their carrier, it was found that, 34.48 per cent of the respondents would like to join in the Corporate Sector. 21.83 per cent would prefer to join the Government Services. Teaching as a carrier was accounted by 16.09 per cent of the respondents, which is followed by Business 13.79 per cent of the respondents. The other responses were joining N.G.O's 8.04 per cent and joining Army/Defence by 5.74 per cent.

An enquiry made from the respondents regarding their attitude towards marriage. To this, 78.16 per cent of the respondents reported that they prefer love marriage and only 21.83 per cent reported for arranged marriage.

We also tried to find out from our respondents that, would they like to make new friends. In response to this, 100 per cent of the respondents are of the view to make new friends, as friendship broaden one's mind and breaks all the barriers. Further an enquiry was made from the respondents about their visit to Restaurants. To this also, 100 per cent of the respondents have replied that they visit Restaurants regularly for tasting the different food items and also it is good for them to discuss on various things/issues among the friends in the Restaurants.

The entertainment and relaxation are essential to life. The means of entertainment keeps changing with time and circumstances. In Shillong city there has been significant change in means of entertainment as a result of urbanization. By keeping this view, we enquired from the respondents who are the youths about their entertainment. In reply to this query, it was found that 41.37 per cent of the respondents prefer entertainment in the family. Respondents who prefered professional entertainment accounted for 33.33 per cent. And another 25.28 per cent of respondents said that they prefer entertainment outside the family.

Enquiring about the health consciousness of the respondents, it was found that 90.80 per cent of the respondents are consciousness about their health and only 9.19 per cent of the respondents have reported that they are not conscious about their health. Moving further it was found out that, 86.20 per cent of the respondents even visit Ladies and Men's Parlor on regular intervals for keeping themselves fit.

Advertisements are important today, as indicators of social and economic progress. The ever expanding markets for goods and their unchallenged assault through advertisements is flooding the society with information and ideas, attitudes and imagery which is difficult to control and assimilate. This is affecting the young minds to a great extent. Youth's are fascinated by advertisements. They react to these glamorous advertisements. Now a days Television advertising had entered into daily life of the youths.

Thus, we were interested to know from our respondents whether they are inflicted with the advertisements which are shown in the Television. The response to this, was that 86.20 per cent of the respondents admitted that they are inflicted by advertisements like Bikes, Mobile Phones, Cosmetics, Dress Materials, Soft Drinks, Chocolates etc. which are shown in the Television. Whereas 13.79 per cent of the respondents have responded that they are not inflicted by any advertisements.

To conclude, the study shows that urbanization changes the attitudes, beliefs, values and the behavior pattern of the youths in Shillong city, which in turn changes the life style of the youths. The impact of urbanization of the life of youth has been observed in many aspects such as education, recreation, behaviour pattern, attitudes etc. It was also observed that urbanization in Shillong has been creating an atmosphere which influences the psychology of the youths and also their behavior pattern.

REFERENCES

Bajpai, Pramod, K., 1992, Youth, Education and Unemployment, Ashish Publishing House, New Delhi.

Berry, B.J., 1962 'Some Relations of Urbanisation and Basic Patterns of Economic Development' in F.R.Pits (eds)., Urban Systems and Economic Development, Eugene, Orengan.

Castell, M., 1977, The Urban Question, Translated by Alan Sheridan, The MIT Press, Cambridge.

Chandna, R.C. and M. Sidhu, 1980, Introduction to Population Geography, Kalyani Publishing, Ludhiana.

Chandna, R.C., 1986, A Geography of Population, Kalyani Publishers, New Delhi.

D'Souza. V.S., 1974, 'Urban Studies: A Trend Report' In a Survey of Research in Sociology and Social Anthropology, Vol. 1, Popular Prakashan, Bombay.

Friedman, F.G., 1971, Youth and Society, MacMillan, London.

Gibbs, J.P., 1966, Measures of Urbanization, Social Forces, Vol. 45 (2).

Goswami, B.B., 1978,Caltural Profile of Shillong, Anthropological Survey of India, Calcutta.

Gunguly, J.B., 1995, Urbanization and Development in North-East India,Deep & Deep Publications, New Delhi.

Gupta, R.C., 1968, (ed)., Youth Ferment, Sterling Publications, New Delhi.

Hollingshead, August, 1949, Elmtown's Youth, John Willey and Sons, New York.

Houser, P.M., 1965, (eds)., The Study of Urbanization, New York.

Kulkarni, P.D., 1985, Youth and Development, University News, AIU Publication, New Delhi.

Mehta, Prayag, 1971 (ed)., The Indian Youth: Emerging Problems and Issues, Sommaiya Publications, Bombay.

Nair, P.S., 1989 (ed)., Indian Youth: A Profile, Mittal Publications, New Delhi.

Pakem,B., (ed)., 1984, Shillong: 1971-1981, Research India Publications, Calcutta.

Prakash, Rao, V.L.S. and V.K.Tiwari, 1986, 'Urbanization in India' In Urban Geography (ed)., P.D. Mahadev, Heritage Publications, New Delhi.

Rao, M.S.A., 1974, Urban Sociology in India, Orient Longman, New Delhi.

Redfield, R., 1941, The Folk Culture of Yucatan, University of Chicago Press.

Riessman,L., 1964, The Urban Process, New York.

Sandhu, R.S., 2003, Urbanization in India, Sociological Contributions, Sage, New Delhi.

Sarlkwal, R.C., 1978, Sociology of a Growing Town, Ajanta Publications, New Delhi.

Sen Gupta, Surojit, 2006, Urban Social Structure — A Study of A Hill City, Akansha Publishing House, New Delhi.

Simmel, G., 1950, The Metropolis and Mental Life, Free Press, New York.

Sinha A.C., 1993, (eds)., Hill Cities of Eastern Himalayas, Indus Publishing Company, New Delhi.

Sovani, N.V., 1966, Urbanization and Urban India, Asia Publishing House, New Delhi.

Tonnies, F., 1957, " Gemeinschaft and Gesellschaft", et al. (eds)., Theories of Society, Vol. 1, Free Press, New York.

Weber, Max, 1961, " The Urban Community", In Theories of Society, Vol. 1, Free Press, New York.

Wirth, L., 1938, Urbanism as a Way of Life, American Journal of Sociology, XLIV.

Toddler Anemia in Rural *A Challenging Threat to West Bengal*

Kaniska Sarkar

ABSTRACT

This study is based on the child anemia in rural areas of Wet Bengal. The main issue of the study is the problem of child anemia and the reason behind of it. This problem is very much related with excessive growth of population, mal-nutrition, scarcity of occupation, scarcity of opportunity for good agricultural facility, scarcity of business, and overall scarcity of financial growth. Weak source of income, lack of education and awareness, superstitions, is the main cause for the family planning problems which are the main reasons for child anemia. Present status of the problem and its effect on society will be discussed. Graphical presentation will be shown to clarify the nature of problems in the study area. The main part of this article shows how to fight against anemia to overcome from this big social barrier. So necessary remedy from the point of health awareness will also be discussed.

Introduction

Anemia is the principal nutritional dearth in the world and it especially affects children and pregnant women in developing countries. Nutritional Anemia according to the WHO is a state in which the hemoglobin concentration in the blood is lower than levels considered normal for the age, gender, physiological state and altitude, as a consequence of shortage of essential nutrients, independent of the cause of this deficiency. Nutritional anemia includes lack of nutrients such as iron, folic acid, vitamin B12 and copper, vitamin C and E and vitamin A. In West Bengal with more than 65 per cent of the population engaged in agriculture and allied sectors is primarily an agrarian state. Among the farmers more than 90 per cent are poor, small and marginal. It is also an accepted fact that in the state, the performance of the agriculture sector influences the growth of the economy. The prosperity of the rural economy is also closely linked to agriculture and allied activities. Slow growth in agriculture with no significant decline in labor force has created a serious disparity between agriculture and non-agriculture. In West Bengal, improving the viability of smaller farm holdings by providing access to technology, inputs and credit remain a big challenge. So it is very much clear that bad effect of toddler anemia in rural areas is not possible to protect very easily. Financial weakness, lack of education, lack of awareness is the main reason not to fight against anemia.

Methodology

Toddler anemia is very much related with social and economic factors. So methodology has been taken from the field of social science. Here data collection has been done through primary research to enable proper interpretation about the factors behind the anemia. The focus on the study is more pronounced due to the paucity of information about this social factor. Mainly two types of data are collected for the study (*i*) Primary data: Special concentration is given on field work which is conducted through questionnaire interview to the parents as well as the doctors of the toddler patient. (*ii*) Secondary data got from literature (reports), unpublished reports, conference abstracts, news paper articles, media coverage, information accessed through the internet, data from different offices, health centers, NGOs, Government departments and data of census.

Data Collection

Nutritional status and its prime determinants and risk factors are assessed from the data, collected in the household schedule. Assessment of vitamin deficiency is also done in the selected adolescents by investigators trained for this purpose. A Cross sectional study is conducted among a sample of effected children selected from the requisite number of villages from the selected Gram Panchayats in the selected blocks like Kalinagar Gram Panchayat in Sandeskhali –I of North 24 Parganas district, Bidhannagar Gram Panchayat in Matiali of Jalpaiguri district and Gangmuri Joypur Gram Panchayat in Rajnagar of Birbhum district.

Need of the Study

Anemia among the toddler is taking a big place which will be a threat to West Bengal. In our state child mortality is very high only for due to high spreading of anemia. Before discussing the need of the study on toddler anemia, we need to know about the anemia diseases. Anemia is usually diagnosed when Pediatrician does a routine blood test at a well child visit, usually at or before the nine month old checkup and again in adolescence. If this blood test is low, it may be told that child has a 'low iron level' or that 'his iron is low,' but that usually isn't totally accurate. What is usually being checked is child's hematocrit, which is low in children with anemia. If a CBC (complete blood count) was done, then there are other clues that would favor a diagnosis of having a low iron level, including having a low MCV (micro cytic anemia), which measures the size of the red blood cells, a high RDW (which measures the variability in the size and shape of red blood cells) and a low red blood cell (RBC) count. By checking the reticulocyte hemoglobin content, iron deficiency may also be diagnosed earlier. The reticulocyte hemoglobin count drops very early in iron deficiency, often before the child is even anemic. Another common cause of mild anemia in children, especially with a normal MCV and no other symptoms, is a recent infection, such as an ear or sinus infection, which can cause decreased production of red blood cells for a short period of time (usually about a month). The most common cause of iron deficiency is having a diet that doesn't have enough iron in it. This can be caused by using a low iron formula, not supplementing breast milk or formula with an iron fortified cereal, not eating foods that are rich in iron and most commonly, by drinking too much milk. Regular cow's milk does not contain very much iron in it and it can actually prevent the child from absorbing other sources of iron in his intestines. These features are very much common in children of West Bengal especially in rural areas. For example we can show the poor condition of anemia in three districts of West Bengal. Here selected rural areas of North 24 Parganas, Jalpaiguri and Birbhum are taken to show the condition of anemia. Comparing among these districts' scenario, whole West Bengal can also be measured. In this regard reason behind the toddler anemia in practical field and necessary preventive steps is highly required to find out.

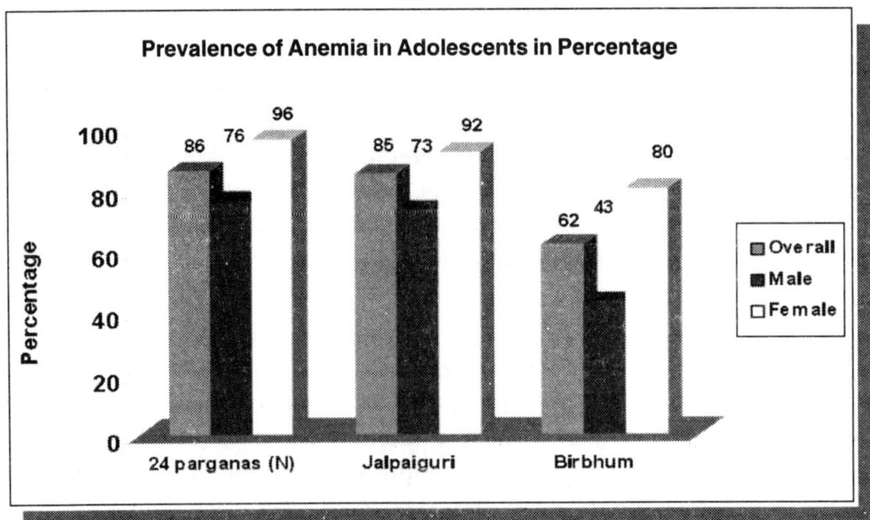

Fig. 21.1

Symptoms of Toddler Anemia

Iron deficiency anemia most commonly affects babies 9 to 24 months old. Different types of symptoms are found during anemic stages:

1. Easy fatigue and loss of energy
2. Unusually rapid heartbeat, particularly with exercise
3. Shortness of breath and headache, particularly with exercise
4. Difficulty concentrating in learning or others
5. Dizziness
6. Pale skin color (pallor)
7. Leg cramps
8. Insomnia
9. Blue-tinged or very pale whites of eyes
10. Blood in the stools
11. Brittle nails
12. Decreased appetite
13. A hunger for strange substances such as paper, ice, or dirt (a condition called pica)
14. Upward curvature of the nails, referred to as koilonychias
15. Soreness of the mouth with cracks at the corners

Nature of the Problem in West Bengal

To analyze the ration between effected and non-effected children, a few samples have been taken for testing. The below medical survey on effected rural children will show the present status of toddler anemia in West Bengal. Total of 437 pre-school children are covered for the estimation of blood hemoglobin levels. Results: A majority (81%) of the rural children of West Bengal are anemic, and the prevalence is significantly (p<0.001) higher among 1-3-year-old (91%) as compared to 4-5-year-old (74.6%) children. A significantly (p<0.01) higher proportion of 1+ and 2+ year children and those belonging to lower socio-economic Scheduled Caste and Scheduled Tribe communities are at risk for anemia.

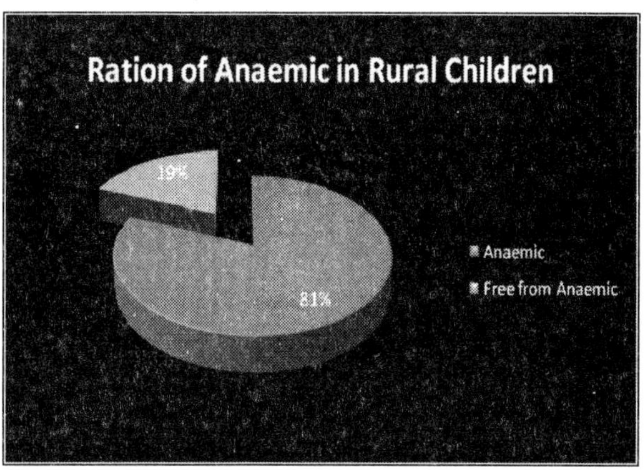

Fig. 21.2

Related Factors

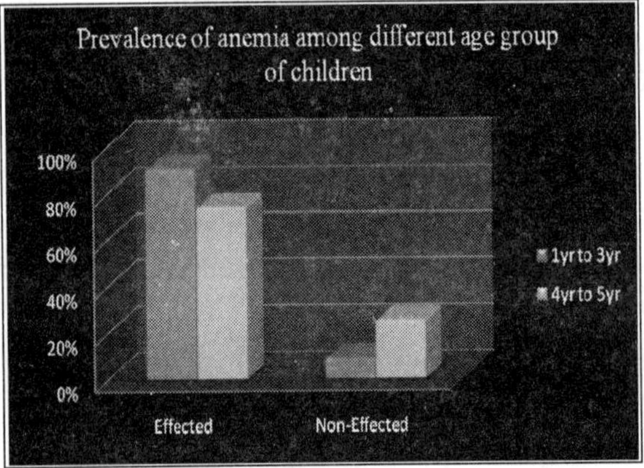

Fig. 21.3

The occurrence of anemia due to iron deficiency is the most common nutritional disorder in infancy, and it affects communities not only in developing nations but also in highly industrialized countries. The main factors involved for anemia in children are the iron reserved at birth, growth rate, diet and iron loss. In children, loss also occurs due to blood in the feces and by the use of whole milk in liquid form during the first year of life. Another possible cause of iron loss is the presence of intestinal parasites (round worm); although several studies have shown that the majority of parasitic diseases have secondary importance in the cause of iron deficiency anemia in under 5-year olds.

Food and Iron Absorption

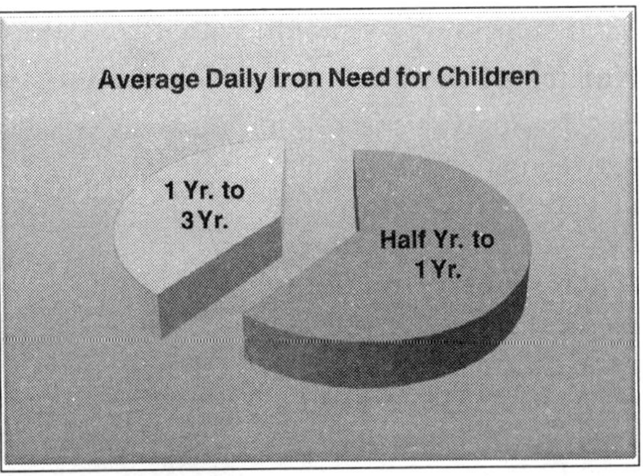

Fig. 21.4

The most significant weight gain and storage of iron by the fetus occurs during the last trimester of pregnancy. Premature births, intrauterine growth restriction and multiple pregnancies are factors that lead to iron deficiency anemia within the first six months of life, caused by low stocks of iron at birth. The average daily iron needs are from 0.72 mg to 0.46 mg for children from five months to one year old and from one to three years old, respectively. Among the iron absorption stimulation factors in the diet are citric fruits (oxalic acid). Among the iron absorption inhibitory factors are fibers, whole grains and beans (phytic acids), spinach and beetroot (oxalic acid), tea, coffee and chocolate (tannin). Calcium, which is present in milk and dairy products, and other minerals that are close to iron in the periodic table, which compete with the same intestinal absorption, also inhibits the absorption of iron. Hence there should be a gap of 4 hours between food containing iron and dietary supplement containing inhibitory factors. That is why citric fruits are advised to take after lunch that helps in early absorption of iron from diet. For full-term newborn babies, the iron deposits at birth provide the needs for this mineral until four to six months of age. In spite of the low iron content of human milk (0.26 to 0.73mg/L), the iron in mother's milk has high absorption (around 50%). Because of the greater physiological requirements within the first two years of life it is rare that the child will manage to ingest the recommended daily amount of iron. Thus, preventive iron supplements are usually necessary for this age group.

Method of Prevention and Conclusion

We all know that anemia is the Global health problem. Our study reveals that poor nutrition is the main cause of anemia. Apart from socio-economic barriers, lack of awareness also results in low-intake of nutrientrich natural food stuffs. It has been suggested that nutritional anemia can be improved by balanced diet selecting items from the locally available resources. In case of hereditary anaemias, it is advisable that carriers must be detected and individuals, who have family history of hereditary anaemias, their family and first degree relatives, should be screened. Everyone should know their carrier status of hereditary anemia (haemoglobinopathy) at least before marriage. If both husband and wife are carriers of any haemoglobinopathy, chance of the birth of an affected child is 25 per cent. Screening is essential to prevent the birth of affected child for hereditary anaemias. It is suggested that before marriage carrier status of hereditary anemia should be known and if possible individuals can marry with non-carriers. Babies are born with iron stored in their bodies. Because they grow rapidly, infants and children need to absorb an average of 1 mg. of iron per day.

Since children only absorb about 10 per cent of the iron they eat, most children need to receive 8-10 mg. of iron per day. Breastfed babies need less, because iron is absorbed 3 times better when it is in breast milk.

Cow's milk is a common cause of iron deficiency. It contains less iron than many other foods and also makes it more difficult for the body to absorb iron from other foods. Cow's milk also can cause the intestines to lose small amounts of blood. The American Academy of Pediatrics (AAP) recommends that all infants be fed breast milk or iron-fortified formula for at least 12 months. The AAP does not recommend giving cow's milk to children under 1 year old.

Anemia is a common but potentially serious illness. While some forms result from a genetic condition, the most common variety is caused by a lack of available iron in the diet. Women and athletes must be especially vigilant to prevent this condition, as prevention is easier than treatment. The following steps will help to prevent anemia.

STEP - 1

Determine if there is any risk by checking risk factors. Risk factors include:

1. A strenuous workout routine
2. A vegetarian diet (especially vegan)
3. Any other dieting
4. Inadequate vitamin C intake
5. Family history
6. Recent surgery
7. A serious injury

STEP - 2

Eat a diet rich in iron and vitamin C. Good sources of available iron include:

(a) Animal proteins (especially red meat)

(b) Beans, Spinach, Dark chocolate

STEP - 3

Avoid excessive dieting or over-exercising, which can trigger symptoms in someone who is already at risk.

STEP - 4

1. Exclusive breast feeding up to 12 months of age.
2. Fortification of cheap and easily available foods and the diversification of foods promoted by education programme by health organizations.
3. Supplementation with ferrous sulfate, either intermittently or weekly, is one short-term strategy that can be applied in wide-reaching programmes.
4. Food fortification should be utilized as a prophylactic measure, choosing specific foods regularly consumed by the population.
5. Domestic drinking water has also been used for fortification purposes, giving good results in children.
6. Dietary guidance is a strategy that should be simultaneously implemented with some other type of programme, with the aim of improving the bioavailability of iron.
7. To improve iron absorption, meat ingestion should be encouraged, instead of higher intake of iron containing plants, because it is rich in bioavailable iron, and/or vitamin C should be included when the diet offers low bioavailable iron.

REFERENCES

World Health Organization, Nutritional Anemia: Report of a WHO Scientific Group. Technical Report Series, No. 405, Geneva: WHO; 1968.

De, Maeyer EM, Dallman P, Gurney JM, Hallberg L, Sood SK, Srikanta SG. Preventing and Controlling Iron Deficiency Anemia Through Primary Health Care. A Guide for Health Administrators and Programme Managers. Geneva: WHO; 1989.

De, Morais MB, Suzuki HU, Corral JN, Machado NL, Neto UF, Asymptomatic Giardiasis does not Affect Iron Absorption in Children with Iron Deficiency Anemia. J. Am Coll Nutr. 1996; 15(5):434-8.

World Health Organization, United Nations Childrens' Fund, United Nations University, Indicators for Assessing Iron Deficiency and Strategies for its Prevention (draft based on a WHO/UNICEF/UNU Consultation, 6-10 December 1993). Geneva: WHO; 1996.

22

Influence of Demonstration and Exposure Trip for Development of Beneficiaries by NGOs in Nagaland, India

M.N. Odyuo, N.K. Patra, S. Das and **L.Y. Longchar**

ABSTRACT

Development practitioners, government officials and foreign donors considered that, the NGOs by virtue of being small scale, flexible, innovative and participatory, are more successful in reaching the poor and in poverty alleviation. This consideration has resulted in the rapid growth of NGOs in initiating and implementing rural development programmes. Thousands of NGOs are engaged in the state of Nagaland for all round development of the resource poor peoples of urban and rural area. Types and characteristics of NGOs are varied and different from one to others. Their way of activity and consideration of issues related to social problems is varied greatly. Potential adopters of a new idea are aided in evaluating an innovation if they are able to observe it in use under conditions to their own. Such observation often occurs naturally, when one individual views another's experience in using the innovation. Facilitators may try to increase the observability of an innovation. Farmers, and particularly farm women, in less developed State like Nagaland, are not fortunate enough to visit other towns and cities on their own, so they enjoy the opportunity to join such exposure trips conducted by different development agencies. Simultaneously, in this State NGOs are playing vital role in development sector particularly in all round development of the rural people. Accordingly, this study is intended to explore the inception and positivity about the different identified development tools viz. Demonstration and Exposure trips by NGOs for smooth and faster development of their beneficiaries.

Introduction

The Non-Government and Voluntary Organizations have been a part of the historical legacy or rural development in India. In 19th and 20th centuries, several voluntary efforts started in development programmes. The NGOs came to prominence after independence, especially after 1970s. This was partly because of the limited success of past development policies pursued by the government. Development practitioners, government officials and foreign donors considered that, the NGOs by virtue of being small scale, flexible, innovative and participatory, are more successful in reaching the poor and in poverty alleviation. This consideration has resulted in the rapid growth of NGOs in initiating and implementing rural development programmes.

Development basically means, advancement of an area, revealing, unfolding or opening up something which is latent and a change that is desirable. It is referred to as a continuous and rigorous process of progress, mobilizing the people towards self reliance, assuring and/or ensuring equitable distribution or benefit of opportunity, resource and social justice among all sections of the society. According to Mondal et al.(2007), 'Development is the process of creating and maintaining a situation in which all citizens of the country can lead a desirable and satisfying life'.

In development sector, non-government organizations (the organizations which are outside the direct control of government agencies or autonomous bodies and are engaged in providing financial and non-financial services to the community are called NGO or Voluntary Organization) are playing major role in the development of different target groups since time immemorial.

Thousands of NGOs are engaged in the state of Nagaland for all round development of the resource poor peoples of urban and rural area. Types and characteristics of NGOs are varied and different from one to others. Their way of activity and consideration of issues related to social problems is varied greatly.

"Developmental roles" such as; socio-economic improvement of small and marginal farmers in rural area, safe guarding national food grain production, development of eco-friendly sustainable agriculture, resource conservation, empowerment of farm women and training of farmers, human resource development, health service and awareness, disease control, eradication of drug addiction, conflict management etc. are quite impossible to tackle only by Government development machinery. Recent development in the global scenario has also facilitated the emergence of private agencies, commercial firms, NGOs etc. in the area of rural development and agricultural extension.

Potential adopters of a new idea are aided in evaluating an innovation if they are able to observe it in use under conditions to their own. Such observation often occurs naturally, when one individual views another's experience in using the innovation. Facilitators may try to increase the observability of an innovation, and thus speed its rate of adoption, by organizing a demonstration of the innovation.

The term 'Demonstration" has been in use since the mid-19th century, as was the term 'monster meeting', which was coined initially with reference to the huge assemblies of protesters inspired by Daniel O'Connell in Ireland (Wikipedia, 2011). However it is used to explain in several events.

Demonstration may stimulate farmers to try out innovations themselves, or even may replace a test of the innovation by the farmer. Demonstrations can show the causes of problems and their possible solutions without complicated technical details. It involves showing by proof, explaining or making clear by use of examples or experiments. People can communicate values and ideas through demonstrations (G.L Ray, 2011).

Result Demonstration is a method of motivating the people for adoption of a new practice by showing its distinctly superior result. The demonstrations are conducted in the farm home of selected individuals and are utilized to educate and motivate groups of people in their neighbourhood. This is a very effective method for the transfer of technology in a community (G.L Ray, 2011).

Further, Van Den Ban (1996) stated that, 'Action Demonstrations' try to show that large sections of the population desire changes in government policy or in their society. However, 'Method Demonstration' is given before a group of people to show how to carry out an entirely new practice or an old practice in a better way. It involves seeing, hearing, participating and practicing in a group which shall stimulate interest and action (G.L Ray, 2011).

The best part of conducting demonstration is to see how an innovation works in practice. It gives opportunity to the participants for learning by doing and giving them more scope of acquiring the know-how about the technology to be disseminated. The uniqueness of the demonstration is such that the whole demonstration is carried out by the participant himself with the presence, guidance and advice of the facilitator.

Exposure trip is a teaching method in which a group of interested farmers accompanied and guided by an extension worker, goes on tour to see and gain first-hand knowledge of improved practices in their natural setting like research farm, demonstration farm, institution or farmer's field. Field visit, field work, camp study, educational tour, study tour etc are a few synonyms for this practice of seeing an improved performance or results of a practice in actual situations (R.R Chole et al, 2010).

In exposure trip, a group of people having a common interest, along with a guide goes to some other places with an aim to visit new places, research stations, farms and fields etc and also to study and learn significant improvement in farm and home elsewhere. Such exposure trips motivate the visitors by observing with first-hand knowledge on what others have been able to achieve thereby stimulates interests among the group members. It also convinces the visitors about their unexplored potentialities of achieving great results by seeing and believing what others could accomplish in other villages and thus stimulates action.

Farmers on exposure trip moves out of their neighbourhood to visit farms and experimental fields of other village, towns or cities. Such activity gives them a good platform to gain vast knowledge on both on-farm and out-of-the farm sectors. When the farmers are exposed to the success of diverse farm practices being followed in other places, they are motivated and with more knowledge their confidence level is boosted. Having a first-hand experience in the farms and fields, they have more memory retention capacity which ultimately stimulates action to adopt new beneficial farm practices.

Both, Exposure Trips and Demonstrations allow the farmers to observe the effects of different newly adopted farm practices as well as it gives them the opportunity to discuss about the pros and cons of the practices with other experienced farmers.

Farmers, and particularly farm women, in less developed State like Nagaland, are not fortunate enough to visit other towns and cities on their own, so they enjoy the opportunity to join such exposure trips conducted by different development agencies. Simultaneously, in this State NGOs are playing vital role in development sector particularly in all round development of the rural people.

Accordingly, this study is intended to explore the inception and positivity about the different identified development tools viz. Demonstration and Exposure trips by NGOs for smooth and faster development of their beneficiaries.

Materials and Methods

Nagaland State was inaugurated as the sixteenth State of India on 1st December, 1963. It is bounded by Assam in the West, Myanmar on the East, Arunachal Pradesh and part of Assam on the North and Manipur in the South. The State approximately lies between 25°6′ and 27°4′ latitude; North of Equator and between the Longitudinal lines of 93°20′and 95°15′E. Geographical area is 16527 sq km and total population is 19,80,602 (as per 2011 census). Average annual rainfall ranges from 2000-3000 mm and temperature ranges from 4°C to 31°C. The topography of the state is undulating, full of hill range which breaks into wide chaos of spurs and ridges. The altitudes vary between 194 to 3840 meters above the mean sea level. The state has a beautiful landscape and it consists of 11 administrative districts viz., Kohima, Dimapur, Kipheri, Longleng, Mokokchung, Mon, Peren, Phek, Tuensang, Wokha and Zunheboto. Out of the total 11 districts, 6 districts have been selected purposively for the present study, namely, Dimapur, Kohima, Mokokchung, Peren, Tuensang and Wokha.

Out of total 85 NGOs identified by obtaining list from reliable sources, 45 NGOs were finally selected. From every selected NGO, one respondent from the higher level of employees and minimum one respondent from the lower level of employees were considered as respondent. Higher level of employees of NGOs includes top level functionaries, like Director, Secretary, Topmost functionaries of sub-office of the large NGOs. A lower level employee of NGOs includes those which are not designed in higher level of position and directly involved in grass root level implementation of work. Accordingly, 45 higher level of employees and 75 lower levels of employees were interviewed as respondents (total 120) which were selected as the final respondents.

In this study, the NGOs were classified into various ways and categories. According to the working places, i.e. some NGOs are working in only one Block of District and at the same time, some NGOs are working in numbers of countries; accordingly, all NGOs were classified into four categories- International, National, State level and Local Level. Further, in this study, researcher has considered extent of conducting demonstration and exposure trips by higher and lower level of employees of the NGOs and performance of the employees according to their status of the organization, during the last one year of period.

Result and Discussion

Organizing Demonstration for Beneficiaries

Demonstration is a widely accepted extension method and tool to mobilize and motivate the people for dissemination and adoption of innovation amongst the target group. It also offers the scope of 'seeing is believing' and target group can see the method of operation or how to carry out the operation and simultaneously getting the opportunity to see the performance and relative advantage of the innovation. In this study researcher has considered demonstration as an important method or tool to disseminate the innovation and implementation of developmental activities for proper and further upliftment. In this regard researcher has considered extent of conducting demonstration by higher level and lower level of employees of the NGOs and performance of the employees according to their status of the organization, during the last one year of period.

Table 22.1: Organization of Demonstrations for Beneficiaries by Higher Levels of Employees of NGOs.

Organized Demonstration for Beneficiaries	Total	%	Local	%	State	%	National	%	Inter-national	%
Not Organized	18	40.00	11	40.74	4	33.33	2	66.66	1	33.33
Upto 3	7	15.55	6	22.22	1	8.33	0	0	0	0
Upto 6	3	6.66	2	7.40	1	8.33	0	0	0	0
Upto 10	4	8.88	2	7.40	1	8.33	0	0	1	33.33
Upto 15	4	8.88	1	3.70	2	16.66	0	0	1	33.33
Upto 20	3	6.66	2	7.40	0	0	1	33.33	0	0
Above 20	6	13.33	3	11.11	3	25	0	0	0	0
Total	45	100.00	27	100.00	12	100.00	3	100.00	3	100.00

Table 22.1 shows the information about organized demonstration by the higher level of employees of NGOs for their beneficiaries during the last one year. Table explains that 40 per cent of higher levels of employees of NGOs did not organize any demonstration for beneficiaries during last one year whereas remaining 60 per cent of employees had organized demonstration during last one year. Table clearly shows that 16 per cent of employees had conducted upto 3 demonstrations only for beneficiaries during the last one year period whereas another 6 per cent each conducted demonstration upto 6 and upto 20 numbers respectively. Table also shows that 9 per cent each of employees from higher level had conducted upto 10 and upto 15 numbers of demonstrations respectively for their beneficiaries and remaining 13 per cent of employees conducted demonstration more than 20 numbers during the same period.

Taking into consideration of the status of the NGOs, 41 per cent of employees of local level of NGOs had not organized any demonstration and followed by 33 per cent employees each from State and International level of NGOs and 67 per cent of National level of NGOs' employees had not conducted any demonstration programme. In connection with local level of NGOs, 22 per cent of employees conducted demonstration upto 3 numbers and 7 per cent each conducted upto 6 numbers, upto 10 and upto 20 numbers of demonstration respectively during the period of last one year. It is clear in case of local level of NGOs, a considerable numbers of employees i.e. 11 per cent conducted demonstration more than 20 times and a negligible percentage of employees i.e. 4 per cent conducted upto 15 demonstrations during the last one year of period. Further table shows that 8 per cent each of employees of State level of NGOs conducted upto 3, upto 6 and upto 10 numbers of demonstrations respectively during the period of last one year. Whereas 33 per cent of employees of National levels of NGOs conducted demonstration upto 20 in numbers and 33 per cent each of International levels of NGOs conducted upto 10 and upto 15 in numbers of demonstrations for their beneficiaries during the one year of period.

Table 22.2: Organization of Demonstrations for Beneficiaries by Lower Levels of Employees of NGOs

Organized Demonstration for Beneficiaries	Total	%	Local	%	State	%	National	%	Inter-national	%
Not Organized	51	68	29	65.90	13	68.42	5	71.42	4	80
Upto 3	12	16	6	13.63	4	21.05	2	28.57	0	0
Upto 6	6	8	4	9.09	2	10.52	0	0	0	0
Upto 10	5	6.66	4	9.09	0	0	0	0	1	20
Upto 15	1	1.33	1	2.27	0	0	0	0	0	0
Upto 20	0	0	0	0	0	0	0	0	0	0
Above 20	0	0	0	0	0	0	0	0	0	0
Total	75	100.00	44	100.00	19	100.00	7	100.00	5	100

Table 22.2 contains the information about organized demonstration by the lower level of employees of NGOs for their beneficiaries during the last one year of period. Table shows that 68 per cent of lower levels of employees of NGOs had not organized any demonstration for their beneficiaries during last one year whereas remaining 32 per cent of lower levels of employees had organized demonstration during last one year. Table clearly shows that 16 per cent of lower levels of employees had conducted upto 3 demonstrations only, for beneficiaries during the last one year of period where 8 per cent of employees had conducted demonstrations upto 6, and 7 per cent of employees conducted upto 10 numbers of demonstrations; and a negligible number of NGOs i.e. 1 per cent had conducted demonstration upto 15 in numbers for their beneficiaries.

Table also shows that 66 per cent of lower levels of employees of local levels of NGOs had not conducted any demonstration and only 34 per cent of employees from lower level were conducted demonstration, and out of this 34 per cent, only 14 per cent of employees had conducted demonstration upto 3 only; and 9 per cent each conducted upto 6 and upto 10 numbers of demonstration respectively and a negligible numbers i.e. about 2 per cent of employees had conducted upto 15 numbers of demonstrations during the last one year of period.

It is clear from the table that, 68 per cent of lower levels of employees of State level of NGOs had not conducted any demonstration where remaining 32 per cent conducted during the last one year of period, and of which 21 per cent conducted upto 3 numbers of demonstrations and 11 per cent conducted upto 6 numbers of demonstration during the period of one year.

Further table depicts that 71 per cent of employees from lower levels of National level of NGOs and 80 per cent of lower level of employees from International levels of NGOs had not conducted any demonstrations and remaining percentage of employees of National level of NGOs i.e.29 per cent had conducted demonstration upto 3 only and same way remaining 20 per cent of employees of International levels of NGOs had organized upto 10 numbers of demonstration for their beneficiaries during the last one year of period.

Exposure Trip

Exposure trip is an important concept of extension in gaining first-hand experience and knowledge about new innovation or practice. In exposure trip, participants are getting first hand opportunity to know about technology by seeing it in the real situation, either in research station or other farmer's field which they can implement in their own situation. The main purpose of exposure trip is to mobilize and motivate the participants or visitors by showing others achievement.

In this regard researcher has tried to explore the degree and extend of acceptability of exposure trip by different levels of NGOs' employees for mobilization, modernization and improvement of their beneficiaries.

Table 22.3: Organization of Exposure Trip for Beneficiaries by High Levels of Employees of NGOs

Organized Exposure Trip for Beneficiaries	Total	%	Local	%	State	%	National	%	Inter-national	%
Not Organized	23	51.11	15	55.55	5	41.66	2	66.66	1	33.33
Upto 3	19	42.22	9	33.33	7	58.33	1	33.33	2	66.66
Upto 6	3	6.66	3	11.11	0		0		0	
Total	45	100.00	27	100.00	12	100.00	3	100.0C	3	100.00

Table 22.3 contains the information about organized exposure trip by the higher level of employees of NGOs for their beneficiaries during the last one year of period. Table shows that 51 per cent of higher levels of employees of NGOs had not organized any exposure trip for beneficiaries during last one year of period whereas remaining 49 per cent of employees had organized exposure trip during last one year of period. Table clearly shows that 42 per cent of employees had conducted upto 3 numbers of exposure trips for their beneficiaries during the last one year of period whereas another 7 per cent organized exposure trips upto 6 times for their beneficiaries.

Taking into consideration of the status of the NGOs, then 56 per cent of higher level of employees of local level of NGOs had not organized any exposure trip and followed by 42 per cent of employees from State levels of

NGOs, 67 per cent of employees of National levels of NGOs and 33 per cent of employees of International level of NGOs had not conducted any exposure trip. In connection with local levels of NGOs, 33 per cent of employees had conducted exposure trips upto 3 times and remaining 11 per cent conducted exposure trips upto 6 times during the last one year of period, whereas 58 per cent of employees of State levels of NGOs had conducted upto 3 times of exposure trips for their beneficiaries during the last one year of period. Further table shows that 33 per cent of employees of National levels of NGOs and 66 per cent of employees of International levels of NGOs conducted exposure trips upto 3 times respectively, during the period of last one year.

Table 22.4: Organization of Exposure Trip for Beneficiaries by Lower Levels of Employees of NGOs

Organized Exposure Trip for Beneficiaries	Total	%	Local	%	State	%	National	%	Inter-national	%
Not Organized	54	72.00	29	65.90	16	84.21	5	71.42	4	80
Upto 3	20	26.66	14	31.81	3	15.78	2	28.57	1	20
Upto 6	1	1.33	1	2.22	0	0	0	0	0	0
Total	75	100.00	44	100.00	19	100.00	7	100.00	5	100

Table 22.4 contains the information about organized exposure trips by the lower level of employees of NGOs for their beneficiaries during the last one year of period. Table shows that 72 per cent of lower levels of employees of NGOs did not organize any exposure trips for their beneficiaries during the last one year; whereas remaining 28 per cent of employees were organized exposure trips, which is further distributed into 27 per cent of employees those organized exposure trips upto 3 times and remaining about 1 per cent of lower levels of employees organized upto 6 exposure trips for their beneficiaries during the last one year of period.

Table also shows that 66 per cent of lower levels of employees of local levels of NGOs had not conducted any exposure trips and only 34 per cent of employees from lower level organized exposure trips, and out of this 34 per cent, 32 per cent of employees organized exposure trips upto 3 times only and remaining 2 per cent organized upto 6 times.

It is clear from the table that 84 per cent of lower levels of employees of State level of NGOs did not conduct any exposure trips, whereas remaining 16 per cent conducted exposure trips upto 3 times during the last one year of period.

Further it also depicts that 71 per cent of employees from lower levels of National level of NGOs and 80 per cent of lower level of employees from International levels of NGOs did not conduct any exposure trips while remaining percentage i.e.29 per cent of employees of National levels of NGOs and 20 per cent of lower level of employees of International levels of NGOs had organized exposure trips upto 3 times only during the last one year of period.

Summary and Conclusion

Demonstration and Exposure tour are considered as important activities for the development of beneficiaries or the target groups of NGO's, because both may stimulate the participants to carry out innovations themselves, or even may replace a test of the innovation by them. Conducting demonstrations with own hands shall encourage the participants to act on a scientific basis rather than something which is magical. Exposure tours motivate the visitors by showing what others have been able to achieve. It stimulates interests among the group members. It also induces healthy competition by showing the accomplishment in other villages and also convinces people utility of a practice and stimulates action.

In development sector, non-government organizations (the organizations which are outside the direct control of government agencies or autonomous bodies and are engaged in providing financial and non-financial services to the community are called NGO or Voluntary Organization) are playing major role in the development of different target groups since time immemorial.

Study depicted the information about organized demonstration by the employees of NGOs for their beneficiaries during the last one year of period and shows that 60 per cent and 32 per cent of employees from higher and lower levels had organized demonstration during the last one year. Study also depicted that 16 per cent each of employees from higher and lower level conducted upto 3 demonstrations, where another 6 per cent of employees from higher level and 8 per cent from lower level conducted demonstration upto 6 and a considerable percentage of employees from higher and lower level conducted more numbers of demonstration for their beneficiaries during the same period.

Study also explored about organized exposure trip by the employees of NGOs for their beneficiaries during the last one year of period and shows that 49 per cent of employees from higher level and 28 per cent from lower level of employees organized exposure trip during last one year of period. Study also shows that 42 per cent of employees from higher level and 27 per cent from lower level of employees conducted upto 3 numbers of exposure trips for their beneficiaries and remaining percentage of employees from both the levels conducted exposure trip upto 6 times during the last one year of period.

Study showed that the higher level of employees of the NGOs had conducted demonstration and exposure trips sufficiently during the last one year of period. Further, from the study it can be concluded that demonstration is more preferred tools compared to exposure trips. Performance about conducting the demonstration and exposure trips by lower level of employees were not upto the level of satisfactory. It is apparently obvious that expenditure for organizing exposure trips by any organization is more, but conducting demonstration is comparatively less expensive. Further, it is important that role of lower level of employees for conducting demonstration is vital and in spite of that the performance of conducting demonstration by the lower level of employees of NGOs was not upto the mark. So concern authority may take corrective initiative accordingly.

REFERENCES

Census of India 2011a, "Rural Urban Distribution of Population (Provisional Population Totals)", *http://censusindia.gov.in/2011-prov-results/paper2/data_files/india/Rural_Urban_2011.pdf*

Chole R.R., P.R. Deshmukh and P.S Kapse (2010), 'Transfer of Agricultural Technology' Scientific Publishers, Jodhpur, India.

Mondal Sagar and G. L.Ray (2007), 'Text Book of Entrepreneurship and Rural Development'. Kalyani Publishers, Ludhiana, India.

Ray G.L. (2011). Extension Communication and Management. Kalyani Publishers, Ludhiana, India.

Van Den Ban A.W. and Hawkins H.S (1996), 'Agricultural Extension' Longman Scientific and Technical, England and Blackwell Science Ltd., London.

www.wikipedia.com access on 02.11.13

Index